Muslim Schools and Education in Europe and South Africa

Religionen im Dialog

A series edited by the
Academy of World Religions
at Hamburg University

Volume 5

Waxmann 2011
Münster / New York / München / Berlin

Abdulkader Tayob
Inga Niehaus
Wolfram Weisse (Eds.)

Muslim Schools and Education in Europe and South Africa

Waxmann 2011
Münster / New York / München / Berlin

Bibliographic information published by the Deutsche Nationalbibliothek
The Deutsche Nationalbibliothek lists this publication in
the Deutsche Nationalbibliografie; detailed bibliographic data
is available in the Internet at http://dnb.d-nb.de

Religionen im Dialog, volume 5

A series edited by the Academy of World Religions
at Hamburg University

ISSN 1867-1292
ISBN 978-3-8309-2554-5

Postfach 8603, 48046 Münster

www.waxmann.com
info@waxmann.com

Cover design: Plessmann Design, Ascheberg
Cover image: © Orhan Çam – Fotolia.com
Typesetting: Stoddart Satz- und Layoutservice, Münster
Print: SDK Systemdruck, Köln

Printed on age-resistant paper,
acid-free as per ISO 9706

Printed in Germany

Contents

Abdulkader Tayob, Inga Niehaus and Wolfram Weisse

Introduction

Islamic education has become a highly contested and controversial topic in many societies across the globe. It is often associated with radical Islamic politics, invariably linked with the Taliban (literally, students in Urdu) in Afghanistan or with alleged terrorists who may have spent more or less time in a *madrasah* (educational institute) (Hefner 2007, 1). Typically, this has meant occasional attendance at some lectures or participation in a short course. This "tangible" association is avidly presented as a hard fact in a subject that is overwhelmed by conjecture, secret cells and sinister dealings. Evidence is hard to come by but Islamic education in its peculiarity provides an outlet of some sort, and terrorism is given a place and a shape. This not only applies to Islamic educational institutions in Asia and the Middle East, but since the bombings in London in July 2005, also to Islamic schools and *madrassahs* in Great Britain and other European counties which were suspected to be the birthplace of "home-grown" Islamic terrorist cells (Mandaville 2007, 226).

The reality of Islamic education and the *madrasah* as the ultimate *jihād* factory is very different from this public perception. *Madrasahs* in all their variety are places of learning in Islamic culture and history. They are highly complex social institutions which have their fair share of challenges and opportunities. This has also been vividly illustrated in Indonesia, where Islamic schools (*pesantren*) have been accused of promoting and training extremists. A detailed study showed that the *Pesantren* offer a variety of Islamic educational models, including some which support women's rights and interreligious dialogue (Pohl 2009). Such a case therefore further illustrates the necessity of detailed academic research dealing with themes of public interest, where more information may better inform public discussion, which are too often dominated by emotions and ambivalent, or even wrong positions. Islamic educational institutions represent the religious convictions and aspirations of Muslims in everyday life. On the one hand, they may threaten the integration of Muslims in a national society and promote isolation and self-marginalization. On the other hand, Islamic education has the potential to enable Muslim children to gain a strong understanding of their own tradition in order to face the challenges of a secular pluralistic society (Aslan 2009, 12). This may occur especially in contexts where Muslims are in the minority which is the case in European countries and in South Africa.

This collection of essays is a close examination of such challenges and opportunities within Islamic education in Europe and South Africa in recent times.

Islamic education has been the subject of intense discussion and innovation within Muslim societies and communities in the modern period (Qadi al 2006). Modernization has impacted on the content and pedagogy of education, affecting the subjects taught, method of delivery, organization of syllabi and general philosophies. A number of positions have been taken on these issues, and at least two very clear poles of a wide spectrum may be identified: a commitment to preserve and transmit a body of knowledge increasingly regarded as religious and sacred; and a commitment to modern scientific education as the bedrock for development and progress (Waardenburg 1965; Rahman 1982; Zaman 2002). An inevitable bifurcation of education from these two extreme poles has been a cause of concern among many Muslims, but persists into the most recent developments in Europe and South Africa.

Like other social developments, Islamic education also needs to be put into context. Plank and Sykes (1999) contend that since the 1980s, there has been a global trend towards privatizing education for a diverse set of reasons. In liberal societies, this trend coincided with greater demand by parents to take basic education into their own hands; with claims of greater efficiency against state systems; and with the liberal state's willingness to outsource key functions previously regarded as central to national development. Islamic education should be contextualized within the trend of private education, which in turn is part of a dominant liberal paradigm of the state. In South Africa, this trend coincided with the demise of apartheid and the demand for middle classes to maintain privileges against a new democratic government (Fiske & Ladd 2003). Not surprisingly, Britain leads the pack in private schooling in the European context, but there are similar but clearly limited trends in France, Germany and the Netherlands (see Niehaus and Weisse here).

This edited collection presents Islamic education in South Africa and a number of countries in Europe in this new educational context. It brings together general concerns of education among Muslims, together with current and unique developments in each country. Given the place of Islamic education in public debate, the collection includes a variety of contributions that respond to the goals and future of Islamic education, the context of terrorism and counter-terrorism, the place of religious education in the context of secular education and the role religious education plays in promoting or hindering social cohesion. It includes reflections on where Muslims should be directing education in the next few years to make it socially relevant and contribute to the democratization of society (Waghid, Nadvi), as well as some comments on the unfortunate but real crosscurrents in educational policy and counter-terrorist initiatives (Scott-Bauman). In between, it contains some reflective essays on the uniqueness and commonalities of Islamic education in various countries (Niehaus), on unexpected and unknown outcomes (Fataar), and on new philosophies of education (Tayob). In fact, the essays may be seen as critical contributions on at least four themes that are debated in the public sphere and within these schools.

The first of these themes touches on the religious-secular divide within society and within the schools themselves. Islamic education in the modern period has been split between the provision of religious knowledge and values, and support for employment in so-called secular sectors. The secular and religious domains are mutually exclusive as argued by Asad, and inherently antagonistic (Asad 2003). In fact, the antagonism is ever present within a number of Muslim educational contexts. And yet, closer study reveals some interesting twists to this general theme. Waghid's contribution presents a case for a critical philosophy of education where the division between the religious and the secular are overcome. His is a recovery and re-invention of key educational processes that destroy the clear divisions between the secular and the sacred, in favour of a creative, inquiring approach to education and personal development. On the other hand, closer study of purely Islamic educational establishments reveal that sectarian traditions are still dominant and thriving. Sayed's detailed documentation of higher Islamic institutions in South Africa points to their old and new sectarian nature. Internal debates among Islamic theologies dominate the spread and proliferation of such schools, where modernist/secular orientations play a minor role if any. The real place of the secular and religious is present in Niehaus' essay, comparing Islamic schools in South Africa, Britain and the Netherlands. This is not surprising, given the role of the modern secular state in her case studies. In each of the countries studied, the state is a dominant role player that establishes the meaning of the secular in terms of a neutral public space, a space for interreligious dialogue and the promotion of democratic values. In all these countries, the establishment of Islamic schools was favoured by an educational system that supported denominational schools – especially Christian – for decades. The article critically assesses how Islamic schools followed this model, whilst providing an Islamic ethos and identity within the broader national context. All the schools do the basics: meeting the requirements of the national curriculum (secular), and creating an Islamic atmosphere. They differ, however, on the relationship they cultivate between religious and national and democratic ideals in each context.

In the context of schooling, the secular and religious tension reflects schooling that alternatively serves the nation and the specific religious communities. Schooling for the nation is considered to be secular, whilst schooling for a specific religious community is religious. From this perspective, the secular and religious divisions become clearer and may be further specified. The nation is interested in citizenship and democratic participation, while the religious community favours participation in a cultural world that appears to make demands in very specific and intimate ways. It may appear that the nation is a much larger group than the specific religious community which it has to accommodate. Most of the papers in this collection make this assumption, and show the relationship between the larger and dominant national social order within which religious groups thrive. The national order sets the rules, which religious groups follow, or with which they accommodate themselves. However, Reetz's contribution highlights another important dimension of the social world of religion, pointing to the production of an alternate globality inscribed by Deobandi educational institutions. Religious communities occupy and take shape within very specific national social contexts, but their global impact and connections should not be forgotten. The tension between the secular nation and the religious community, then, relates to competing commitment to social spaces from the community to the nation and to global formations.

It is not surprising that integration occupies an equally second important theme in these papers. The secular and religious may be mutually and antagonistically divided, but basic education brings them together. Integration is a term that addresses this demand for conversation and dialogue. Integration is clearly the dominant issue in European public debates with regard to Islam in general and Islamic education in particular. Muslims are often presented with a choice of isolation, integration or assimilation. The difference between the last two is often not so clearly articulated, leaving the choice only between isolation and assimilation. Most of the articles in this collection on European case studies address this issue, but Hieronymus addresses this matter in Hamburg with some depth. His contribution brings out the complexity of the matter, adding the reality of discrimination among all groups that stand in the way of healthy integration in the city. Weisse, Kiefer and Mohr and Niehaus bring out the challenge of integration in the very different political contexts of Europe. Their contributions bring out the very unique contexts in each country, region or city with regard to religious education, attitude towards religion, and the particular meaning of nation and citizenship. Europe might appear homogenous, and may often speak in one voice, but closer attention to the specific circumstances of Islamic schools brings out the variations. The controversial debates, even in Germany, show the importance attributed to the question of the rights of religious communities to have an “own” religious education in public schools. Whether, for Muslims, this leads to a successful way of getting the same opportunities as Christians, or whether a separated Muslim education paves the way for an “own”, but exclusive system, is still in discussion. There are also alternatives which exist to these options, whereby Muslims have an opportunity for religious education whilst participating as part of a comprehensive religion education, as Weisse shows in his article. The debate on integration will continuc, but it might be best to see it as part of a long-term process that does not necessary head in one direction. The articles in this collection show religious education showing both challenges and opportunities for integration.

By considering the South African perspective, the papers also point to other sites of integration within Islamic schools, often neglected in European debates. Thus, in the South African context, the essays by Fataar and Tayob point to racial integration concerns after many years of apartheid. Fataar’s contribution shows how Islamic schooling provided an opportunity for upward mobility for Black African working class learners. At the same time, according to Tayob, Islamic schools continue to perpetuate racial differentiation and class interests. The particular location of Islamic schools within South Africa with respect to race, class and economic status play a significant role. Occupying the middle ground between Black and White schools, Islamic schools lead to unexpected and unintended consequences. These contradictory tendencies are reflected in various schools in Europe as well: upward mobility for those who do not have other opportunities or suffer discrimination, and self-isolation in other respects. With regard to Islamic education, the difference between Europe and South Africa also brings out another important consideration. Whilst Muslims constitute minorities in both situations, Muslims in South Africa enjoy a long history of institution formation. Islamic schools under study in Fataar and Tayob are part of a history of modern Islamic education, and are continuing as suggested by Waghid and Nadvi. Any perspective on Islamic schools in Europe and their potential for integration should take into consideration their relatively shorter history, their transformation and, more importantly, inevitable change.

Multiple terrains of integration in Islamic schools are closely related to a third thematic tension in Islamic education as attested to in this volume. In particular, Islamic schools are self-consciously defined by their religious identity, and most of them exhibit this in one way or another. However, looking more closely at the religious nature of these schools reveals a gap between the theory of education promoted and reality (praxis). Islamic schools are ambitious in their attempt to promote both religious learning and secular knowledge. As shown in the articles by Tayob and Niehaus, the philosophy of Islamization in some cases is promoted to provide the conceptual glue with which to bind the two fields of educational activity. Reality is often more complex than the theory proposes. The theory of Islamic education promotes religious identity and commitment, the reality reveals however, that it is also the site where secular knowledge is entrenched, mobility and social advancement provided, and ethnic identity deepened. This gap between Islamic education and its ideals is not unique. Modern schooling is designed to provide equal schools for all citizens, but hardly ever succeeds as it also perpetuates class and ethnic/racial differences, marginalization and discrimination. Thankfully, as these essays on Islamic schooling attest, education also leads to emancipation and development. The gap between theory and praxis recalls the gap between religious claims and observance. While it may be a problem for theologians to justify, it is a gap that has some potentially beneficial and adverse outcomes. We may have to recognize that the theory of Islamization has a necessary function for the discussion of priorities in the whole set of education theory, but not necessarily as dominant background for Islamic schools only.

The fourth theme covered in these papers relates to the social space in which education takes place, and which it inscribes. Education takes place in locations and spaces that have very specific characteristics. They may be community-based organizations (such as the *Dār al-ʿulūm* or seminaries), or they may be institutions that fall under direct or indirect government supervision (such as most schools). These spaces as geographic locations are easily described and specified with respect to legal and economic conditions. Islamic schools, for example, usually conform to laws governing general schooling in a country. They also need a certain level of finance to support and sustain themselves over time. There is no doubt about the extent of contextualization of schools in Europe and South Africa where theses institutions try to adapt to – and sometime confront – the state-supervised educational system. This collection is a clear testimony of this phenomenon.

At the same time, education also inscribes intangible social spaces through the rituals and myths that permeate institutions in one way or another (Chidester 1994). Most of the educational institutions are in this sense national schools, serving the nation in direct or indirect ways. But they are also committed to their class, religious and ethnic identities. More controversially for nation-states, religious institutions and schools are both smaller and larger than them. They support both sub-national and supra-national social formations. Sub-national groups refer not only to Muslims in the various countries studied in this volume. Muslims are internally divided along theological and ethnic lines, and schools reflect these tensions. Schools seem to be serving these more narrowly defined interests and theological directions. Since the modern state in recent times seems to recognize the religious nature of minorities, and not racial identities as in the past, schools are now becoming more clearly identified through religion. A case may be made for the development of national Muslim identities through these various school projects. Such a development should not be seen as a natural outcome of the aspiration of Muslims, but an innovative development within nation states.

National and sub-national groups are not the only social spaces inscribed by Islamic education. Global connections and concerns cannot be ignored. In modern Islamic education, Islamization and Deobandi globalities define at least two very different forms of global connections that are examined closely here. Deobandi globality as defined by Reetz suggests a very interesting development in Islamic religious learning. Riding on the back of a globalization led by the flow of capital, ideas and people, Deobandism has managed to break out of its South Asian borders and founded a chain of institutions in the English-speaking world. Variations are clearly present, but they self-consciously map out the field in the same way that fast-food chains have spread around the globe. Islamization in schools is a different form of globality. It is not as successful and efficient, but it too represents a globally shared idea. However, Islamization is not an institution that can be duplicated from one context to another. It represents a set of ideas available to Muslims to implement in a local context. National and trans-national bodies support and develop ideas of Islamization through workshops, conferences and seminars. Deobandism is a form of globalization that duplicates a tested model in a new context, whilst Islamization provides the basis for a contextual appropriation of a global non-territorial concept. Islamic education represents both of these forms. Not surprisingly, Islamic schools represent Islamization but they are often served by Deobandi or Deobandi-like religious teachers that support a different mode of global Islamic practice.

The articles in this volume are the product of two conferences which took place within the collaborative research programme “Muslims in Europe and their societies of origin in Africa and Asia” (2006-2009) coordinated by the Centre for Modern Oriental Studies in Berlin[1]. A sub-project of this larger programme was looking at Islamic private schools in South Africa, Great Britain and the Netherlands. The study with the title “Between participation and disengagement. The Muslim minority and its schools in South Africa and Europe” was carried out by Inga Niehaus under the leadership of Wolfram Weisse. Of particular interest were the links and parallels, as well as the differences and divisions between Islamic schools in South Africa and those in Europe. For the dissemination of the research results, one symposium was conducted in Cape Town/South Africa in October 2008 and another in Hamburg/Germany in May 2009. Both events

1 See http://www.zmo.de/muslime_in_europa/. The collaborative project was coordinated by senior lecturer Dr. Dietrich Reetz at the Centre for Modern Oriental Studies (ZMO) in Berlin. Six studies investigated the role of religious Muslim groups, movements, and institutions in European countries in an attempt to understand the extent to which Muslims will shape emerging European identity

brought together academics and practitioners in the field of Islamic education in general and Islamic private schools in particular. Researchers, representatives of educational institutions, school teachers and school principals as well as religious leaders debated relevant issues with regard to Islamic education in societies where Muslims are minorities. Most of the authors in this volume attended one of these two conferences and contributed with their discussions and feedback to the result of the study whose outcomes are in part presented in the Niehaus' article.

The research carried out by Inga Niehaus was closely linked to a large-scale European research programme led by Wolfram Weisse with the title "Religion in Education. A contribution to dialogue or a factor of conflict in transforming societies of European Countries" (REDCo). In this interdisciplinary research programme, researchers from different countries cooperated in order to gain better insight into how European citizens of different religious, cultural and political backgrounds can live together and enter into dialogue of mutual respect and understanding.[2] One of the publications from this research programme focussed on Islam in education in European Countries (see Alvarez Veinguer et al. 2009).

Both projects and programmes illustrate the increased research interest into the role of religious education in general and Islamic education in particular on a European level and beyond. The results are contributing, through methodologically grounded qualitative and quantitative data, to answering questions regarding the potential contribution of religious education to social cohesion in pluralistic societies. The research shows that in spite of a secular school system, religion in education does play an important role in many societies and does respond to the needs of students, parents and educators who demand value-based education, where religious identities are acknowledged and an understanding of one's own tradition is promoted, in order to enter into an intercultural dialogue. The renowned Dutch philosopher of education, Wilna A.J. Meijer, reminds us that education in general and Islamic education in particular "is about striking a balance between tradition and enlightenment: about transmitting culture in such a way as to stimulate critical reflection on that culture" (Meijer 2009, 15).

It is our privilege and honour to thank those who have supported this publication in one way or another. Nabowayah Kafaar at the University of Cape and Anna Körs at Hamburg University supported the conferences in 2008 and 2009. Jihad Omar worked closely with the text, editing and correcting the articles as they came from the authors. Beate Plugge effortlessly managed the coordination with the printer and publisher. And last but not least, each one of the authors deserve thanks for responding with speed and patience.

References

Aslan, Ednan. 2009. Preface. In *Islamische Erziehung in Europa. Islamic Education in Europe*, ed. by Ednan Aslan, 11-12. Wien, Köln and Wimar: Böhlau Verlag.

Alvarez-Veinguer, Aurora, Gunther Dietz, Dan-Paul Jozsa, and Thorsten Knauth, (eds.) 2009. *Islam in Education in European Countries: Pedagogical Concepts and Em-*

2 See http://www.redco.uni-hamburg.de/web/3480/3481/index.html

pirical Findings. Vol. 18, *Religious Diversity and Education in Europe*. Münster: Waxmann.

Asad, Talal. 2003. *Formations of the Secular: Christianity, Islam, Modernity. Cultural Memory in the Present*. Stanford: Stanford University Press.

Chidester, David. 1994. The Poetics and Politics of Sacred Space: Towards a Critical Phenomenology of Religion. In *Analecta Husserliana*, ed. by A.T. Tymieniecka, 211-31. Netherlands: Kluwer Academic Publishers.

Fiske, Edward B., and Helen F. Ladd. 2003. *Balancing Public and Private Resources for Basic Education: School Fees in Post-Apartheid South Africa*. In SAN03-03, Terry Sanford Institute of Public Policy.

Hefner, Robert W. and Muhammad Qasim Zaman, eds. 2007. *Schooling Islam. The Culture and Politics of Modern Muslim Education*. Princeton and Oxford: Princeton University Press.

Mandaville, Peter. 2007. Islamic Edcuation in Britain: Approaches to Religious Knowledge in a Pluralist Society. In *Schooling Islam. The Culture and Politics of Modern Muslim Education* ed. by Robert W. Hefner and Muhammad Qasim Zaman, 224-241. Princeton and Oxford: Princeton University Press.

Meijer, Wilna A.J. 2009. Tr*adition and Future of Islamic Education*. Münster: Waxmann.

Pohl, Florian. 2009. *Islamic Education and the Public Sphere. Today's Pesantren in Indonesia*. Vol 12 of Jugend-Religion-Unterricht. Beiträge zu einer dialogischen Religionspädagogik, Münster: Waxmann.

Plank, David N., and Gary Sykes. 1999. How Choice Changes the Education System: A Michigan Case Study. *International Review of Education / Internationale Zeitschrift für Erziehungswissenschaft / Revue de l'Education* 45 (5/6): 385-416.

Qadi al, Wadad. 2006. Education in Islam – Myths and Truths. *Comparative Education Review* 50 (3): 311-24.

Rahman, Fazlur. 1982. *Islam and Modernity: Transformation of an Intellectual Tradition*. Chicago: University of Chicago Press.

Waardenburg, Jacques. 1965. Some Institutional Aspects of Muslim Higher Education and their Relation to Islam. *Numen* 12 (2): 96-138.

Zaman, Muhammad Qasim. 2002. *The Ulama in Contemporary Islam: Custodians of Change*. Princeton: Princeton University Press.

Inga Niehaus

Emancipation or Disengagement?

Muslim Minorities and their Islamic Schools in Britain, the Netherlands and South Africa

Introduction

The past two decades have seen an expansion of private Islamic schools in various non-Muslim countries like Britain, the Netherlands and South Africa.[1]

Most Islamic schools are independent faith schools which offer primary and some also secondary education like many of the private Church schools in these countries. These schools largely follow the national curriculum and offer special Islamic instruction.[2]

The motivations to establish Islamic schools were manifold: Muslim educators and parents intended to provide high quality education for children in an Islamic environment and to affirm and strengthen the Islamic identity of children. Furthermore, they wanted to ensure that Muslim pupils are protected from what they regard as un-Islamic or secular influences within the society and that Muslim children are taught in single-sex schools at puberty.

In Europe the establishment of Islamic schools was a post-migration phenomenon and an expression of the increasing institutionalisation and public visibility of Islam in the 1980s and 1990s. In South Africa, on the other hand, the majority of Islamic schools emerged at a time when the general education system was experiencing a deep crisis in the 1980s. Due to national school boycotts and the dismantling of apartheid, hardly any formal education was taking place at public schools. The founders of the South African private Islamic schools intended to reinstate discipline, regular school lessons and ensure high academic performance.

The status and organization of Islamic schools varies considerably in the three countries. It depends on the structure of the education system, the legal and political settings, the relationship between church and state, the integration policies as well as the mobilisation and self-organization of Muslim minorities (Fetzer & Soper 2005, 147).[3] In Britain, the Netherlands and South Africa, the establish-

1 Britain has 125 Islamic schools (11 are voluntarily aided), the Netherlands 43 and South Africa around 70. These schools cater only for a small percentage of Muslim children (one to two percent of the school going Muslim population); http://www.education.gov.uk/schools/leadership/typesofschools/b0066996/faith-schools und http://www.deisbo.nl/?cat=1.

2 The research project focuses on the accredited Islamic schools, which teach in the national language and which offer the national school leaving certificates. There are a number of independent Islamic schools in various European countries which have been established to serve certain ethnic groups and which offer foreign school leaving certificates.

3 Fetzer and Soper (2005, 147) see the church-state relationship as the decisive factor which determines the institutionalisation of Islam: “In each country Muslims inherited

ment of Islamic schools was favoured by education laws and an educational system which supported denominational schools – especially Christian – for decades.

This article assesses critically how Islamic schools are mediating the ideal of creating a distinct Islamic ethos on the one hand, and meeting the requirements of the national curriculum and challenges of a multi-cultural society on the other hand. The leading questions will explore in which ways Islamic schools promote democratic citizenship education and how principals, teachers and learners perceive their role within society. Taking the aims of citizenship education into account, it is argued that faith schools in general are permeated by a religious ethos based on certain values, such as tolerance, and that they have put a particular emphasis on communicating their beliefs in the broader society (Parker-Jenkins et al. 2005).[4] For Farid Panjwani (2008, 292) the key question is what role education plays vis-à-vis citizenship in "minimizing any possible tension between national and religious – particularly Muslim – identities". Merry (2007, 56) states, that "Islamic schools claim to actively promote dual citizenship: one to the global Muslim community and one to the local culture".

In answering how citizenship education is implemented in Islamic schools and in which ways religious and civic identities are expressed, the article gives particular voice to educators, but considers primarily the learners, who are the recipients of a faith based education. The analysis is based on empirical research conducted in Islamic schools in South Africa, Britain and in the Netherlands.[5]

Religious identity formation within Islamic schools – creating an Islamic ethos and teaching Islam

In Britain, the Netherlands and South Africa the emphasis of Muslim schools is on educating children according to the values, norms and traditions of Islam as interpreted by the respective governing bodies, principals and teachers. This is achieved by, among others, offering special Islamic instruction, praying together, introducing special dress codes and by observing the Islamic calendar. Islamic schools in these countries are highly heterogeneous in terms of internal regulations and Islamic practices. Conservative schools often impose strict dress codes; they insist on complete gender separation and are orientated on a certain school of thought within Islam which permeates into school policies. In so called "liber-

---

a web of church-state interactions based on constitutional principles, legal practice, historical precedent, and foundational conceptions of the appropriate relationship between church and state. This combination of factors eventually determined how each state accommodated Muslims on the issues of religion in public schools, state aid to private Islamic schools, and, in part, mosque building."

4 Theoretically the article refers to discourses on the role of democratic citizenship education in multi-cultural societies and relationship between faith schools, especially Muslim schools, and social cohesion (see Jackson 2003; Merry 2007; Short 2002; Berkeley 2008).

5 The data collection was carried out between July 2006 and June 2009.

al" schools, the wearing of the headscarf is not compulsory and co-education is pursued while the National Curriculum is taught without exception.[6]

The Islamic subjects play a central role in creating a religious ethos and shaping religious identities at the schools. Islamic studies often include the transmission of basic knowledge of the practices and history of the faith, without elaborating on different schools of thought within Islamic theology and law. To give an example, the religious instruction syllabi of two Islamic high schools in Britain and South Africa which took part in the research, are developed by the religious teachers of the schools themselves, and are based primarily on the *Qur'an* and the *Sunnah*. Because of the different Islamic and cultural background of learners, the schools avoid teaching according to particular law schools (*madhāhib*). The emphasis lies on what they regard as 'basic Islamic knowledge' and on stressing the commonalities and not the differences of religious practices. The teaching material for Islamic Studies is drawn from various sources such as Muslim organizations and research institutes in England, the United States and South Africa, where Islamic schools exist and developed in a Muslim minority context.[7] One British high school recently introduced published, modern textbooks for Islamic studies which are designed for Muslim children in the West. Here, the learners are introduced to topics which support a plural and tolerant approach towards intra-Islamic differences, other religions and culturally diverse societies. Sections deal with among others, intra-Muslim differences (Shīʿa versus Sunni Islam), Muslim political participation and resistance against unjust governments, as well as rights and responsibilities of Muslims living in non-Muslim countries.[8]

In the Netherlands, the umbrella body for Islamic schools, ISBO (Islamitische Scholen Besturen Organisatie), was part of an initiative to improve the subject of Islamic Studies. The organization has produced a new curriculum for Islamic instruction integrating modern teaching methods and featuring an interactive and dialogical approach, which was introduced in the schools in 2007.

Religious instruction in many Islamic schools seems to be oriented towards the experiences of the children who live in a multicultural society and the subject includes aspects of citizenship education. To give one example: in one lesson in a British Islamic high school, the learners were taught that one of the principles of Islam, giving charity, has to be applied to all human beings, and learners were

---

6 In an early study Shadid and van Koningsveld (1992) distinguish in the Dutch context between conservative schools and liberal schools. Most of them were founded by local ethnic groups which where in a few cases affiliated with particular Islamic organizations.

7 The organizations which produce educational material used by the school for the Islamic studies syllabus are from the Islamic Foundation in England, IQRA in the United States and the Islamic studies syllabus developed in South Africa by the International Board of Educational Research and Resources. Those curricula follow a classical, rather conservative approach and do not include comparative religion or learning about different movements and school of thoughts within Islam.

8 See Ruqayyah Waris Maqsood: "Textbook Islamic Studies. Examining Religions: Islam", Heinemann Education, 2008 and "Islam in Today's World, revised Edition, Series: Religion in Focus: Moral Issues and ultimate Questions, Hodder Murray, 2008

encouraged to assist not only people in their faith community but also needy non-Muslim compatriots.[9]

The subject of Islamic studies within Islamic schools has two aims: Firstly, to unify those learners who come from different cultural and ethnic backgrounds into an imaginary *ummah* of same-believers. Secondly, the subject intends to prepare learners for the challenges they face within a plural society which often contradict their Islamic belief system.

Another area in which the distinctly religious character of the schools are promoted, is the attempt to Islamize the secular curriculum, or to teach it from an Islamic perspective. Popularised by Muslim academics and organizations in the late 1970s, the concept of the "Islamization of Knowledge" influenced founders of Islamic schools in Europe and South Africa. The aim was basically to reverse the domination of Western educational traditions and to bring Islam into secular subjects by re-writing textbooks and materials for teaching. There have been some initiatives by Muslim organizations like the International Board of Educational Research and Resources (IBERR), to produce material and guidelines for Islamic schools in the West, but most schools are, for various reasons, orientated towards teaching the respective National Curriculum. In many instances they are legally obliged to do so, such as in the Netherlands, where all Islamic schools are state funded and so too in Britain with the "voluntarily aided" Islamic schools. Most of the independent schools in Britain who would be able to determine their own syllabi for the subjects follow the National Curriculum since they have to take part in national exams and offer school leaving certificates. Nevertheless, there are considerable variations of how the National Curriculum is applied and in most subject areas it allows flexibility in terms of omitting aspects which are regarded as "un-Islamic" by some Muslim educators. The more conservative schools for example do not allow the teaching of music, dance and figurative arts which is part of the respective National Curricula. There are many example of how the National Curriculum is adapted to the Islamic context of the schools. In the Islamic high schools in Britain and South Africa, the teachers try individually to incorporate the Islamic or Muslim perspective into the secular subjects. An English teacher stated that she does it in two ways: she either chooses poems or literature which were written by a Muslim author or, if she has to teach the prescribed texts, like Shakespeare's Romeo and Juliet, the role and behaviour of the figures in the literature will be discussed from an Islamic perspective and related to the learners' experience of living in a Western society as Muslims.[10] Even in the South African schools, culturally and religiously sensitive literature is introduced, but from an Islamic angle. An English teacher explains: "...We try to introduce it in a different way. We say: 'Now this is how we are going to look at it' and bring in the Islamic viewpoint" (MK-3)[11]. Many Islam-

9 Participatory observation of a Religious Instruction class at an Islamic high school, 24 May 2007.

10 Interview with an English teacher of an Islamic high school in Great Britain, 24 May 2007.

11 Names of teachers, principals, learners and experts as well as schools are withheld to protect the identity of the interviewees. Personal details of the interviewees are documented by the author. The interviews were carried out between 2007-2009.

ic schools modify their art and music syllabi. Instead of drawing humans or animals, the learners are taught to do mosaics, design carpets and calligraphy, while in music, they are introduced to the singing of Islamic songs without using instruments, known as *nasheeds*.

Islamizing their lessons, means the teachers therefore primarily follow the National Curriculum and "add on" the Islamic or Muslim references or look for and introduce Islamic alternatives to certain subject topics. According to the principal of an Islamic high school in Britain, the "Islamization of the curriculum" plays no role in the curriculum development in his school, and he promotes a holistic understanding of knowledge. From his point of view, knowledge consists of a cognitive domain and affective domain. The affective side, or the so called "hidden curriculum", is strengthened through school prayers, religious studies and character development. In the principal's opinion the learners are doing well academically and they are also confident in their Islamic identity without the Islamization of the curriculum.[12]

In South African Islamic schools, the Islamization discourse was prominent and in the process of being re-discovered. I observed a renewed interest among directors, principals and teachers in the project to Islamize the curriculum and an emphasis on developing the Islamic ethos of the school. The main reason for this shift was the perceived preference of learners and parents for the so called secular subjects and academic performance over religious subjects. A Religious Studies teacher explains: "… our schools have become too secularized. There is too much emphasis on achieving those results in Maths, Physics … so they can go to university to study Medicine, to become a lawyer, to become an accountant … " (AL-1). According to a recently appointed principal of an Islamic high school in Cape Town, Islamization of knowledge is the "top priority" for him and he envisages an ideal situation where Arabic and Islamic studies have the same status as the secular subjects and Islam informs the syllabi of all subjects.[13]

The Islamization project is a means to lead the school to a distinctive Islamic character and identity which many educators regard as important for the development of the institution. The principal of an Islamic primary school in Durban brings the discourse to a point by stating that besides praying together and dressing in a particular way, "the question arises, 'What distinguishes you from any other school?'" (RJ-4)

Democratic citizenship and social cohesion

In Britain, the Netherlands and South Africa, Islamic schools are required to teach democratic citizenship as part of the National Curriculum. While in the European countries democratic citizenship education aims to enhance social cohesion and the integration of migrant communities, in South Africa it was introduced to support the nation-building process in a deeply divided society.

---

12 Interview with the principal of an Islamic high school in Great Britain, 7 July 2008.

13 See interview with the principal of an Islamic high school in South Africa, 9 October 2007.

Islamic schools in South Africa are obliged to teach democratic citizenship education since it is part of the post-apartheid National Curriculum. It is mainly taught within the subject of Life Orientation and deals with, among others, diversity, religious beliefs, human rights, rights and responsibilities of citizens, and personal issues. Islamic schools teach these topics from an Islamic point of view and remove what seems unacceptable to include, such as HIV-Aids education and sexual relationships between teenagers. In some schools, Life Orientation was combined with Islamic studies to ensure that the subject is taught from an Islamic perspective.

In light of an increasingly diverse, multicultural society, and the public and political 'integration debates', the Netherlands and Britain introduced the new statutory requirement to actively promote democratic citizenship and social cohesion in schools. [14] In the aftermath of 9/11 and the terror attacks in Europe in recent years, Islamic schools are being particularly scrutinised regarding the implementation of citizenship programmes.

Many Islamic schools have responded to these education policies and the negative public image by starting to engage actively in social cohesion programmes and promoting democratic citizenship – especially those which receive state funds. The need to open up to society is also reflected in the self-understanding of educators in Islamic schools. A principal of an Islamic high school, which recently gained voluntarily aided status, explained that he wishes to nurture children as "good citizens" who are confident in their ability to communicate with the broader society.[15] To give practise to this approach the school engages in a variety of exchange programmes with non-Muslim schools and introduced a community outreach programme. The school has also started with so called "extended services" to the community. It is planned to open the sports and recreational facilities to community groups and to offer adult education and religious studies classes (*madrassa*). In order to facilitate inclusion and integration, the school participates in a "citizenship and social cohesion" programme which is compulsory for all state funded schools which includes, among others, long-term exchange programmes with other schools.

In the Dutch case, the issue of Islamic schools and social cohesion is debated in a different way: here the focus lies on keeping up with required academic and pedagogical standards to promote socio-economic integration.[16] Many Islamic schools attracted academically weak and problematic pupils from public schools. The parents hoped that their children would perform better at an exclusively Muslim school. The reason for the under-performance of Muslim children is often insufficient Dutch language skills. The Muslim children who attend Islamic

---

14 A new Bill brought before parliament by the Dutch Secretary of Education in 2006 makes it compulsory for schools in the Netherlands to teach democratic citizenship education. In Britain, the citizenship curriculum was introduced in the schools in 2002 and in 2007 the maintained schools were given the duty to actively promote social cohesion (Education and Inspection Act 2006).

15 Interview with the principal of an Islamic high school in Great Britain, 7 July 2008.

16 In the Dutch context Islamic schools are often referred to as "black schools" since over 90 percent of the pupils are from ethnic minority background. For further discussion on the term "black" and "white" school see Vedder 2006.

schools are mostly the children of second or third generation Turkish or Moroccan immigrants and Dutch is hardly spoken at home. The acquisition of language skills is therefore the priority of most of the educators at Islamic schools. In many Islamic schools in the Netherlands a gradual shift occurred, from focusing on identity formation, to improving academic standards and quality of education.[17] In the Dutch situation, the question of social cohesion is therefore not primarily a question of religious identity and democratic citizenship, but rather a question of socio-economic status and integration. In order to promote social cohesion and prevent the "ghettoization" of Islamic schools, a small number of Islamic schools in the Netherlands are part of a so called "broad schools" which means they share a building with other non-Muslim schools. Broad schools offer new opportunities for teachers, parents and pupils to enter into an institutionalized exchange with those who are not part of their religious, cultural or ethnic community.

Democratic citizenship education and interfaith issues in South African Islamic schools are primarily dealt with in an abstract and theoretical way and only have a practical dimension if the school engages in exchange programmes with non-Muslim schools or youth and community organizations. In the schools I researched, exchange initiatives were not part of a structured school programme and only happened occasionally. Nevertheless, all of the schools are involved in some kind of charity work. Pupils learn to take responsibility for their co-citizens by distributing food parcels to the poor and assisting at crèches and old age homes. If and in which way a particular school engages with the wider community is primarily dependent on the self-understanding and religious discourses within the school, as well as the socio-political and cultural context in which the school operates.

Religious and civic identity – voices from learners

In research on Islamic schools little emphasis was given to learners' choices, their religious convictions, their attitude towards the Islamic school they attend and the society they live in. As part of the research, questionnaires were handed out to learners, aged 15-17, from Islamic high schools.[18] The answers, nevertheless, do not allow any conclusion of how the religious and civic identities of learners are shaped by the particular school. The home environment, mosques and other institutions are also important sites of religious socialization and transmission of Is-

17 According to the acting director of ISBO, the generation who started Islamic schools in the Netherlands twenty years ago was primarily interested in creating a protected environment for Muslim children where their Islamic identity could develop. This changed over the years and today educators and parents regard the improvement of academic standard as the most important prerogative (interview with the interim director of ISBO, 10 March 2008, Utrecht)

18 Questionnaires were handed out to learners of Islamic schools in South Africa and Britain and the Netherlands (the latter are not yet analyzed). The sample from England consists of 59 questionnaires from one Islamic high school, the sample from South Africa of 120 questionnaires from two Islamic high schools.

lamic knowledge. But the results of the questionnaires show if and in which way learners identify with the school they attend, and whether the mono-faith environment impacts on their experience with people of other or no faith and their attitude towards a plural society. Although the socio-political and cultural context of Islamic schools in Britain and South Africa are very different, the answers of their respective learners are remarkably similar. For most learners, religion is most or very important in their personal lives. Religion is seen as a guide and a means of giving purpose and direction to life. Learners further relate the role religion plays in their personal lives to the Islamic context of the school. Most of the British and South African learners regard the Islamic environment and ethos, or the fact that they can practise their religion, as positive aspects of their school, followed by the good and supportive relationship between teachers and students. For most learners the school seems to be a place where they feel protected and accepted as the following quote from a 15-year old British girl illustrates: "I like my school because we are all of the same religion, we all feel equal and nobody is ashamed or shy of practising their religion" (38MHg11).

As negative aspects of the school, the most frequently raised issues among British learners are the lack of school outings and extra-mural activities. Therefore it is not so much what is happening within the lessons and regular school hours, but more what is not happening that is of concern to learners. It is furthermore an indication that the schools are not enabling learners to engage in activities outside of school and prescribed lessons out of lack of resources or internal policies. In the South African context it was instead the lack of facilities in school as well as the performance of certain teachers which were critically evaluated by learners.

Pupils in both countries recall diverse experiences with people of other faiths – positive as well as negative. Some of the encounters relate to personal experiences, but other learners would make general statements and reproduced stereotypes. Many learners state that they have a positive relationship with their neighbours and people in their community in particular. A South African learner recalls the following experience: "I never thought that they would be so friendly and accommodating, but they are. All my neighbors are non-Muslims and they are extremely friendly and understanding. When we have get-togethers they don't bring any alcohol and the food is kept separately" (24AFf11). Learning from one another and discussing religious issues with people from different faith backgrounds are further mentioned as positive experiences by British as well as South African learners.

Regarding their negative experiences with people of other faiths, the most frequently recalled incidents by British students are acts of racism and Islamophobia, as well as stigmatization and discrimination. Often these experiences are brought into a political context and related to the negative public image of Islam since 9/11 and 7/7. The stigmatization is felt by pupils in particular in public. One British learner criticizes the reactions by others when they see her veiled mother: "My mum wears a purdah and covers her face, and when she goes into the town centre people stare at her like she's some sort of (an) alien. It is very annoying and uncomfortable. I feel people do this because they don't have knowledge about Islam" (23MHg11). In the South African context, learners mentioned disrespectful and discriminating incidents as well, but more important was the different lifestyle and values systems of people of other or no faith. A student from South Africa states: "When you tend to have friends in other religions they are allowed to do stuff that you are not allowed to do in Islam and that is the only downside when having friends from other religions" (6AFf11).

Regarding their civic identity, most British and South African students state that they have a sense of belonging in the society they are living in. The reasons given predominantly relate to a perceived strong Muslim community which they are part of as the following quote by a British learner indicates: "There are a lot of Muslims living in this society and there are mosques which we attend" (31MHg11). A South African pupil even states that he has a sense of belonging "because the society is made up predominantly by Muslims" (21AFm11). Taking into account that the Muslim population of South Africa does not even account for two percent of the general population, it seems that the learner in his interpretation of the term equates "society" with "community".

British learners' attitudes are strongly shaped by the multi-cultural and multi-faith environment of the community or city they are living in. When asked whether they believe that people of different faiths can live together peacefully in one society, one learner responded: "(This city) is a multi-faith society and (it) shows that people from different religions can live together" (3MHb11). There were only a few learners who were sceptical about the possibility of living together peacefully in a multi-cultural society. One pupil was critical of the ability of society to cope with plurality: "I think that society needs to be taught how to be tolerant of other religions. Then only will we be able to live together and integrate. Society is still wary of differences" (16MHb11). Although learners from South Africa recalled positive situations where people of different religious and ethnic backgrounds live peacefully together in a neighbourhood, the question was answered in a more hypothetical approach. Many learners placed the possibility of living together under certain preconditions, for example, that religious groups respect and do not judge each other. South African learners were also more critical, and a number of them did not believe that people of different faiths could live together peacefully, arguing that such a situation would lead to conflict and fighting.

To sum up the results of the questionnaire; the learners show a strong attachment to collective identities formed along religious lines. This finds its expression in their relationship with the Islamic school they attend where "sameness" and the feeling of "being one family" is emphasised, but also in the society at large where a sense of belonging primarily arises in the context of a visible and strong Muslim community and the existence of Muslim institutions and places of worship which provide for religious and communal needs.

The relationship and experience with people of other or no faith is ambivalent. There are positive relationships with personal friends and neighbours which are characterized by mutual respect, tolerance and support. On the other hand there are experiences of conflict and confrontation which are shaped by being discriminated against, being treated disrespectfully and, especially in the British context, being exposed to racist or anti-Islamic attitudes and attacks.

Conclusion

The British, Dutch and South African Islamic schools which were part of the research have in common an openness to fully participate in the plural society they are part of. But one has to bear in mind that the institutions I gained access to, are those which already hold more liberal and progressive views in terms of religious attitudes and pedagogical practice. There are also those schools which are more secluded and do not promote exchange with the larger society. But the schools which were part of the research hold prominent positions within the national umbrella bodies of Islamic schools and therefore one can regard them as being part of the mainstream. Their views and examples of good practice most likely permeate through to other schools.

Regarding the voices of the learners in the questionnaires, the answers vary considerably, but there are certain tendencies which became visible in the analysis: experiences of learners with people of other or no faith takes place mainly outside the schools on the streets and mostly in the neighbourhoods. This is an indication that the school is not yet a place of inter-religious exchange and learning. The need to create forums for inter-religious and inter-communal dialogue and exchange is further reflected in the learner's responses: The students feel predominantly positive about the multi-cultural community or society they are living in, regarding it as a site of learning about and from each other as well as building friendships and establishing good relations with fellow citizens. But at the same time, due to the negative public image of Islam, many of them feel victimized and discriminated against. For the South African learners it is less the negative public responses which affect their civic identity, but more feeling alienated by norms and values of a majority society they cannot completely identify with. Many learners seem to be ambivalent about their role within society: On the one hand they regard their school and community as a "safe haven" where religion can be lived and practised without compromises and where they are protected from discrimination and stigmatization. On the other hand they want to be active citizens of a plural society. The question is, whether they are able to merge their religious and civic identities and develop their multiple belongings within the multi-cultural and multi-faith environment they are living in.

In which ways Muslim schools are able to create an Islamic ethos and promote Islamic values and norms is primarily dependent on the educational policies of the specific country, as well as on the ideological and religious orientation of the governing body, principals and teachers. In terms of creating a distinct Islamic identity, the research shows that the Islamic schools are diverse in their religious approaches, which are visible in the particular rules and regulations that pupils and teachers have to follow as well as the educational goals the schools are pursuing. Dutch Islamic schools often find it difficult to create and uphold an Islamic ethos due to the fact that a high percentage of teachers are non-Muslim.

On the other side, these schools seem to equip their pupils better to engage with the broader society since inter-faith dialogue happens on a daily basis between Muslim learners and non-Muslim teachers. The British and South African Islamic schools on the other hand, are more homogeneous with most of the children and teachers being from South Asian backgrounds. Culturally and religiously the South Asian heritage is important for the syllabi of the subjects which are taught, including Islamic studies.

Regarding the concept of Islamizing the curriculum, the British and Dutch schools in this study do not perceive it as a priority of their activities. The curriculum at these schools does not differ much from that at public schools. Instead of Islamizing the entire syllabi and teaching materials, it seems to be important for educators in all disciplines to use Islamic references and examples in the context of secular subjects. The emphasis of the schools is clearly to provide Muslim children with a sound academic education which enables them to cope with the requirements of a professional life or to proceed to further and higher education. This indicates that there has been a shift in discourses within Muslim educational organizations and institutions from religious identity formation to providing an excellent academic education within or oriented toward the mainstream education system. Integration into society and the labour market seems to be the priority for Islamic schools, at least for those who actively promote social cohesion. The Islamic environment of the school is not seen anymore as a means to protect children's religious identity against the un-Islamic influences of the larger society, but as a tool to prepare them for their role as active citizens and the challenges they are going to face in the larger society.

In the South African Islamic schools, which are less publicly scrutinised in terms of integration efforts than their European counterparts, the development of a distinct Islamic curriculum and ethos is a prominent part of their internal endeavours in an attempt to uplift the status of religious and spiritual education.

The case studies show that Islamic schools are sites of ongoing discourses where religious traditions and practices are debated, reviewed and changed to respond to the local or national context and to the educational requirements of the specific society. The school boards, which consist of members from different ethnic background and Islamic traditions, are required to develop a vision of the school and determine the religious ethos the school intends to pursue. In doing so, they need to overcome differences related to their cultural and religious backgrounds. These processes are important in promoting emancipation and integration into the society by developing a localized understanding of the 'Islamic way of life' which they want to live and pass on to Muslim children. Often, the debates which take place within Islamic schools are being carried into the broader Muslim society and initiate new discourses which support emancipation processes of religious minorities.

References

Berkeley, Rob with Savita Vij. 2008. *Right to divide? Faith schools and community cohesion.* London: The Runneymede Trust.

Fetzer, Joel S., and Christopher J. Soper. 2005. *Muslims and the state in Britain, France and Germany*. New York: Cambridge University Press.

Jackson, Robert. 2003. Citizenship, religious and cultural diversity and education. In *International perspectives on citizenship, education and religious diversity*, ed. Robert Jackson, 1-28. London and New York: Routledge Falmer.

Merry, Michael S. 2007. *Culture, identity and Islamic schooling. A philosophical approach*. New York: Palgrave & Macmillan.

Panjwani, Farid. 2008. Religion, citizenship and hope: civic virtues and education about Muslim traditions. In *Sage handbook of education for citizenship and democracy*, ed. James Arthur, Ian Davies and Carol Hahn, 292-304. London: Sage Publications.

Parker-Jenkins, Marie, Dimitra Hartas and Barrie A. Irving. 2005. *In Good faith. Schools, religion and public funding*. Aldershot: Ashgate.

Shadid, Wasif, and Pieter Sjoerd van Koningsveld. 1992. Islamic primary schools. In *Islam in Dutch society: Current developments and future prospects*, ed. Wasif Shadid and Pieter Sjoerd van Koningsveld, 107-122. Kampen: Kok Pharos.

Short, Geoffrey. 2002. Faith-based schools: A threat to social cohesion? *Journal of Philosophy of Education* 36 (4): 559-572.

Vedder, Paul. 2006. Black and white schools in the Netherlands. *European Education* 38 (2): 36-49.

Yusef Waghid

Critical Islamic Pedagogy

Possibilities for Cultivating Democratic Citizenship and Cosmopolitanism in Muslim Schools

On some of the limitations of a philosophy of Islamic education

I proceed from earlier works (Waghid 1996a, 1996b) which specifically dealt with a distinctive conception of a philosophy of Islamic education for three reasons: First, the word *falsafa* (philosophy) does not appear in the Qur'an (the primary source for Islamic education); second, a philosophy of Islamic education does not contain only a body of knowledge which embeds the ontological, epistemological and ethical premises of Islam, because philosophy can also be considered an activity which addresses major problems which one can then explore for their implications for pedagogy; and third, if a philosophy of Islamic education were to exist, it would have to comprise multiple derivatives, as there is not one universal, absolute understanding of Islamic theory and practice – in this sense one would have to refer to philosophies of Islamic education. My understanding of a philosophy of education as an activity is situated in the view that Muslim thinkers throughout Islam's intellectual epochs used particular modes of inquiry to pursue exegeses, whether through *tafsīr* (exegetical analysis), *ta'wīl* (deep exploration) and/or *ijtihād* (rigorous mindful action). In a way, the latter practices can be considered as constitutive of a philosophy of education, because through these actions major problems or issues are examined and then their pedagogical implications can be determined.

However, I do not wish to talk about a philosophy of Islamic education for the reasons stated above. Rather, I want to answer the question as to what education can do to remedy some of the problems and/or challenges we encounter today, with specific reference to doctrinaire thinking. And, if through education one hopes to come up with plausible reasons as to why certain practices ought to be enacted, then I cannot delink such a discussion from what it means to embark on critical education. This brings me to the issue of what constitutes a critical Islamic pedagogy.

Towards a critical Islamic pedagogy

My use of the word 'critical' has some connection with a transformative, liberatory politics. To put it differently: a critical pedagogy requires one to look at a situation often dominated by exclusion, marginalisation and repression, and then to offer possibilities to change such a distorted situation. This is what the Prophet of Islam did through his *Sunnah* (lived experiences). His concern with the oppression of some of the Arabs by exploitative aristocrats made human freedom, a yearning concern for liberation and equality for all, a priority. So, formulating a critical Islamic pedagogy implies that in the first place teaching and learning have to be empowering, liberatory and deliberatively engaging. Invoking a critical pedagogy essentially implies that one has to move away from taking things at face value, or to be satisfied with some metaphysical explanation of an event. Instead, becoming critical means that one has to engage the other in an ongoing conversation – a conversation that would eventually secure the participants' right to initiate free speech and choice in the topics of the conversation, the right to take into question what has been said, and the right to do things not dismissive of the other's presence. It is for this reason that I now show how concepts which have been traditionally associated with Islamic education, namely *tarbiyyah* (nurturing), *ta'līm* (instruction) and *ta'dīb* (good action) can lead to different ways of human action when guided by a critical pedagogy.

Firstly, following a critical pedagogy, *tarbiyyah* (nurturing) cannot just be narrowly connected to the nurturing and rearing of children according to an ethics of appropriate or good conduct. This is an aim in itself. But cultivating young people according to a liberatory ethics goes along with inculcating in them respect for the probable strength of reasons, the readiness to challenge ill-conceived ideas, and a willingness to listen to the views of others, while simultaneously taking one another's points of view into systematic controversy (MacIntyre 1988). When one acts in such a respectful manner, one is said to have acquired the virtue of respect, that is, *tarbiyyah*, which would then enable one to act on the basis of a concern for human freedom. Often *tarbiyyah* is wrongly associated with excessive rote learning and memorisation. I am not denying the transformative potential of rote learning – often, committing a verse of the Qur'an to memory could hasten its critical implementation. For instance, the verse which deals with Muslims having to interact with one another could result in actions which can lead to an improvement in human relations. But focusing on rote learning only could also retard or reduce an emphasis on critical, transformative action – one is too busy committing several verses to memory to allow sufficient time for critical reflection.

Moreover, if respect is central to the exercise of *tarbiyyah* (nurturing), then having a critical approach to respect brings to the fore that a learner cannot just be satisfied or agree with everything he or she has been taught. If it makes sense to respect a person for being a teacher then it equally makes sense to respect the reasons that person proffers. And, if these reasons are perhaps not convincing or if at times they are ill-conceived, then respect demands that one holds the other person accountable for the unconvincing arguments being offered. Not doing so would be to treat someone with disrespect, that is, to consider his or her views uncritically. Thus, having a critical approach to *tarbiyyah* (nurturing) implies that a teacher should engender in learners a spirit of open questioning, disagreement and dissonance. In this way nurturing would be respectful, open and critical. Here I have in mind learners being reared to adopt questioning attitudes, to develop the ability to disagree after being socialised with some aspects of Islamic epistemology, and to oppose an unconvincing position. This links up with my second point.

Secondly, on reconceptualising *taʿlīm* (instruction), it is clear that it cannot solely be linked to narrow instruction for that in the first instance would subvert the dialectical relationship between teaching and learning. Teaching cannot just be about instruction or transmission, because that would assume that students are dead subjects who do not construct or even have the ability to construct meanings. In fact, to 'bank' information is tantamount to simple transmission which does not prepare learners for the demanding tasks of an ever-changing world. This is so because the information which is being transmitted is supposed to be consumed by passive people who are told mostly to consider the world from others' points of view. However, when students construct meanings, they engage with the thoughts of others, including those of their teachers. They (learners) are afforded the pedagogical spaces to break with what is supposedly fixed, certain and completed. In this way teaching and learning, or rather pedagogy, becomes a deliberative process. Hence *taʿlīm* (instruction) can most saliently be reconceptualised as reflective and deliberative engagement, which in many ways has a concomitant link with *shūrā* (mutual interaction). But then, following a critical pedagogy, such deliberative encounters are not just policed conversations between teachers and students. Often provocations that can lead to distressful and belligerent moments in the deliberations can ensue (Callan 1997). Such a situation would then allow teachers and students to explore other multiple possibilities during meaning constructions, because belligerence would allow all parties the possibility to take more risks than before. Being prepared to engage in more risk-taking behaviour is exactly what a critical pedagogy has in mind. This is because taking risks implies that the boundaries are more relaxed and participants in the deliberation are more willing and open to achieve the unexpected or the improbable. In short, actions such as *tafakkur* and *tadabbur* (the two specifically mentioned in the Qur'an) would acquire a more reflective orientation. That would imply that teachers and students would explore one another's points of view more openly and freely. Imagine a teacher creating conditions in a classroom whereby students engage with more freedom and belligerence. In such a situation the possibility for the expression and cultivation of more enriched views arises, because students are not constrained or limited in their encounters with others. I am not suggesting that teachers and students should have unconstrained freedom, for that *per se* would invariably jeopardise the endless possibilities risk taking can effect. Imagine that learners in a *madrassah* (school) should be taught to develop the capacity to look at things differently and actually conjure up ways to condemn selectively the atrocities perpetrated against Muslims but do not learn to be outraged by harmful actions inflicted on non-Muslims. This kind of freedom should not be permitted on the grounds that justice cannot be partially applied. In fact, as soon as an injustice is done towards other people, freedom of action and thought can no longer be left unhindered. In any case, ensuring that justice is done to all persons irrespective of their religious or cultural orientation is in fact to develop a kind of critical stance with respect to them as persons.

Thirdly, *ta'dīb* (good action) cannot just be exclusively associated with doing good without raising human consciousness about and against injustices. This in turn implies that one recognises injustices and actually does something about changing, rectifying or modifying a situation – that is, transforming it. Thus, when *ta'dīb* (good action) is considered as the discipline of the body, soul and mind in order to act with justice and to ensure that everything is in its right and proper place (Al-Attas 1991), then such a view in itself cannot be divorced from performing acts of universal justice. In this way, *ta'dīb* (good action) becomes a form of social activism, which is an idea not foreign to the Qur'anic injunction (*'amal al-ṣāliḥāt*, the doing of righteous deeds) to be of benefit to society at large. By implication, what is learned in a Muslim school is in fact enacted in the broader society with the aim of transforming a distressing situation – a matter of recognising a societal ill and actually doing something about changing it. Nowadays, the world is witnessing unacceptable human rights violations and atrocities committed against human beings. *Ta'dīb* (good action) seems to be a desirable practice which can raise the consciousness of people against forms of human rights violations and atrocious acts perpetrated against humanity. Certainly in some communities on the African continent societal ills such as perpetual genocide, rape, mass enslavement, political dictatorships, xenophobic violence and religious intolerance are calling for some educative intervention which in (Muslim) schools would teach some of Africa's people about what it means to act with compassion and justice.

In essence, the above-mentioned concepts do not have to be practised in isolation. In fact, a coherent and interdependent enactment of them would be more viable to achieve some of the most salient aims of Islamic education, such as engendering in people an affinity for responsible action (*'amal al-ṣāliḥāt*), preparing people to engage in civic deliberation and criticism (*shūrā*), and attuning people to the requirements of achieving social and universal justice (*'adl*). Understandably, these goals of Islamic education can most appropriately be achieved through a critical pedagogy. I shall now explore the implications of such a critical Islamic pedagogy for schooling, in particular by showing how such pedagogy can engender a defensible ethics of democratic citizenship and cosmopolitanism.

On the possibility of cultivating democratic citizenship and cosmopolitanism in Muslim schools

Now that I have shown that a critical Islamic pedagogy can be lived out through *tarbiyyah* (responsible action), *ta'līm* (deliberative and reflective engagement) and *ta'dīb* (social activism) – note the change in meanings – I turn my attention to a discussion of the possibility of engendering democratic citizenship and cosmopolitanism.

The question arises: what constitutes democratic citizenship education? On the one hand, to act democratically implies doing so in relation to and in association with others. One does not act alone. One is governed by a justification of one's views to others who might find one's views either acceptable or unacceptable. Similarly others' enactments are determined by persuasions to the self. In other words, to act democratically is to exercise one's individualism in association with others' subjectivities and *vice versa.* In a way, to act democratically is to do things in an inter-subjective way without necessarily denying the subjectivity of the self. On the other hand to be a citizen is to be governed by norms of society and the world. This means that one exercises one's rights in relation to the society or group to which one belongs and simultaneously to universal norms of appropriate ethical conduct.

Following this, democratic citizenship education takes into account the following actions: Firstly, students are taught to respect the life-worlds of others, which involves demonstrating a judicious tolerance of ways of living that are perhaps deeply threatening to one's own. Subsequently, students are taught to find a civil space for the sharing of commonalities and disagreements. Respecting the life-worlds of others involves trying not to impose one's own view of the world and how it should be lived out by others, but rather to recognise that others have a right to be different and to live their differences. The point about respecting the life-worlds of others is that it involves experiencing them as they present themselves and not fitting them into some kind of preconceived picture of one's own imaginings – that is, what others should be like.

Secondly, students are afforded opportunities to engage in public deliberation. They are taught about their right to engage in various speech acts, to initiate new topics and to ask for justification of the presuppositions of the conversation (Benhabib 2002, 107). Public deliberation takes place when students speak their minds (but only up to the point where injustice to others begins) and no one has the right to silence dissent (Callan 1997, 215). Public deliberation is different from debate and discussion or conversation. Although debate involves offering arguments for or against points of view it does not necessarily imply that people should reach some consensus or dissensus about the topic under scrutiny of a debate – that is, a debate does not necessarily have a fixed outcome. Similarly, discussion or conversation can go on endlessly without participants reaching any form of conclusion. In fact, participants in discussion do not have to be attentive to one another's points of view. The point about public deliberation is that there can be a temporary conclusion, whether consensus or dissensus, with the possibility that something new and different can emerge. In a way a public deliberation is reflexive in the sense that there need not be any fixed, final or conclusive outcome. The possibility should always exist for new meanings to unfold.

Thirdly, students are taught about their right to the protection of life, liberty and property, the right to freedom of conscience and certain associational rights (Benhabib 2002, 163-164). Students are taught that, to enjoy these rights, they should accept appropriate responsibility for the rights of others, and not just make a fuss about their own rights (Callan 1997, 73). Thus to be educated as a democratic citizen involves being initiated into a process of recognising the legitimate rights of others, whether they are social, cultural, political or economic rights. The point about recognising these rights is concomitant with the responsibility to ensure that these rights are attained and that one does not merely give lip service to them. For instance, Muslim learners should not just be taught that their religious right of practising Islam is important but also that they should uphold these rights.

And, what does cosmopolitan education entail? It seems as if the democratic citizenship education agenda is restricted in the sense that it considers action only from the vantage point of individuals or groups that need to respond to other individuals or groups in a national context. So the question remains: how can cosmopolitanism extend the democratic citizenship education agenda? Whereas democratic citizenship functions mostly within the boundaries of its memberships, emphasising citizens' duties and responsibilities towards other individuals and groups, cosmopolitanism recognises the rights of others to 'universal hospitality'. Simply put, others have the right to be treated hospitably. For Benhabib hospitality, in a neo-Kantian sense, "is not to be understood as a virtue of sociability, as the kindness and generosity one may show to strangers who come to one's land or who become dependent on one's act of kindness through circumstances of nature or history; hospitality is a right that belongs to all human beings as far as we view them as potential participants in a world republic" (Benhabib 2006, 22). Such a right to hospitality imposes an obligation on democratic states and their citizens not to deny refuge and asylum to those whose intentions are peaceful, particularly if refusing them would cause them harm (Benhabib 2006, 25). So, if the intentions of immigrant entrepreneurs are peaceful, it would be considered their right to be treated hospitably and it would be seen as the democratic citizens' obligation to ensure that these immigrants enjoy such a right.

I shall now look in more detail at what such a cosmopolitan approach to Islamic education entails. Firstly, considering that cosmopolitanism involves the right to temporary residence on the part of the "stranger who comes to our land" (Benhabib 2006, 22), it follows from this that Muslim schools cannot deny access to children of immigrant communities. Secondly, "the right to have rights" prohibits states from denying individuals citizenship rights and state protection against murder, extermination, enslavement, deportation and other inhumane acts such as persecution (whether political, cultural or religious) (Benhabib 2006, 25). So, if immigrant children wish to wear their headscarves in public schools, following "the right to have rights" notion, these children cannot be discriminated against. Asking these children to remove their scarves, which they might consider as important to their religious and cultural identity, would be a matter of treating them unjustly on the grounds that their right to be different would be undermined. Thirdly, to act as a cosmopolitan implies not just exercising democratic iterations – those linguistic, legal, cultural and political repetitions-in-transformation (Benhabib 2006, 48). A democratic iteration is characterised by acts of reappropriation and reinterpretation. One simply has to engage in an unending debate with others through democratic self-reflection and self-determination and public defensiveness. It is a profound sense of democratic reflexivity which appeals to recursive questioning and reiterated justifications. For instance, consider the "scarf affair" which Benhabib uses to expound on democratic reiterations in France in 1989 which started with the expulsion of three scarf-wearing Muslim girls from their school (Benhabib 2006, 49). Seven years later there was a mass exclusion of 23 Muslim girls from their school. Throughout the 1990s and well into the twenty-first century confrontations between school authorities and young Muslim girls and women continued. Although the intervention of the French authorities to ban the wearing of the veil in the schools at first seemed like an attempt of a progressive state bureaucracy to modernise the backward-looking customs of a group, this intervention cascaded into a series of democratic iterations: from the intense debate among the French public about the meaning of wearing the scarf, to the self-defence of the girls involved and the re-articulation of the meaning of their actions, to the encouragement of other immigrant women to wear their headscarves to the workplace.

Basically women have learned to 'talk back [to the state]' – a matter of engaging and contesting the meanings of the Islamic practices they want to uphold. To my mind, democratic iteration is precisely what we require in Muslim schools to make sure that the education system has been subjected to democratic reflexivity and recursive justifications, which means listening to the views of those involved in the implementation of the education system and then to 'talk back'. Only then can doctrinaire thinking in education be avoided, because performing democratic reflexivity and recursive justifications would render the educational project as a narrative which is always in the making, to borrow a formulation from Maxine Greene (1995). Talking back does not have to be non-belligerent or non-distressful just because we think we need to continue the conversation. Sometimes we can articulate our reasons with a sense of roughness and distress, even to the extent of making the other feel uncomfortable; otherwise our conversations would be unduly policed (by ourselves and others) and often frivolous or useless mediations. Hence, the notion of doctrinaire thinking does not sit easily with democratic iterations, because the latter always subjects the self-mastery and mastery of the subject to incredulity (that is, an inability to believe) or a loss of faith in the regimes of mastery. Rather than being a route to mastery (a form of doctrinaire thinking), Islamic education might be better considered as a condition of "constant apprenticeship" (Rikowski in Edwards 2006, 277). If Islamic education could be considered to be the continuous perpetuation of apprenticeships, iterative learning communities would evolve in which teachers and learners engage in meaningful work; subjects studied would generate new understandings; and learning would be mediated through active experimentation (Alexander in Gray 2006, 320). In fact, learners would be encouraged to be reflective about why their way of thinking is desirable (or not), and these communities would be performing teaching as opposed to training, and engaging in genuine learning as opposed to mechanical learning (Alexander in Gray 2006, 321). Through such a cosmopolitan imaginary, teaching would be understood as a moral activity that seeks to strengthen the moral agent within, empowering students to make moral choices more intelligently on their own, which may involve some training but should culminate in understanding and independence that are expressed concretely (Gray 2006, 321).

In essence, cosmopolitanism and its concomitant agenda of hospitality and democratic iterations which ought to be afforded to other human beings (especially from immigrant communities) in many ways complement the duties and responsibilities associated with the activities of democratic citizens. Unless countries and their peoples recognise the rights of others to be treated with dignity and respect, without suppressing their rights, the achievement of justice will remain remote from the minds and hearts of people.

Now the question arises: What seems to be wrong with doctrinaire thinking? Doctrinaire thinking is a technologically deterministic view of education which reduces the purpose of education (as we find in outcomes-based education in South Africa today) to a regime of "mastery" (Edwards 2006, 277). Mastery represents a form of completion, an end to learning, and points towards a position of finality and closure. Moreover, attempts at mastery (such as through outcomes-based education) – increasingly inscribed in discourses of standards and targets – only point to the inability to master (Edwards 2006, 277). Nowadays one often witnesses the escalated promotion of some Muslims to the position of religious leaders because their performances are deemed excellent through the game of audit – that is, having the ability to recite the Qur'an, to communicate in the Arabic language, and to offer devotional prayers at important Muslim ceremonies. Yet it is nevertheless true that some of them (simplistically put) might not even be able to convincingly articulate a coherent argument or even a sentence, or to critically and playfully engage with the untidiness and complexity of the current Islamic education situation. They fail to destabilise (or what Lyotard refers to as to paralogise) performative language games in an imaginative way (Lyotard 1984). They attempt to master Islamic discourses, but actually fail in their attempt to do so. How many learners have left our Muslim schools having being told that they have mastered the outcomes, yet they go into the world with an inability to contend with the challenges of modernity and postmodernity? Here I specifically think of learners who might have acquired the prowess of reciting the Qur'an and offering invocations in Arabic, yet do not know how to engage in forms of public deliberation or even what it means to respect the dignity of other human beings.

With such an understanding of democratic citizenship and cosmopolitan education in mind, one may well ask how a critical Islamic pedagogy can engender such virtues in Muslim schools with reference to reflexive actions such as *ummah* (community), *shūrā* (public deliberation) and *ʿaql* (contemplative thought).

Reflexive actions and their implications for the virtues of democratic citizenship and cosmopolitan education

I have argued that a critical Islamic pedagogy could cultivate democratic citizenship and cosmopolitan education. With reference to *ummah* (community), *shūrā* (public deliberation) and *ʿaql* (contemplative thought) I shall now show how reflexive actions can frame such a critical Islamic pedagogy in Muslim schools, primarily because these concepts are considered to be constitutive of any form of Islamic education, whether *tarbiyyah* (nurturing), *taʿlīm* (instruction) or *taʾdīb* (good action).

Firstly, *ummah* (community) entails that individuals are actively engaged with the unending struggle and responsibility for the improvement of the economic, social and political aspects of life (Alibasic 1999, 234). In this sense *ummah* is concerned with a long-term and inconclusive commitment to the improvement of human conditions, with maintaining "the freedom and duty of criticism and monitoring of government", accepting "criticism in good spirit", facilitating "peaceful change", and with remaining united through consensus and disagreement (Alibasic 1999, 237 – 42, 292) – a clear indication of a community's obligation to be critical, to develop self-critical attitudes, and to live peacefully. Moreover, community or *ummah* is also concerned with a plurality of human ideas and not denying the rights of others (Alibasic 1999, 249, 271) – thus indicating its tolerance of difference. Considering that both the cultivation of community or *ummah* and a critical Islamic pedagogy have in mind the achievement of responsible, just action it can be argued that community or *ummah* can be a means through which a critical Islamic pedagogy can be realised.

Secondly, the Qur'an does not only encourage people to act justly as a global community, but it also suggests a way of *shūrā* (public deliberation) as to how people ought to engage. What does the Qur'an say about *shūrā*? In fact, an entire chapter (*sūrah*) of the Qur'an is devoted to a discussion of *shūrā*. The core verse which relates specifically to *shūrā* is as follows:

> And those who respond to their Lord and keep up prayer, and their rule is to take counsel [*shūrā*] among themselves and spend out what we have given them. (Qur'an, 42: 38)

The value attached to *shūrā* is so profound that Allah Almighty connects the practice to prayer (*ṣalāh*) and alms-giving (*zakāh*). Throughout the chapter Allah speaks about the importance of engaging others justly (Qur'an, 42: 15), that is, with patience, forgiveness and courage (Qur'an, 42: 43). To my mind these qualities constitute virtues of public deliberation (*shūrā*), which would hopefully encourage and persuade people to act justly. In the first instance, public deliberation cannot happen without the patience required for listening to the viewpoints of others, even if they are in conflict with one's own. The point is that public deliberation cannot happen unless we listen attentively to others' justifications and, in turn, give to others an account of our own justifications. Only then can we safely talk about deliberation.

Moreover, in the second instance, the Qur'an also states:

> Call [engage others] to the way of your Lord with wisdom and goodly exhortation, and have disputations with them in the best manner; surely your Lord best knows those who go astray from his path, and He knows best those who follow the right way. (Qur'an 16: 125)

Whereas public deliberation ought to involve different and contending parties listening to one another's views, it also needs to invoke disputations. This means that people should also have the courage to take one another's views into some kind of systematic controversy. In other words, we should not be concerned merely with listening to what others have to say and then agreeing with them, but we should also treat one another's truth claims critically without, of course, exceeding the limits (Qur'an, 7: 55). In this sense, exceeding the limits refers to insulting and demeaning people. However, it does not mean that one cannot fervently disagree with another person's view. In this sense disputations do not only have to be weak. Rather, arguments can be articulated ardently without alienating others, more specifically without excluding them from public deliberation. And, for the reason that public deliberation (*shūrā*) and a critical Islamic pedagogy have in mind the achievement of inclusive action, public deliberation (*shūrā*) can most appropriately be considered as a means towards attaining a critical Islamic pedagogy.

Thirdly, the use of *ʿaql* (contemplative thought) can be considered as an important means to achieve a critical Islamic pedagogical discourse on the basis that contemplation can be regarded as a necessary condition for critical action. The following Qur'anic verses attest to such a consideration:

> And He has made subservient for you the night and the day and the sun and the moon, and the stars are made subservient by His commandment; most surely there are signs in this for a people who ponder. (Qur'an, 16: 12)
>
> And of the fruits of the palms and the grapes – you obtain from them intoxication and goodly provision; most surely there is a sign in this for a people who ponder. (Qur'an, 16:67)
>
> (It is) a Book We have revealed to you abounding in good that they may ponder its verses, and that those endowed with understanding may be mindful. (Qur'an, 38: 29)

The use of contemplative thought (*ʿaql*) is connected to always asking: 'What is at stake?' It is a kind of contemplation that allows us to take more risks, to deal openly with the radical incommensurability of the language games that constitute our society, and invites new possibilities to emerge. Contemplation, and more specifically critique, is a matter of enhancing the possibility of dissent and diversity of interpretations (Burik 2009, 301); of complicating what is taken for granted, pointing to what has been overlooked in establishing identities (Burik 2009, 302); it is an active opening up of one's own thought structures that is necessary for other ways to find an entrance (Burik 2009, 304). In a different way, it is performing a critical Islamic pedagogy, because the latter is innately concerned with creating possibilities for dissent, diversity of interpretations, complicating the taken for granted and opening up to the other.

Now that I have looked at how reflexive actions are conceptually and pragmatically intertwined in a critical Islamic pedagogy, I finally turn my attention to the cultivation of such a pedagogy in Muslims schools.

Conclusion: Cultivating a critical Islamic pedagogy in Muslim schools

Firstly, teachers should engage students through activities which lend themselves to democratic iterations. This means that students should be taught to 'talk back'. In learning to talk back students should be encouraged to engage with and contest the meanings of the Islamic practices they want to uphold. To my mind, democratic iteration is precisely what we require in our Muslim schools to make sure that the curricula implemented have been subjected to democratic reflexivity and recursive justifications, which means listening to the views of those involved in the implementation of the education system and then to 'talk back'. Talking back does not have to be non-belligerent or non-distressful just because we think we need to continue the conversation. Sometimes we can articulate our reasons with a sense of roughness and distress, even to the extent of making the other feel uncomfortable; otherwise our conversations would be unduly policed (by ourselves and others) and often frivolous or useless mediations. In this way, students would be taught a form of *ta'līm* which is very much attuned to democratic iterations.

Secondly, teachers should teach students that all people have a cosmopolitan right (a virtue of hospitality), a right that belongs to all human beings insofar as we view them as potential participants in a world republic. Teachers go on to teach students that states should be prohibited from denying refuge and asylum to those [immigrants] whose intentions are peaceful, and especially if refusing them sojourn would lead to their demise. This implies that states can no longer treat immigrants as foreigners or resident aliens, but should recognise their rights as co-citizens. Students in Muslim schools are taught that the desired aspirations of immigrant students are legitimate and that they should not be treated as aliens who do not have a right to education. For me, this is what *tarbiyyah* connotes in kind because students are taught to respect the rights of others.

Finally, students should be taught to become social activists – a matter of becoming *mu'addibūn* or those educated to act against forms of injustices. Often what is learnt in Muslim schools is not really connected to making a contribution to changing undesirable situations in society. In this way what is taught in Muslim schools is separated from actual societal developments. What I have in mind is that students should be taught to make constructive contributions to changing situations in society. For instance, when students are taught to challenge any form of repression (with reference to their primary sources, namely the Qur'an and *Sunnah*), they actually do something about, for example, the exclusion of marginalised people from activities in the society. Here I specifically think of subverting gender inequality in a patriarchal society.

In conclusion: a critical Islamic pedagogy has the potential to engender an ethics of responsible, reflexive action, if notions such as *tarbiyyah, ta'līm* and *ta'dīb* are reconceptualised so that they go beyond nurturing to cultivating respect for the other and others' reasons, from uni-directional instruction to deliberative engagement, and from doing good to cultivating acts of social activism.

References

Al-Attas, Syed Muhammad Naquib. 1991. *The Concept of Education in Islam.* Kuala Lumpur: The International Institute of Islamic Thought and Civilisation.

Alibasic, Ahmet. 1999. The right of political opposition in Islamic history and legal theory: an exploration of an ambivalent heritage. *Al-Shajarah* 4(2): 231-295.

Benhabib, Seyla. 2002. *The Claims of Culture: Equality and Diversity in the Global Era.* Princeton: Princeton University Press.

Benhabib, Seyla. 2006. *Another Cosmopolitanism.* Oxford: Oxford University Press.

Burik, Steven. 2009. Opening philosophy to the world: Derrida and education in philosophy. *Educational Theory* 59(3): 297-312.

Callan, Eamonn. 1997. *Creating Citizens: Political Education and Liberal Democracy.* Oxford: Oxford University Press.

Edwards, Richard. 2006. All quiet on the postmodern front? *Studies in Philosophy and Education* 24(5): 273-278.

Gray, Kevin. 2006. Spirituality, critical thinking, and the desire for what is infinite. *Studies in Philosophy and Education* 24(5): 315-326.

Greene, Maxine. 1995. *Releasing the Imagination – Essays on Education, the Arts and Social Change.* San Franciso: Jossey-Bass.

Lyotard, Jean-François. 1984. *The Postmodern Condition: A Report on Knowledge.* Translated by Bennington, G, and B. Massumi. Vol. 10. *Theory and History of Literature.* Minneapolis: University of Manchester Press.

MacIntyre, Alasdair. 1988. *Whose Justice? Which Rationality.* London: Duckworth.

The Koran: An Electronically Scanned Version of M. H. Shakir's English Translation of the Holy Qur'an, as Published by Tahrike Tarsile Qur'an, Inc. http://quod.lib.umich.edu/k/koran/ (accessed April 24, 2011).

Waghid, Yusef. 1996a. *Ta'dib:* restatement of Islamic education. *Muslim Education Quarterly* 13(4): 32-45.

Waghid, Yusef. 1996b. In search of a boundless ocean and new skies: Human creativity is a matter of *a'mal, jihad* and *ijtihād. American Journal of Islamic Social Sciences* 13(3): 353-365.

Abdulkader Tayob

Islamization for South African Muslim Independent Schools

Islamic education has come in the spotlight of Western public debate and academic research for at least two interrelated reasons. The large number of Muslims in Europe and North America and their public visibility has coincided with fundamental questions about the place of culture and identity in a globalizing world. Many of these countries are (re)discovering the fissures and cracks that lay buried under powerful and apparently coherent national identities. Muslims in these countries were themselves discovering or tenaciously holding onto their own identities and religious mores. Religious markers and subjectivities sat uneasily in Western publics ideally defined in terms of a clear separation of public and private sensibilities. The sheer multiplicity of identities in the public sphere was enough of a problem for Muslims, if not compounded by the threat that radical groups, albeit small and isolated, openly and actively challenged local and foreign policies of these countries. These groups were turning away, sometimes with extreme violence, from a shared consensus of values in public life. In the light of both pluralism and radicalization, then, questions have been posed of values and loyalties generated within Muslim communities in Europe and North America.

Of particular relevance to this article, questions were being asked as to where anti-social values were developed and nurtured in the heart and ghettoes of Western cities within Muslim communities. In particular, Islamic education has been identified as one of the conduits of radicalism or ghettoization. Research and policy developments have been proposed to address the challenge, and find ways of developing antidotes towards eradicating or minimizing anti-social behaviour and radicalization (Johnson 1980; Shadid and van Koningsveld 1992; Perko 2000; Zine 2001; 2005; McGlyn 2005; Starret 2006; Alvarez-Veinguer et al. 2009). This attention to Islamic education has come under critical scrutiny. Among others, Starret (2006), one of the leading authorities on schooling in Muslim societies has questioned the assumptions underlying the attention of policy makers to implement and impose changes in Muslim curricula on a global scale. He cautioned against the tendency to see schooling as an effective and efficient way of changing society, pointing to the complex relation between education and society. For this particular article, the caution is necessary for another reason. Western political and social concerns about Islamic education are obscuring a much larger debate on modern Islamic education. Islamic education is quintessentially presented as traditional, crying out for modernization and adjustment for Europe. Such an assumption ignores the fact that Islamic education has been the site of a complex debate and restructuring since the nineteenth century. The Western debate can scarcely ignore this much longer development.

In this particular contribution, Muslim schools founded in South Africa since the 1980s are examined in this longer historical context. The main purpose of this article is focused on how Islamic education is defined within schools. Schooling here is distinguished from confessional religious education imparted in homes, mosques and religious institutions. It refers to institutions that offer both religious confessional subjects and modern 'secular' subjects such as mathematics, natural sciences, history and other humanities and social sciences. The definition of Islamic education and schooling is scrutinized in relation to these new subjects. Given the need and desire to meet educational and curricular standards set by governments, how do Muslim schools formulate and present Islamic education? Given the divergent ways in which education is conceptualized in modern scientific learning and theological learning, how do teachers of religious subjects define the core curriculum and knowledge outcomes? Given the diverse range of Islamic trends in any specific locality, how do religious teachers reflect these and cope with them? These were some of the questions posed to religious educators in South African Muslim schools. For this article, one of the schools, the first of such schools founded in 1984, is put in the centre of analysis. Its founder, Mawlānā Ali Adam, has been the leading spokesperson for Islamization. His views will be compared and contrasted with the other persons who have been interviewed.

Modern Islamic education and schooling

Since the Ottoman and other Muslim political powers started sending delegations to the West to learn its ways and its strengths, Muslim societies have debated on how to integrate these newly acquired sciences into the educational framework inherited from the past. Scholars examining this encounter have pointed to the dichotomization of education as a chief outcome of this engagement. In a general review of higher Islamic educational institutes, Waardenburg has pointed to the bifurcation in knowledge between teaching orthodoxy, and adopting Western knowledge traditions (Waardenburg 1965).

Modern Muslim intellectuals have been particularly concerned about this bifurcation, and hoped to overcome it in one way or another. Rahman, among many others, lamented the bifurcation of society between a scripturalism devoid of ethics, and a technicalism derived from Western knowledge (Rahman 1982:45). Ismāʿīl al Fārūqī (d. 1986) was also concerned about this bifurcation, and launched a project in the 1980s called the Islamization of knowledge to overcome it (Al Faruqi 1406). The concept of Islamization was initiated at an international congress held in Mecca in 1977, followed by five other conferences that explored the problem of Muslim education and the need to find a comprehensive and integrated solution. A number of universities have been established on the basis of the vision, the most well-known being the International Islamic Universities in Malaysia and Pakistan. The American-based International Institute of Islamic Thought, founded by al Fārūqī and his colleagues, may be regarded as the think-tank for this project.[1] Muslim schools are on the coalface of this challenge of bifurcation of knowledge and education. Whilst intellectuals and theo-

1 Various individuals proposed this integration in the 1960s and 1970s, but Islamization of knowledge is closely associated with the late Ismāʿīl al Fārūqī (d. 1986) (Alatas

rists have developed interesting formulas and projects of integration, schools set up to project this integration might tell us much more as they translated these into practice. In fact, a number of them in English-speaking countries have adopted the Islamization of knowledge as a framework for integration. The final international conference on Islamization took place in Cape Town in 1996, and it was specifically dedicated to producing curricula and workbooks for Muslim schools.[2] Schools are an important place to examine these theories and intellectual projects.

The bifurcation of education in Muslim educational practice has not closely examined the transformation of the two components that make up the antagonistic pair. Both Islamic and modern education are assumed to be occupying two mutually separate epistemic universes. Waardenburg's thesis seems to suggest that Islamic knowledge has entered the modern world without being affected by the epistemologies and the changed political contexts. The teaching of orthodoxy takes its place in Islamic schools alongside the new imported subjects. This is also the unstated assumption of Muslim intellectuals who accepted the dichotomization of education and knowledge, and see the need for re-examining traditional education and knowledge frameworks for the modern world. Theirs was a modernist approach to education that presented traditional education as unchanging and constant. Halstead, comparing Islamic and liberal education in recent troubled times, has also adopted this view of Islamic education, unchanging from the time of the medieval scholar al-Ghazālī to the present (Halstead 2004). This perspective of Islamic education is not supported by those who have closely examined modern knowledge and educational practices. Zaman has followed the reception of Western (particularly British) knowledge systems among South Asian *ʿulamāʾ* (theologians). Adopting the distinction between useful and non-useful knowledge promoted by the British, Muslim theologians emphasized the usefulness of what they increasingly came to define as religious (*dīnī*) knowledge (Zaman 1999). In this insightful analysis, Zaman pointed to the creation of a new idea of knowledge, and thus education, around the value of usefulness. This South Asian response may be compared with Islamic schooling in Mali in West Africa studied by Brenner. Brenner traced the transformation of Islamic education from an esoteric hierarchical episteme to a rational episteme. Scientific subjects introduced by French colonizers impacted upon religious subject in a fundamental and transformative manner (Brenner 2000). Eickelman's extensive work on education in the Arab world has also focused on this transformation; he has called attention to the objectification of Islamic knowledge in modern societies (Eickelman 1992). Euben's characterization of Islamization of knowledge may also be put alongside these reflections. She has defined it as an epistemological critique of both Western and Islamic sciences, and the creation of an integrated body of knowledge (Euben 2002). All these studies point to the complex

---

1995; Euben 2002; Dangor 2005). See also http://www.iiit.org/, accessed September 30, 2010.

2 Some of these schools have also founded a research institute, the International Board of Educational Research and Resources (IBERR), to realize the goals of Islamization (http://iberr.co.za/, accessed September 30, 2010). The date of its formation is not given, but it was already active by 1999.

creation of a new approach to knowledge. The bifurcation of education impacted fundamentally on the idea of Islamic education and knowledge systems.

In this article, this complexity and transformation of the knowledge of Islam is kept in focus in the study of Islamization. With a particular focus on one educator, the vision of South African Muslim private schools is placed in local context. The article examines Islamization as a vision of the integration of subjects in actual practice, keeping in mind some of the demands for schooling in South Africa. It also takes into consideration a changing context, from the end of apartheid to democracy and globalization. Moreover, it argues that there was a major gap between the new philosophy of education, and the practice of education as conceived by school principals. The vision of Islamization was upheld as a framework of education, but the actual practice was guided by the racial and institutional context of Muslim schools.

Islamic schooling in South Africa

The Schools under investigation were part of a broader array of educational institutions founded in South Africa since the first arrival of Muslims in the 17th century. The first Muslim schools were established at the end of the nineteenth century, the demand being driven by the discovery of rich mineral deposits in the country. Such developments pushed the country on a path of rapid industrialization and modernization. Muslim children and students were not the earliest beneficiaries of modern schooling. Both the British colonial and Afrikaner state policies were highly inadequate and discriminatory. Missionaries were the main channel through which these opportunities were provided to those on the margins of the society.

Ajam has documented the initiative of Cape Muslim community to provide own schooling from 1913. They were called Moslem Mission Schools, following similar Christian Mission Schools in name. By 1956, fifteen such schools were founded throughout the city of Cape Town (Ajam 1986; Ajam 1989). The schools provided jobs for Muslim teachers who had qualified at teachers' colleges but who could not get jobs at Christian-dominated schools, and for Muslim children whose parents were concerned about the dominant Christian ethos at both state and missionary schools. The newly-arrived Indian communities also built such schools, almost as they arrived from 1860s on (Calpin 1949:72; Maharaj 1979). Indian religious communities sometimes established separate schools, and provided space for religious education in the afternoons or weekends. Muslims also followed this pattern, and established a number of such so-called state-aided schools. The communities provided buildings, while the state provided teaching infrastructure. The communities were free to develop religious education within these structures. In this context, a dichotomization of knowledge and education took root as elsewhere in the world.

From the 1980s, a new type of private Muslim schooling was introduced, first in Cape Town and in the rest of the country. Such schools have proliferated throughout the country since the 1990s, taking advantage of new legislation after the end of apartheid. They are loosely organized in the Association of Muslim Schools.[3] These Muslim schools were clearly motivated and informed by culture, and should be put alongside well-established and privileged groups in South Africa who took a particular approach to the challenges of education in the country.

These Islamic schools were not unique in South Africa. In a quantitative study of independent schools, Du Toit reports that independent schools had significantly increased in South Africa since 1990 (du Toit 2004). In 2002, there were 1287 independent schools with 391,248 learners. Of these, 61.1% registered after 1990. Of these, under half (565) were religious schools. Another interesting feature is the high number of girls in independent schools in du Toit's study (17:1). And the number of African learners was higher than other groups at the top-fee schools, indicating the preference of the middle classes for independent schooling. Muslim schools in contemporary South Africa have embraced the concept of independent schools in terms of the 1996 South African Schools Act. They are very active in the association representing independent schools in South Africa in general. Some of the leaders in the Association of Muslim Schools hold places on these national bodies. The secretary general of the Association of Muslim Schools, Rashied Chopdat, was an office bearer of the national association of independent schools in 2006.

The proliferation and development of Muslims schools seems to converge with culture-specific independent schools analyzed by du Toit. These new Muslim schools dramatically increased after 1990, as parents were concerned about the racial and religious profile of the schools. Muslim children had attended racially segregated school during apartheid, and their religious identities were also clearly inscribed among coloured and Indian schools. After 1990 and the liberalizing reforms, they 'perceived' an influx of African children into their schools. Identifying better schooling opportunities in previous white schools, many parents chose to move their children to these schools. Parents who were particularly concerned about the religious needs developed and chose Muslim schools. The new Schools Act of 1996 facilitated this process on an institutional level. The Act made provision for only two types of schools: public and independent schools. All previous state-aided schools had to chose between becoming public schools or independent schools status. Muslim state-aided schools, as many others, opted for becoming independent schools, with the support of Paragraph 48 which ensured some state subsidy. It seems that this provision significantly increased the number of Muslim schools, and their economic viability, in Indian Muslim areas.

The following figures for Muslim schools were collected towards the end of 2006, and they reveal some interesting trends. There were a total of 74 independent Muslim schools. Using du Toit's figures, they formed a very small percentage of the total number of independent schools (5.74%), but higher than the proportion of Muslims in the population as a whole (1.5%). Even more significantly, they constituted a larger percentage of independent schools (12.8%) based on religion. Although we did not get specific numbers of girls in Muslim schools, we did get an impression that girls were over-represented. Muslim schools also rep-

3 http://www.ams-sa.org/, accessed September 30, 2010.

resent the aspirations of middle classes for independent schools, and to maintain the racial profile of schooling. These aspirations only need some qualification.

Table 1: Muslim Schools (2006)

Province	Number of Schools	Number of Teachers	Number of Students	Teacher/ Student Ratio
Western Cape	22	331	8417	25
Gauteng (TVL)	24	860	21000	24
Kwazulu Natal	28[4]	700	15000	21
	74	1891	44417	23

The majority of learners in Muslim schools come from Gauteng, while the Western Cape had the fewest number of learners. The Western Cape has about half of the Muslim population in the country, but only 19% of the total number of learners at Muslim schools. The Kwazulu-Natal province also has a larger number of Muslims than the Gauteng, but the number of learners was significantly lower than Gauteng. Gauteng was the economic capital of the country, and also the source of capital for Muslim institutions such as mosques and schools. This class basis of Muslim schools needs some qualification. There was definitely a tendency to provide education outside of the state schools to families who were able to afford it. However, an examination of the fees at the schools indicate that they were offering independent schooling at rates much lower than other similar schools in the country. Fees at Muslim schools were supplemented with fundraising activities on a large scale. Fees charged were often much lower than those found in former white public schools. These latter schools largely maintained their own cultural ethos, and charged higher fees, with the support of well-organized school governing bodies.

The choice of Islamic schooling seemed to perpetuate the racial identities of the past. Muslim schools were overwhelmingly Indian and Coloured, and even these were maintaining racial profiles among learners. At most, in Cape Town, one or two schools were bringing Indians and Coloureds together. In 2006, the secretary-general of the Association of Muslim Schools told me that one of the biggest challenges at Muslim schools remains attitudes towards race. Sometimes, as with the Islamiyya school in Cape Town founded in 1984, there was a desire to introduce Muslim schools to the black African communities. Also, in Fataar's study, an attempt was made in Cape Town to found a school in the black township. The latter closed down due to a dispute in management between the Imam on whose premises the school was founded, and its middle-class funders (Fataar 2005). The overwhelming trend of Muslim schools preserved the established racial profile of Muslims in the country.

4 http://www.ams-sa.org/about-ams/kzn-region/64-kzn-school-list.html. December 7, 2009.

Defining Islamic education

Most Muslims schools justified their existence on the delivery of a good integrated Islamic education. For some, Muslim schools provided a better management of time. Both religious and secular subjects were taught in one school, and under one management. Other schools were more ambitious, and attempted to develop an integrating programme like Islamization. In fact, the Association of Muslim Schools adopted the Islamization of education as the main objective of the school, and organized various workshops for teachers. But the adopted was uneven, and Islamization needs to be appreciated as one among a number of strategies to achieve integration. We now look closely at Adam's vision for Islamiyya as an ideal and practice that he presented to our research. We will draw comparisons with some of the other schools visited.

Ali Adam: Islamization, identity and moral discipline

Mawlānā Ali Adam may be regarded as the foremost ideologue of Islamic independent schooling in South Africa. He grew up around his family business in rural Transkei in the Eastern Province of South Africa. His family traced this business to at least 1890. Adam went to India to pursue higher Islamic education. He spent ten years at the Nadwat 'l-'Ulūm in Lucknow, mainly in the service (*khidma*) of its well-known founder and Indian reformer Abu 'l-Ḥasan 'Alī Nadvī (d. 1999). Adam informed us that he only completed three years of formal education, but imbibed the value of education during the service offered to his mentor. The reform of Islam, as Adam learnt fron Nadvī, was not going to come from leading people in mosques but by improving the level of education within society. Soon after his return, he worked hard to realize this vision of working for the education of Muslims. Interestingly, another Nadwa graduate who was an Imam at a local mosque, Mawlana Qutb al-Din Kajee, beat him to a public announcement of the formation of such a school in a Friday sermon in late 1983. Adam had been contemplating this idea since the breakout of anti-apartheid uprisings in 1976. Nevertheless, the two Nadvis (Adam and Qutb al-Din), another Indian-trained scholar Malānā Yusuf Keeran and a businessman Sulayman Bhayat came together and founded the Islamiyya High School in 1983 with 7 girls. In 1984, the school opened its door on the premises of the Habibiyya Mosque. For the next 15 years, Adam was its principal and led its growth and fame. At the time of the interview in 2006, he was what he called its "non-executive director." Many believed that Adam was always the power and ideologue of the school, and also that of independent Muslim schools in South Africa. He had also established a reputation in other English-speaking Muslim communities in the United Kingdom, North America, Australia and the Gulf region.

Adam was inspired by Nadvi, but considered himself a student of Al Fārūqī as far as the Islamization of Knowledge was concerned. He was instrumental in ensuring that the sixth conference on Islamization was held in Cape Town, and also played a leading role in the research institute dedicated to providing guidelines for teachers, principals and governing bodies. In an extensive interview, Adam elaborated on his understanding of Islamization (Adam 2006).

A heuristic distinction may be made between an Islamization programme pertaining to knowledge, and an identity and ethos that accompanied it. The Islamization programme was shared to some extent by the schools through the Association of Muslim schools. At the same time, one could not ignore the unique identity and ethos that existed at individual schools. This ethos was partly informed by the theological and visionary orientation of each school, and partly by the particular construction of a new identity connected to the particular location, formation and history of the school. More importantly, the specific meaning of Islamization at each school depended on this identity. In the following analysis, both aspects will be highlighted.

Adam's understanding of the Islamization as a knowledge project may be divided into three components that he emphasized in various ways in the interview. These were convictions or principles shared by others that have embarked on Islamization, or other integrating projects. Firstly and predictably, Islamization was a commitment to break the dichotomy of the sciences. Adam believed that "Muslims originally never separated subjects" and "taught *fiqh* [jurisprudence] alongside medicine, physics". Moreover, "all subjects, *fiqh*, geography, *uṣūl* [principles or roots of jurisprudence]... is (sic) all one and the same; [and] should be done in one institution with different faculties." He was "uncomfortable" with the word "secular" and felt that this was a term that Muslims should not be using. The "dichotomy" present in Muslim education "should be broken." This was the one common conviction echoed at all schools. They all combined secular and religious subjects in one location. It is important to note that there were schools that met some opposition to combine the religious and secular subjects. In one of the Muslim schools in Pretoria, some of the *ʿulamāʾ* in the community were appalled. As the head teacher of Islamic education. Mawlānā Yusuf Abed (Abed 2006), recalled in 2006:

> ... few of the *ʿālims* felt very insulted that you giving Western education [preference] over *dīnī taʿlīm* … there were counter allegations and *fatwās* [juridical opinions] that were moving around, you know, questioning the *ʿulamāʾ* who were involved for the school, their *imān* [orthodoxy] was questioned. You can't believe it! It was just in 1990.

It seemed the school had since 1990 overcome this suspicion, but the foundation of a school combining Islamic and "Western" subjects was not considered the most obvious path at the time.

The second aspect of Islamization was also shared among schools but with some important variations. According to Adam, Islamization was a unique perspective of subjects taught and studied at school. It was not a distinct body of knowledge, covering theology, jurisprudence or exegesis. Thus, IBERR (the research institute dedicated to Islamization) was preparing a "broad curriculum of skills for life." This broad set of guidelines would be "a vehicle to Islamize all the other subjects" on the basis of which teachers would be able to work: "every teacher will draw from the book [prepared by IBERR]; it is not a text book to teach them as a subject but it is a textbook to teach guidelines. What can I draw from this reading material? The math teacher will say what can I draw from it. So, it is like a resource material for Islamizing subjects without Islamizing every subject." In another segment of the interview, Adam clarified this point by saying that the goal of the school was to produce learners who will "be Islamically highly knowledgeable – thinking wise." Parents should teach children all that is necessary for daily rituals, but "in school" they must be given "an Islamic thinking package more than a *fiqh* package". When asked about the state of Islamization practices at schools, Adam lamented that it was "loosely" applied. He also used the same term (loosely) when referring to the materials that IBERR would be presenting to teachers in 2007 (interviewed in 2006). And when asked about how non-Muslim teachers would implement Islamization, he first answered: "Because it is very loose (Islamization), it does not matter!" He then quickly corrected himself by saying "There is no formal Islamization programme". These responses perhaps suggest that Islamization was a framework for studying other subjects. The framework was derived from Islamic teachings, but these were not as clearly formulated and presented in any concrete form. Adam offered one example of what exactly Islamization might mean, namely, in the teaching of Shakespeare's Romeo and Juliet:

> We are going to teach Shakespeare, but we will bring in an Islamic *bias* to it. For example, what we are already doing, when you teach Romeo and Juliet. We will deal with suicide as a concept in Islam! We are not going to teach and leave it at that! So they committed suicide! That is their *understanding*! So when you finish Romeo and Juliet, you glorify suicide! That is your *feeling*, because of the way it's taught. So we will counter that. It [Romeo and Juliet] is okay, it could act as part of literature, but as Muslims we cannot. It is a *thinking* exercise, it is not incorporating Madrassa [religious confessional school] work into school. It is an attempt to create a *thinking* Muslim. That is the ... objective.

I have emphasized the italicized words in this quotation (bias, understanding, feeling, thinking). This single example illustrates the point that Islamization was not conveying a body of knowledge from the sources of Islam. It was a call for a change in orientation or outlook on the same material studied in other schools. This body of Islamic knowledge was certainly not abandoned, but assigned to the home and perhaps to the mosque.

Some of the teachers and principals at other schools felt that Islamization was not clear to them. In spite of attending the workshops organized by the Association of Muslim Schools, they had little idea of how Islamization should work. Khamissa was a former principal at Islamiyya and often led these Islamization seminars. He said that Islamization only provided a good broader vision but not clear guidelines in the classrooms.[5] Some teachers, we were told, simply inserted verses of the Qur'an here and there in the syllabus, but felt that there was something missing. Abed at the Tswane Muslim School in Pretoria waited for more guidance to come from the Association, but then adopted the syllabus of

5 Interview with Idris Khamissa, November 21, 2006 (Cape Town).

the theologians in the area. In contrast, Amod at al-Falah was very positive about the support provided by the Association and implemented the programme of Islamization in an innovative way (Amod 2006). Both Abed and Amod confirmed Adam's view of Islamization as a perspective, and not a body of information. Amod's called this subject "applied Islam" which seemed to echo Adam's "thinking package":

> … at Al Falah we always say that we do not want to promote a certain school of thought, but what we would like to do is to bring that learner, as close as possible to *think* [my emphasis] via the Qur'an, the Sunnah.

Amod did not reject any particular view, but he defined the process of education as one led by questioning, scenario building and role-playing. In comparison with Adam and Amod, though, Abed had more to say about the foundation provided at lower levels. He too, however, defined the goal of the school in this broad, non-specific way:

> The ethos that we are trying to create here, where we are trying to find a balance between *dīni*, as well as other sciences.

He did mention that such general analyses were presented only at higher grades (10,11, 12):

> (then) you would not just restrict yourself to the *ṣalāt* and all that, you speak about … abortion and all those (you know) what we call *jadīd masā'il* [new issues] …, new type of things, you know, equip them with the reality … [of] babies, same-sex –change operations, homosexuality, all those things are, so that's one advantage at that level.

Abed also intimated that parents were not really interested in this aspect of education. They were happy for the school to provide the primary foundation; some even sending their children to more expensive private schools afterwards. There was more than a hint here that parents were not that enthusiastic about the new issues and 'balance' that the school was aiming to achieve. Abed himself said that they were not committed to the vision of the school. In general, I would like to propose that Adam, Amod and Abed were trying to ensure a broad orientation and vision among the learners.

This particular feature of Islamization seems to echo the theory of Islamization propounded by Al Fārūqī. He too focuses on the "malaise" of the Muslim *umma* and the important role for education. However, he too argued essentially for a change in vision within Muslim societies.

> There is no genuine search of knowledge without spirit; and spirit is precisely what cannot be copied [from the West]. It is generated by the vision of self, of word and reality; in short, by religion. Muslim word education lacks this vision. It does not have the vision of the West by necessity; and it does not have the vision of Islam by choice, i.e. by ignorance, laziness and unconcern (Al Faruqi 1406:7).

His workplan for the Islamization of discipline is developed around this vision. It attempts to critique and re-organize the disciplines of knowledge in terms of this vision.

The third aspect of Islamization revealed by Adam was directly related to some of the hesitation felt in Tswane with the integration provided by the school. In Adam, it was expressed in terms of how the Islamization programme was competing with the demands placed on teachers engaged in the teaching of 'secular' subjects. Adam was sympathetic to serving these demands, even if this meant that Islamization would be de-prioritized: "We are Islamising, but very slowly, almost unseen, because we cannot be unrealistic, they have to write those exams. We should be very cautious when Islamizing." The Islamic framework could not jeopardize the success that parents and learners expected from schooling. And this schooling referring to a very separate sphere of educational activity as revealed in the following segment:

> … we have to be realistic. These children have to write the national exams. Because they have to go to University and they have to have careers; you cannot impose a new curriculum or over-Islamize and make them unable to make them highly successful in the exams. *So there is almost like a dual thing going on* [my emphasis]. We are Islamizing but very slowly, almost unseen.

It is surprising that Adam here makes provision for a duality that he generally rejected in pursuit of Islamization. He did not use the objectionable and uncomfortable term 'secular', but it is clear that Islamic schools felt compelled to accommodate the demands of schooling for a world that needed basic information and skills in math, literature, geography and other subjects. In another segment, he also mentioned the extent to which Islamic schools through IBERR were working with a University in Gloucestershire (England) in improving the standards and skills, particularly in Maths and Science. Similarly, he looked forward to Oxford and Cambridge accreditation for Islamic schools on a global level. Adam related with pride what prestige that such global, Western accreditation would bring to Islamic schools. Careful attention to the interview shows that the accreditation was given to the "secular" offerings of the Islamic schools: "IBERR associated with Gloucestershire University for 4-5 years with regards to teacher training of Muslim teachers, especially in Maths and Science." These projects reveal the primacy and importance of general education, dare one say 'secular' education, that Muslim schools provided for learners and parents. Islamization acted as a vision over these skills and bodies of information, providing just enough leavening to leave an impression. Success in the world, though, had to be measured on a more objective and consensual level, determined by English universities that Muslims globally accepted.

Not surprisingly, this lack of integration between subjects was evident in other schools as well. Abed summarized this succinctly:

> So basically, what it is, Muslim schools actually, what .. they've done actually is they've taken the afternoon component which we used to know as *madrassa* or *maktab*, and they have inserted it into the school curriculum.

The defacto bifurcation took place in most schools where Islamization was not clearly understood or implemented. The traditional confessional education (*madrassa, slamseskool*) was distributed across the working week.

Islamization as a knowledge project, then, may be summarized as a project that brought all knowledge acquired by Muslims on one premises. Overtly, it was a call to reject the dichotomization brought on by modernization. On a more substantial level, integration was not achieved. A clear duality was maintained within the activities of the schools. This duality might be justified by the demands placed on the school, as Adam told us, or the resistance experience by religious leaders and parents as presented by Abed. The effect of this accommodation, however, reinforced the second aspect of Islamization. Duality emphasized the role and meaning of Islam in these schools as a general perspective and framework. Islamization was not a new theology or exegesis or similar body of information that derived ultimately from the revelation given to the Prophet Muhammad. Rather, it was a general perspective that interrogated the values and attitudes presented in secular subjects like literature, math and history. Learners needed science to pass an exam, but they needed an Islamic perspective to live as Muslims.

This particular understanding of Islamization raises questions about the perspective presented in the subjects, and thus to the ethos and identity of the school. Given the many different traditions within Islam, which one was chosen to study Shakespeare's Romeo and Juliet, or other issues that come up in the study of geography, biology and economics? Was the school guided by a theory, an orientation or a contemporary Islamic trend? Muslim Schools in South Africa were indeed oriented to their theological founders and funders: Tablighi, Deobandi, Barelwi, Salafi, neutral, and Islamist. Our interviews, however, revealed a blurring of the boundaries as far as these theological trends are concerned. All the schools stressed their unwillingness to imprint these theological lenses implicitly or explicitly in school. But there were clearly differences among the schools that could not be denied. Each school may be identified for its unique identity, constructed and changed in the view of its founders, principals, teachers, parents, governing bodies and learners. We might even expect a complex of competing identities within each school. Within the scope of this article, the full complexity cannot be examined. However, the identity that was closely related to the meaning of Islamization may be highlighted. The study of English literature and history were not Islamized through an epistemological critique of novels, plays and literature, but by a reorientation. Listening to this orientation given in Adam's interview, the following identity is proposed for Islamiyya.

Adam presented a number of pointers to how he and perhaps the founders of the Islamiyya school projected an identity of the school. The most important component of this identity seemed to be related to sexual propriety and its challenge to 'morals' of the learners and society. This was the raison d'être of the foundation of the school and has continued to define its identity and its limits in a number of ways. In the 1970s, Adam and his colleagues were alarmed at the "looser trends and downward morals [that] were creeping in" during the schools uprisings. They founded the school for girls in order to prevent or arrest this moral deterioration. Based on the frank interview with Adam, and general observations over the years, I would venture to say that the school has maintained this original ethos. Or more accurately, one might say that Adam and the governing body have tried to ensure that this focus was maintained.

Adam admitted that the school had not been able to stem the tide of moral deterioration. He was aware that moral scandals connected with the school had been reported in the local press. He identifies the failure to maintain this moral compass due to a lack of "discipline of our pupils". This deficiency was related to the high "level of permissiveness" and "too much freedom, because of mixing" (of the sexes). Mobile phones and other media were the source so that "our children, even in the big Muslim homes, are no more protected – they do get exposed" – a condition for which Islamiyya and other Muslim schools were unprepared. This preoccupation with morality and its relentless tide reinforced the self-image of a school built to defend the young Muslim learner, particular the girl-child, from the threat of moral decadence.

In 2006, the school was preparing to embark on policing this 'immorality' on and off school property. This new approach, according to Adam, would also include a surveillance of the parents. Adam said that the school had decided to screen the parents of children admitted to the school: "If a mother comes to admit her child with a … skirt and no scarf [she would be told] that you do not belong to … Islamiyya." Adam did not think this would be a common occurrence, but the parent would be told in no uncertain terms:

> So we would tell that parent, especially if she is bringing her daughter, or even a son it doesn't matter. Look, you, as a parent, do not belong to this circle.
>
> We have a case of a girl with open belly buttons. So we asked the mother, so she said "I am liberal, my daughter can do what she wants." So that parent does not belong here.

The emphasis on the morality of females (mothers and daughters) is very striking, in spite of the occasional lip-service paid to the boys as well. In general, though, it seems that sexual propriety as represented by dress and behaviour constituted the dominant ethos of the school. Behaviour deemed to project this moral propriety, the dress code of female learners and their mothers, would identify the school.

Sexual morality also featured in how the school identified itself against non-Muslim and Africans. The school was clearly Indian, even though it was Adam's vision to transform it into a Black school. He was at pains to prove that the school had started to abandon its Indian identity by appointing a new Malay principal to take up his post in 2007. He had been appointed against an Indian candidate from Johannesburg or Durban. But the identity of the school, using sexual rhetoric, was strongly inscribed against non-Muslims and Africans. When discussing the presence of Christians in the school, Adam brought up the fact that they would be accommodated, but would have to attend all "moral lessons" at prayer times, and conform to the dress code of Islamiyya. He hardly thought that Christian girls and their parents would tolerate the uniform imposed by the school on girls: "The boys will have it much easier, because it is grey pants, white shirt and a blazer. So they won't have a problem but girls will have a problem … I mean who wants to come and put this uniform on because you cannot have a mini-skirted girl … So that is what keeps them away." The religious ethos of the school is defined against the apparently obvious desire of Christian girls to wear mini skirts.

When discussing the presence (or rather lack) of black African children in Islamic schools, he revealed the same concern for sexual morality. He suggested that some schools in other regions might have had a problem with admitting blacks, but not Cape Town.[6] He suggested a fear of moral standards might have justified these schools. African boys posed a threat to young Indian girls, he declared: "And those boys have no moral values; their values are so different." More alarmingly, he continued, "free mixing, sleeping around ... is not against their culture". "Even if they come in separate classes," he continued, "they will meet in the grounds, they would be overpowering on those little girls – so we must accept that fear of the parents as a reality." And thus, Indian Muslims were justified according to Adam in establishing Muslim schools in order to preserve the purity of their daughters. He recalled one alarming incident when "a Black Muslim girl from a good home gets involved with a Black boy who does not become a Muslim – she goes and lives with him in Soweto! That is a shock for our community."

As represented by Adam, the fear of sexual chaos represents an important part of Islamiyya's identity. Sexuality was intimately woven within the dress requirement of female learners, the chaos promised by black African boys and their culture. This particular representation of the school was shared by parents and other Muslim schools in the country. Coming much later than Islamiyya, Muslim schools in other regions were founded when segregation was broken down. The formation of Islamic schools preserved racial identities, and perhaps also their preoccupation with sexual politics. Based on the interviews, however, I can argue that Abed and Amod projected different concerns and identities. Abed presented his school as one confronted by diversity and complexity. Emerging as a Deobandi school, the Tswane Muslim School blazed a novel path of combining religious (*dīnī*) and secular subjects, against the wishes of religious scholars. On the other hand, it had become a home to people from diverse background. The schools attempted to produce a new identity out of this diversity. Amod was also dealing with a greater diversity at school. Unlike Abed, he was not in a school with a clear theological background and was freer to develop a new approach. My preliminary impression was that he was supporting an approach that focussed on the history of the of the Prophet as a model that could be interpreted and implemented in the lives of his students.

Conclusion

The presentation of Adam's vision of Islamization and its identity presents an opportunity to assess the project in practice. Clearly, the bifurcation of education was felt by most of the founders of Muslim schools in South Africa. However, bifurcation did not necessarily present a major obstacle that the grand theorists

6 At the time of the interview in 2006, there were only 5 or 6 Black African students in Islamiyya school with an enrollment of a 1000.

of modern Islamic education felt. More interestingly, the attempt at integration seemed to be a problem in some quarters. They had accepted the difference between Islamic education and 'Western" sciences, and thus opposed to what they called mixing. Some parents also seemed to restrict the role of religious instruction at the elementary level. Secondly, Islamization in substantial terms was not a new interpretation of religious texts or theology. It was first and foremost an orientation and vision. Islamization could be a critique of modern, Western subjects that Euben argued (Euben 2002). But it is more appropriately defined as a continuing attempt at resolving the contradictions and tensions arising from bringing Islamic and modern bodies of knowledge together. Thirdly and finally, Islamization is also employed to frame identities at different levels of the school experience. Using the conversation with Adam and the history of Islamiyya, I want to argue that moral propriety occupied an important place in this identity. However, our interviews and observations suggest that Islamization may also be employed by other constructions. This particular aspect of Islamization, to my knowledge, has not been highlighted in the literature. And yet, it seems to play as important a role as the frequently publicized and overt goal of combining bifurcated knowledge systems, and a vision that provides an overview of the new sciences. This last aspect of Islamic schools is not doubt more difficult to identify, since it changes from one individual or group to another. Using the material from diverse actors and role-players at schools, however, it seems that the identities of the Islamization programme may be identified.

References

Ajam, M. 1989. Islamic Schools of Cape Town as Agencies of Socialization. *Journal for Islamic Studies* 9: 70-98.

Ajam, M. T. "The Raison De'Etre of the Muslim Mission Primary School in Cape Town and Environs From 1860 to 1980 with Special Reference to the Role of Dr. A. Abdurahman in the Modernisatiion of Islam-Oriented Schools." Phd dissertation, Faculty of Education, University of Cape Town, Cape Town.

Al Faruqi, Ismaīl Rāji. 1406. Islamization of Knowledge: The General Principles and Workplan. In *Knowledge for What? Being the Proceedings and Papers of the Seminar on Islamization of Knowledge, Organized Jointly by the National Hijra Centenary Committee, Pakistan, the Institute of Education, Islamic University, Islamabad, and International Institute of Islamic Thought, Wyncote, Pennsylvania, USA*, 1-49. Islamabad: National Hijra Council.

Alatas, Syed Farid. 1995. The Sacralization of the Social Sciences: A Critique of an Emerging Theme in Academic Discourse. *Archives de sciences sociales des religions* 40 (91): 89-111.

Alvarez-Veinguer, Aurora, Gunther Dietz, Dan-Paul Jozsa, and Thorsten Knauth, (eds.) 2009. *Islam in Education in European Countries: Pedagogical Concepts and Empirical Findings*. Vol. 18, *Religious Diversity and Education in Europe*. Münster: Waxmann.

Brenner, Louis. 2000. *Controlling Knowledge: Religion, Power and Schooling in a West African Muslim Society*. London: Hurst & Company.

Calpin, George H. 1949. *Indians in South Africa.* Shuter & Shooter.

Dangor, Suleman. 2005. Islamization of Disciplines: Towards an Indigenous Educational System. *Educational Philosophy and Theory* 37 (4): 519-31.
du Toit, Jacques L. 2004. *Independent Schooling in Post-Apartheid South Africa: A Quantitative Overview*. Occasional Paper 1, *Human Resources Development Research Programme*. Cape Town: HSRC Publishers.
Eickelman, Dale E. 1992. Mass Higher Education and the Religous Imagination in Contemporary Arab Societies. *American Ethnologist. Imagining Identities: nation, culture, and the past* 19 (4): 643-55.
Euben, Roxanne L. 2002. Contingent Borders, Syncretic Perspectives: Globalization, Political Theory, and Islamizing Knowledge. *International Studies Review* 4 (1): 23-48.
Fataar, Aslam. 2005. Discourse, Differentiation, and Agency: Muslim Community Schools in Postapartheid Cape Town. *Comparative Education Review* 49 (1): 23-43.
Halstead, J. Mark. 2004. An Islamic Concept of Education. *Comparative Education* 40 (4): 517-29.
Johnson, Norris Brock. 1980. The Material Culture of Public School Classroooms: The Symbolic Integration of Local Schools and National Culture. *Anthropology & Education Quarterly* 11 (3): 173-90.
Maharaj, S. R. 1979. Primary and Secondary Education. In *South Africa's Indians: The Evolution of a Minority*, ed. by Bridglal Pachai, 338-83. Washington: University Press of America.
McGlyn, Claire. 2005. Integrated and Faith-Based Schooling in Northern England. *The Irish Journal of Education* 36 49-62.
2005. Nota Weerbaarheid en Integratiebeleid. Netherlands: Ministerie van Justitie: Minister voor Vreemdeingzaken en Integratie.
Perko, F. Michael. 2000. Religious Schooling in America: An Historiographic Reflection. *History of Education Quarterly* 40 (3): 320-38.
Rahman, Fazlur. 1982. *Islam and Modernity: Transformation of an Intellectual Tradition*. Chicago: University of Chicago Press.
Shadid, Wasif Abdelrahman, and Pieter Sjoerd van Koningsveld. 1992. *De Mythe van het Islamitische Gevaar: Hindernissen bij Integratie*. Kampen: Kok.
Starret, Gregory. 2006. The American Interest in Islamic Schooling: A Misplaced Emphasis? *Middle East Policy* 13 (1): 120-31.
Waardenburg, Jacques. 1965. Some Institutional Aspects of Muslim Higher Education and their Relation to Islam. *Numen* 12 (2): 96-138.
Zaman, Muhammad Qasim. 1999. Religious Education and the Rhetoric of Reform: The Madrasa in British India and Pakistan. *Comparative Studies in Society and History* 41 (2): 294-32.
Zine, Jasmine. 2001. Muslim Youth in Canadian Schools: Education and the Politics of Religious Identity. *Anthropology & Education* 32 (4): 399-423.

Interviews

Abed, Yusuf. 2006. Interview by Abdulkader Tayob, Tswane (Pretoria), December 5.
Adam, Ali. 2006. Interview by Armien Cassiem, Cape Town, December 5.
Amod, Irshad. 2006. Interview by Abdulkader Tayob, Durban, December 19.

Aslam Fataar

Identity, Religious Conversion and Spatial Mobility

The Case of Fuzile Ali at a Muslim Community School in Cape Town

This article unfolds against the backdrop of rapidly changing livelihoods in the post-apartheid city; in this case the fascinatingly complex and unequal city of Cape Town, framed by the twin features of sheer geographic beauty on the one hand and devastating poverty and material brutality on the other.

Fuzile Ali (pseudonym) finished high school at the Al-Balaagh high school (pseudonym) at the end of 2008. I first encountered him at an end-of-high school dinner where he was one of three student speakers. Something about Fuzile Ali's *performance* stuck me. He made a well rehearsed speech about his ambitions for his life. He was poised and confident, and said nothing about his conversion or the importance of his adopted school or new religion. His discourse was framed by desire and aspiration. I thought then that his story could pierce open one set of understandings, one key cognitive map about how city life is constituted in interaction with rapidly changing school processes in the city. It is in this light that I present a reading of his story 'against' the normative assumptions that underpin religious conversion. His story requires a conceptual approach that can capture the complex iterations among youthful becoming in differently attributed spatial worlds in light of his religious cultural socialization.

I locate my work at the intersection of educational development and reform, specifically at the point where sociological processes inside schools and other educational institutions interact with, and are shaped by, the normative agendas of the post-apartheid state. My analytical lens is a defamiliarising one which focuses on how people live and experience their schooling, on what they become in interaction with the worlds of the schools they attend. I proceed from the view that city spaces are 'lived spaces' encountered and constituted by those who interact with them. The creative articulation between these lived urban practices and schooling practices is at the centre of my work. Schooling practices such as the ones established by Fuzile Ali are an example of some learners' variegated journeys back and forth across geographic regions of South Africa, across rural and urban spaces, and across the city. The five schools he attended provide the backdrop for his scholarly becoming. His case is not an isolated one but part of a larger urban trend. I completed eight interviews with Fuzile Ali over a three week period. My research assistant and I did a number of peripheral interviews with his family members, friends as well as some of his teachers at the various schools he attended.

He currently attends a madrasah (Muslim religious school) attached to a mosque in Cape Town's southern suburbs where he studies Qur'an reading and Arabic. He lives on the premises of the mosque and does part-time work for a *da'wah* (missionary) organization, "Discover Islam", run by a Saudi-trained North American expatriate. He intends studying law next year at one of Cape

Town's universities. His is a complex story of life in post-apartheid society, a young life that spans five schools in sub-regional context, traversing rural and urban areas across the Eastern and Western Cape provinces of South Africa. I would suggest, following De Certeau (1984), that Fuzile Ali's life can be read as constructions of self in his daily encounters with specific lived spaces. De Certeau's key insight is that people use cities for constructing who they are, producing a narrative of identity. They write the city without being able to read it – and they don't know how their individual paths affect the city as a whole. They make a sentence or a story of particular places in the city, while the city is not available as an overview – the city is the way that it is walked (De Certeau 1984, 91-114).

'Walking' the rural – urban divide

So how does Fuzile Ali 'walk' the rural – urban divide and the city of Cape Town in which he has come to settle? He attended his first school in a rural Eastern Cape village at the age of six years old, conceptually and geographically miles away from the context of his conversion to Islam years later. His first rural school in 1996 and the three schools he subsequently attended, in Cape Town, back in the village in the Eastern Cape, and then back in Cape Town respectively, were historically intended for black Africans.

Fuzile Ali can therefore be said to have established a school desire line across black African space, sutured by the policies of racial separation with their roots in the separatist logics of apartheid. Until his move to Balaagh Institute, he had minimal contact with non-black African people. Theorist of race, David Theo Goldberg (2009), suggests productively that the apartheid / post-apartheid turnover, from a society based on rigid formal racialization to the formal deracialization of public life, can be understood in light of what he describes as the shift from the 'sacralization of race' to the 'secularization of race' (Goldberg 2009, 309-321). He argues that since 1994, South African society has begun to move away from a situation where racial exclusivism and racial oppression of black people occurred on the basis of a political theology of race.

Instead of this 'sacralization', race has now become secularised, wrapped in the politically limiting clothing of neoliberalism, individualism and a weak decentralizing state, which has impacted the re-ordering of the South African social order. South Africa has thus moved from racial exclusiveness to what I would call the flexibilities and limitations of deracialization where post-racial repositionings are articulated by class, space and the vagaries of material access. Fuzile Ali traverses the asynchronous spatialities of the post-apartheid order. He 'walks' through this landscape by drawing on a repertoire of internal and external resources. It is the coming together of these internal psychological resources and the material opportunities of the external environment, a particular individual articulation, which points the way for his subjective becoming. His life is knitted together by contingency and strategic readings trumped by an aspirant desire for mobility. This mobility is inflected by the vagaries of the physical spaces he finds himself in, and his assertion of his own meanings, desires and aspirations in these spaces. His is an example of making space, or in the conception of Lefebvre (1991:7-12), 'representing space' or 'living space'. Fuzile Ali thus develops a complex subjectivity by actively 'walking' through the dissonant post-racial spatial order.

Let me explain: his first school in the rural village in the Eastern Cape is a one-building school with three teachers. Deeply impoverished, the school performs its pedagogical rudiments in the Xhosa language. Fuzile Ali completed Grades One, Two and half of Grade Three when, in 1998, the reach of the decentralizing post-apartheid order arrived and dislodged him from his school world. The post-apartheid state arrived in the rural village by way of its school governance reform legislation, in the form of the South African Schools Act (DOE 1996), which enabled the school to charge R20 per annum for school fees, which, in the depressed local economy of a rural village, was an enormous sum. The school charged user fees to augment a limited state allocation to the school. This reform model in effect dispersed the responsibility for equitable school development onto the rural and urban poor with deleterious consequences for the life contours of youngsters like Fuzile Ali.

He was sent home in July 1998, practically banned from school because of a failure to pay. His maternal grandfather, who was not quite committed culturally to the education of his offspring, was either unable or refused to pay. He commandeered Fuzile Ali to take up the position of looking after his cattle full-time. Cattle play a vital role in the life of such traditional rural communities and at an early age Fuzile Ali had already had his fair share of shepherding, which he had come to hate. Withdrawn from school, he performed his shepherd role dutifully, if ruefully, developing a permanent disdain for this type of work. He nonetheless retained his equanimity, and an image as a respectful and hardworking good boy, who is able to turn adversity into a personal asset, a dimension which characterizes his associations and relationships throughout his life.

Drawing on Erikson's (1968) path-breaking work on youth and identity development, I would argue that Fuzile Ali navigates his life circumstances fundamentally on the basis of simultaneous internal discipline that controls his psychological imprinting, marshalled, sometimes with difficulty, while performing a cheery, forward-looking disposition that endears him to those with whom he comes into contact, specifically his teachers and students at his various schools. Erikson's work suggests that we always have to read young people against the unique historical conditions in which they find themselves (Erikson 1968, 35).

Fuzile Ali has been able to cultivate a number of networks, using them to leverage a productive platform for launching himself into modernity, becoming educated, and accessing particular religious affiliations that position him in ever evolving, physical, conceptual and affective terrains. His networks and relations have nonetheless been unstable, and so has his movement across the geographies of the post-apartheid order. Fuzile Ali was whisked away in January 1999 by his paternal grandfather at the age of nine, to attend a school in urban Cape Town. As an urban itinerant who worked variously as a labourer and security guard in this city, his paternal grandfather was in a position to take Fuzile Ali with him to

Cape Town to live with one of three wives in a black African township. Fuzile Ali felt liberated. He fell in love with the city. Associating his rural village with backwardness and stagnation, he began to associate the city with progress and the chance of becoming educated.

He lived with his grandfather's third wife and her children in a hostel apartment in Langa, the oldest existing African township in Cape Town. Interestingly, his step-grandmother placed him in the only Sotho-speaking school in a predominantly Xhosa-speaking township. The Sotho school was perceived to be a more stable and better quality school and instruction was in Sotho, a language cognate but different to the Xhosa language. At age nine Fuzile Ali was placed back into Grade One after failing an informal aptitude test at the school. Reluctant at first, he quickly immersed himself in his school career. With his grandfather paying his fees, he became a teacher's favourite and completed Grades One to Five, from 1999 to 2003.

The grandfather's decision upon his retirement to take a fourth wife back in his home village in the Eastern Cape led to Fuzile Ali expulsion from the home of the step-grandmother with whom he was living. He found himself back in the rural Eastern Cape in January 2004. The decision was made that he would attend the school in his grandfather's rural village, but instead of going into Grade Six he skipped grades to go into Grade Eight. Grade skipping is a common occurrence among black African children who move back and forth between urban and rural schools. The post-apartheid surveillance state has begun to address this incongruence by introducing a very sophisticated IT-based monitoring system that can pick up this grade-skipping. Fuzile Ali was able to skip grades by presenting the village school a story about a burning shack, not an uncommon occurrence in the city, in which everything, including his report cards, was destroyed. The grandfather's association with the school, as a village elder, helped to secure his place in Grade Eight, which he completed at this school.

Fuzile Ali was by then always looking to the city. The move back to the rural village in the Eastern Cape was painful. He described this period in an interview as a wasted year. Changed family arrangements resulted in a situation where he was able to move back to Cape Town to live with his mother's relatives in Phillipi, another township in Cape Town. He thus migrated back to Cape Town in January 2005 where he attended a black African township school for Grades Nine and Ten. His mother's relatives provided him and his younger brother with a relatively stable environment. He had to do many daily chores and take care of his sibling's homework. Grateful for the opportunity to go to school in the city, Fuzile Ali was able to work the formal and informal networks of this township to his advantage. He became an active member of an evangelical church, attending church services thrice per week, participating fully in its youth programmes, and making use of its social welfare provisions such as the food, health services, and clothing.

The church environment also presented him with the opportunity to become immersed in his long-standing interest in drama classes through a drama programme provided in association with the church. This interest had initially been piqued by his being given a bit part in an American-produced short film on life in the township. His persona as an actor found expression in this new environment.

I would argue overall that Fuzile Ali's life scriptings can be likened to a Butlerian view of performance. Butler speaks of performance as scriptings that embed a form of identity, in reference to the ability of the performer to enact and enable a specific identity relative to his specific affective terrains (Butler 1991). The religiosity on display has to be understood in light of the many associations of which it is a part. Eschatological commitments for Fuzile Ali combine with material need on the one hand, and his youthful navigations on the other, to find sustenance for his aspirations in particular environments and networks. His religious commitments generate certain understandings of life, and the possibilities that inhere in such understandings. It is the specific readings and aspirations that he brings to the exercise of his religiosity that helps explain his youthful subjectivity. The attributions of space are crucial, of being inside specific spatialities that organize, articulate and give meaning to his subjective being and becoming. This understanding can be applied to his Christian commitments, his 'Christianness', in the space of the black township and his 'Muslimness' in the space of a subsequent environment, as I will now go on to show.

The spatiality of Fuzile Ali's 'Muslimness'

His mother, until then relatively absent from his growing up, migrated to Cape Town in the middle of 2006. She initially went to live with her sister in a deeply impoverished township in Cape Town. Fortuitous circumstances led to her obtaining a rudimentary house structure in an area of this township that was hurriedly laid on for victims of a fire in an adjacent squatter settlement. The South African National Zakaah Fund (SANZAF), which became involved in relief work in this area, had set up a social welfare office in response to the needs of the refugees. They also established a madrasah structure where they provided basic Islamic education to those people who converted to Islam.

Fuzile Ali and his sibling were now required to live with their mother in this new area. They had to travel to school by taxi. He was thus somewhat cut off from his Christian-based youth and other social networks, although the church continued to pay his school fees and his taxi fares. He still travels to Phillipi township every Saturday for his drama classes. Clearly, becoming Muslim had not cut him loose from his Christian-based networks. Nor had it alienated him from his Christian and traditionally orientated family and friends who were spread across the Cape sub-region. He visited his family in the Eastern Cape regularly and stayed in touch with his many cousins and friends.

Fuzile Ali became Muslim after three days of attending the madrasah in his mother's township. The madrasah was the only religious structure in close proximity to their home. He speaks of having been under the impression that the madrasah was a church, of people worshipping there, dressed in a particular way, reciting in a somewhat strange language. It seems from my interviews that the madrasah provided an affective religious environment in a very depressed situation. The madrasah assisted people with their immediate social welfare needs. Fuzile Ali and his mother were possibly attracted to becoming Muslim because of the access it provided to symbolic and material sustenance in a deeply ephemeral and alienating environment. He suggested that access to food played a major role in their family's attendance of the madrasah and in their becoming Muslim.

His mother left the faith after three months but Fuzile Ali engaged more actively with the discursive material and opportunities that becoming Muslim in this space offered. He spoke of being moved and inspired in the early days of his conversion by the discipline, unity, and simplicity he witnessed when he participated in a pro-Palestinian march in downtown Cape Town. Donning the skull cap and a white robe, and learning about Islamic rituals and the rudiments of Qur'ānic recitation, provided him access to new symbols and a new language. He began to associate a successful and moral youthful existence with his becoming Muslim.

He explained that his conversion was not based on any strong conviction about the eschatological veracity of his new religion. I asked him at what point he started to fully commit to his new religion and on what basis. His answer was astonishing. I expected a rehearsed answer about the comparative logics of the status of Jesus in both Islam and Christianity, and comparisons between *Tawhīd* (the unicity of God) and the Divine Trinity. Instead, Fuzile Ali replied thus; "... when they told me I would go to Cairo to study, I really became committed. From then on I became so committed. ... I practised so hard to know my lessons, to be a good person." It was thus aspiration tied to the conceptual geographies of Islam, of the promise of travelling, of tying mobility to the desire to self-improve and become someone significant, which fired his imagination and motivated his early Islamic becoming.

Not as distant as the promised study trip to Cairo, his move from the high school in Phillipi to Balaagh Institute in 2007, proved decisive in his Muslim youthful becoming. This move afforded him the opportunity to step out of 'black space' into the cultural and ethnically ambiguous space of a middle class Muslim private school controlled by Indian ethnic interests and attended by Coloured (mixed race) and Indian children (Fataar 2004, 2005) . Children pay about R12 000 in fees per year to attend Balaagh Institute. The school is situated on a newly built and fairly sophisticated campus. The South African National Zakaah Fund and the missionary organization, Discover Islam, active in his new township, had decided that it would be in his educational and religious interest for him to complete his high school years at Balaagh Institute. Viewing him as an asset for their missionary efforts, these organizations decided to secure him a place in the school. He was exempted from the annual fees and the missionary organisation paid his taxi fees to travel to school. He was one of the first black African children to attend this school.

Fuzile Ali's resilience, courage and adaptability were severely tested in this new environment. He struggled to adapt to the expected academic rigour and standards of the school. He had to take Mathematics on the higher grade and English as a first language. It is no secret that the gap in quality between a typical Cape Town township school and a middle class private school such as Balaagh Institute is enormous. His Mathematics level would have been at a Grade Four or Five level compared to the expected Grade Eleven level at which he was expected to perform at Balaagh Institute. His level of English language proficiency would have been similarly discordant.

His teachers spent an inordinate amount of time tutoring him to make up for his educational deficiencies. He attended numerous tutorial support programmes in English and Mathematics after school hours, over weekends and during school vacations. He never wavered in his commitment to his educational improvement. He immersed himself in Islamic Studies, proving much more eager to learn about his new religion than his classmates. This commitment endeared him to his teachers and the school governors, but his presence became unnerving for his classmates who ended up periodically bullying him. They challenged the school about the fuss it was making about a 'stupid black kid' who doesn't pay school fees, wastes the teachers' time asking 'irrelevant' questions, and doesn't deserve to be at the school, let alone command all the attention and time teachers spent on him. Fuzile Ali felt deeply hurt and alienated from this environment when he experienced these verbal and physical assaults. The teachers and school management did not countenance these assaults. They managed to establish a tolerable context for him to complete his studies. He eventually succeeded in making friends with many of the students. He kept his eyes on the ball, remained committed to his educational aspirations, and continued to work hard at accessing the educational resources of the school, all the time figuring out and taking on the appropriate religious and educational comportments necessary for success at his new school and in his new religious environs.

The decision to have Fuzile Ali live in a Muslim family, that of a director of SANZAF, proved to be decisive in his successful completion of high school and his 'Muslim becoming'. He lived as a full member of this stable middle class nuclear family which consisted of parents and three daughters. They lived in a comfortable home within walking distance of the school. The family followed strict domestic etiquette. He initially struggled to adapt to these vastly different domestic circumstances; to be on time for dinner and prayers, to observe the family's table etiquette, and its spatial arrangements based on a relatively strict gender separation. Having mastered the domestic decorum of this middle class religious family, he went on to use the space of his new home to commit himself to his studies, establishing a productive and rigorous routine in its protected confines.

In conclusion, Fuzile Ali's story is much more complicated than what the lens of 'religious conversion' can help explain. The story suggests a complex and layered reading of subjective youthful becoming. Space and context are as important to the story as the ability to move beyond space, of how physical space provides the terrain for subjective engagement, strategic readings, and performance. The religious becoming of Fuzile must be understood in light of the 'sociological stretching' out across time and space, across the post-apartheid geographies of the contemporary Now, as Sarah Nuttall (2004) would say.

Fuzile Ali established one creative path across these asynchronous, differently attributed spaces, 'walking' across them, borrowing, adapting, and creating. His religious becoming, his Muslimness, can only be understood in relation to these social transactions, which are trumped by his desire to access the aspirational heights of the city. Becoming Muslim for him is an expression of a particular kind of urban imagination. It is the city and what he can become in the city that provides the rough material for his subjective becoming, and becoming Muslim was for him a path into his evolving process of becoming.

References

Butler, Judith. 1990. *Gender Trouble*. London: Routledge.

De Certeau, Michel. 1984. *The Practice of Everyday Life.* Berkeley: California Press.

Department of Education. 1996. *South African Schools Act.* Pretoria: Government Printers.

Erikson, Erik H. 1968. *Identity, Youth and Crisis*. New York: WW Norton.

Fataar, Aslam. 2004. Muslim schooling in Cape Town, Exemplifying creative adaptation to the democratic landscape. *Annual Review of Islam in South Africa,* 7: 33-40.

Fataar, Aslam. 2005. Discourse, differentiation and agency: Muslim community schooling in post-apartheid Cape Town. *Comparative Education Review*, 49: 23-44.

Fataar, Aslam. 2007. Schooling, Youth Adaptation, and Translocal Citizenship across the Post Apartheid City. *Journal of Education*, 43: 3-21.

Goldberg, David T. 2009. *The Threat of Race: Reflections on Racial Neoliberalism.* Oxford: Blackwell.

Lefebvre, Henri. 1991. *The Production of Space.* Translated by Donald Nicholson-Smith. Oxford: Blackwell.

Nuttall, Sarah. 2004. City Forms and Writing the 'Now' in South Africa. *Journal of Southern African Studies*. 30(4): 731-748.

Muhammad Khalid Sayed

South African Madrasahs Move into the 21st Century

Introduction

Madrasahs, or *madāris*, are literally "places of study". From the establishment of the Madrasah Nizamiyah in Baghdad during the ninth century A.D, madrasahs have functioned globally as centres for higher Islamic education. Madrasahs were, and continue to be, primarily dedicated to the teaching of subjects necessary for the study and understanding of *sharīʿa* (Islamic law). Madrasahs around the world train *ʿulamāʾ* (religious scholars and leaders) for the religious guidance of Muslim communities, especially in matters of Islamic law and theology (Talbani 1996, 68).

Madrasahs socialize Muslims in the textual, legal and theological traditions of Islam, based on the opinions of revered scholars of the past. Arising from this function, madrasahs mediate common identities and links for Muslims that not only differentiates Muslims from non-Muslims, but also from other Muslims in legal and theological matters. However, the development of many madrasahs in colonial and post-colonial contexts, such as the famous Indian madrasah, Darul Uloom (Deoband), established in 1857, show that this religious socialization and sectarianism often reflects local contexts. Therefore, the nature of the religious socialization and sectarianism is characterized by diversification or transformation. The influence of national political trends, globalization, culture, language, gender, ethnicity and class are important factors in this regard.

The South African social landscape is a diverse and changing one, which has become more apparent in Muslim communities since 1994. "Racial" and ethnic mixing, and globalization have become major elements of influence with regard to religious values in South African Muslim communities. As centres for higher Islamic learning, the dynamics surrounding the madrasahs in South Africa reflect both the established and changing socialization and consequent contestations over values.

As South Africans of Indian origin began to be recognized as permanent South African citizens from 1961 onward, their educational opportunities and economic mobility increased. Vahed and Jeppie (2005) assert that during this period, conservative ʿulamāʾ began to emerge as an influential factor shaping local Muslim communities. The concentration of Indian Muslims brought about by the Group Areas Act also allowed for the practice of Islam in a distinctly Indian environment. Thus, when Islamic revivalism manifested itself amongst Indian Muslims, the masses embraced two opposing sectarian tendencies of India, Deobandi[1] and Sunnī/Barelwi (Vahed & Jeppie 2005, 261).[2]

1 Deobandi Islam took root in India in 1867 with the establishment of the Darul Uloom Madrasah Arabia Islamia in Deoband by Mawlānā Muhammad Qasim Nanautawi (d.1880) and Mawlānā Rashid Ahmed Gangohi (d.1905). This followed their defeat by the British in the 1857 mutiny. The Deoband movement remained aloof from political

It was within this context that young men began going to madrasahs in India and Pakistan to pursue theological training. Arising partly from the logistic and economic difficulties related to this arrangement, the first madrasahs soon thereafter began to be established in the Indian Muslim communities in Natal and Transvaal. Darul Uloom (Newcastle) was established in 1973 in the town of Newcastle in the Northern Natal Midlands. The madrasah was established by Mawlānā Cassim Mohamed Sema (d.2007), a South African graduate of Darul Uloom (Dhabel), a well-known Deobandi madrasah in India (Akoo 2009). Other Madrasahs have been founded in South Africa from the 1980s onward and continue to be established, especially in the Gauteng and Kwazulu-Natal regions.

Leading up to and after the 1994 political transition in South Africa, the social and religious demographics of Muslims appears to be more diverse. Indian Muslims of Gauteng and Kwazulu-Natal are no longer as isolated as before from the "Malay" Muslims of the Cape. There has also been an increase in black conversions to Islam (Vahed & Jeppie 2005, 263). Furthermore, globalization has contributed to the existence of additional sectarian trends. For example, Shīʿīsm and Salafīsm have become identifiable sectarian identities amongst certain sectors in South African Muslim communities. Also, generally, Muslims, like other South African citizens are not isolated from the free-market economy, so religious scholarship and leadership too have begun to be packaged in terms of the demands of the modern economy.

It is with this backdrop that I begin to unearth the historical development of madrasah education in South Africa from 1973 to 2008. I identify transformations that have taken place in the madrasah education landscape of South Africa in the last thirty to forty years. I see this work as largely an exercise in contemporary historical excavation, in which more ethnographic work needs to be done. But this is a beginning on a neglected field. After introducing the features of madrasah education in general, I will introduce the madrasahs which I visited in Gauteng and Kwazulu-Natal. Thereafter I will provide general overviews of the organization and the teaching of *fiqh* at the madrasahs. Finally I focus on the changing face of sectarianism in South Africa.

---

activity and attended to educational and religious needs. They were concerned that "compromises" with Hinduism had resulted in syncretic developments. Deobandis targeted popular Ṣūfī beliefs and practices in this regard, such as visitation of tombs and the belief in the intercessionary role of saints. Deobandi Islam was popular among the Gujarati trading class in South Africa. See Moosa, 1993, p. 48

2 The Barelwi tradition originates in the works of Mawlānā Ahmed Raza Khan (d.1922), the founder of the madrasah Manzare Islam in Barelwi, India. He was a renowned scholar of Ḥanafī fiqh, a theologian, and a writer of Urdu and Persian poetry. Khan sought to defend the popular Ṣūfī beliefs and practices which the Deobandis criticized. In his writings, Khan defined this tradition as "Sunnī". In South Africa this tradition found expression mainly among descendants of indentured Muslims. See Vahed & Jeppie, 2005, p. 261

Features of madrasah education

When introducing the history of madrasah education of the Middle East, Jacques Waardenburg (1965) asserts that madrasah education plays a central role in ensuring the continuation of the Islamic tradition. He argues that this is the case because the religious sciences are studied in order to understand the Qur'an and Sunna (Practices of Prophet Muhammad) in a particular way so as to "guide" Muslims (Waardenburg 1965, 96-97). More closely tied to our current study is the assertion made by Barbara Metcalf (1978) in her overview of the madrasah of Deoband. Metcalf asserts that one of the madrasah's central aims was to "serve the daily religious and legal needs of Muslims in India" (Metcalf 1978, 112).

This particular feature of being a space from which to socialize Muslims in the textual, legal and theological traditions of Islam as interpreted by scholars of the past is more clearly underlined when looking at the standard curricula used at madrasahs globally and in South Asia in particular. The subjects in the curricula are Arabic language, *fiqh* (Islamic Jurisprudence), *uṣūl al-fiqh* (Principles of Jurisprudence), *tafsīr al-Qur'ān* (Commentary of the Qur'an), *tārīkh* (History), *ʿaqīda* (Theology), and *ḥadīth* (Prophetic Traditions). Standard texts authored by scholars of the past have formed and continue to form the core of the madrasah curricula for these subjects. For example, for *fiqh*, books authored by jurists of the past such as *Bulūgh al-marām* of Ibn Ḥajar al-ʿAsqalānī (d.1449) and *Minhāj al-ṭālibīn* of Yaḥyā ibn Sharaf al-Nawawī (d.1277) form part of the core of the curriculum at many Shāfiʿī madrasahs. *Fiqh* is the Islamic normative tradition that Muslims usually follow in their daily religious practice. With regard to the emphasis placed on teaching *ḥadīth*, selected and verified by scholars of the past, the six books of Sunnī *ḥadīth* are most commonly taught in the final year of a student's course. These texts are *Ṣaḥīḥ* of Muḥammad ibn Ismaʿīl al-Bukhārī (d.870), *Ṣaḥīḥ* of Muslim ibn Hajjāj (d.875), *Ṣaḥīḥ* of Muḥammad ibn ʿĪsa al-Tirmidhī (d.892), *Sunan* of Sulaymān Abū Dawūd (d.889), *Sunan* of ʿAbdullah ibn Mājah (d.887) and *Sunan* of Aḥmad ibn al- Nasāʾ ī (d.830) (Metcalf 1978, 117).

Arguably the most standardized madrasah curriculum has been, and continues to be, that adopted by the madrasahs of South Asia. Madrasahs in South Asia teach a curriculum known as the *Dars-e Nizami*. It was first introduced by Mullah Nizamuddin Sihalvi (d.1748) during the eighteenth century. Mullah Nizamuddin was a scholar of jurisprudence and philosophy from the famous Farangi Mahal madrasah in Lucknow. According to Mumtaz Ahmed, almost all South Asian Sunnī Ḥanafī madrasahs, irrespective of whether they are of Deobandi or Barelwi persuasion, follow the same standard *Nizami* course of studies adopted by the Deoband madrasah in 1867 (Ahmed 2004, 103).

Core texts taught over a period of six to eight years form the main subjects in the *Dars-e Nizami*. These texts were authored mainly by revered Islamic scholars of the seventh to fourteenth centuries. While different madrasahs have added texts to the subjects, these texts are merely meant to supplement the core *Nizami* texts, or to interpret the *Nizami* texts in line with particular sectarian approaches of the madrasahs (Ahmed 2004, 105). These are the core texts taught in the *Dars-e Nizami*:

- *Fiqh*: Ḥanafī texts, *al-Mukhtaṣar* – of Abu ʿl Ḥasan al-Qudūrī – (d.1037) and *Sharḥ al-wiqāya* by Mullah ʿAlī Qārī (d.1014).
- *Uṣūl al-fiqh*: *Uṣūl al-shāshī* of Nizamuddin al-Shāshī (d.728) and *Nūr al-anwār* of Mullah Jeevan ibn Sa'eed (d.1717).
- *Uṣūl al-ḥadīth*: *Nuzhat al- nadhr fī sharḥ nuqba* of al-ʿAsqalānī.
- *Tafsīr*: *Jalālayn* of Jalāluddin al-Suyūṭī (d.1505) and Jalāluddin al-Maḥallī (d.1459) and *Fawz al-kabīr* of Shah Wali Allah Dehlawī (d.1762).
- *ʿAqīda*: *Sharḥ al-ʿaqāʾid al-nasafī* of Saʿd al-Dīn al-Taftāzānī (d.1390) and *ʿAqīda al-ṭaḥāwī* of Abu Jaʿfar al-Ṭaḥāwī (d.933).
- *Tārīkh*: *Tārīkh al-khulafāʾ* of al-Suyūṭī.
- *Ḥadīth*: *Mishkāt al-maṣābīḥ* of Abū Muḥammad al-Baghawī (d.1117) and the six core books of Sunnī *ḥadīth* literature.

Reichmuth asserts that by providing common ethical and legal forms for Muslims based on the sciences that are standardized and taught through texts, madrasahs provide a basis through which Muslims can openly distinguish themselves from non-Muslims (Reichmuth 2000). The promotion of *fiqh* as a guideline for daily practice is a salient feature in this regard (Reichmuth 2000, 426).

Madrasah education also serves to differentiate one Muslim group from other Muslims, emphasis placed on the priority of teaching a particular legal school, promoting a particular theology, and articulating arguments against other Muslim sects are crucial. According to Waardenburg, from the ninth century madrasahs in the Muslim world only taught one particular legal school as the standard approach to Islamic law, with particular standard texts from that school being taught (Waardenburg 1965). Furthermore, Waardenburg asserts that the very first madarasah to be established in the Islamic world, the Nizamiyah madrasah in Baghdad, was established as a college specifically for the teaching of Shāfiʿī law and the Sunnī Ashʿarī theology (Waardenburg 1965, 100). In Shāfiʿī madrasahs, ranging from the Middle East to East and Southern Africa, standard Shāfiʿī texts such as *Minhāj al-Ṭālibīn* and *Bulūgh al-marām* form the core of the curricula. Madrasahs such as Darul Uloom (Deoband), who serve Ḥanafī Muslims, tend to teach solely Ḥanafī books of *fiqh* such as *al-Mukhtaṣar* of al-Qudūrī (Metcalf 1978, 125). In West Africa, *al-Mukhtaṣar* of Khalīl b. Isḥāq (d.1366) is the predominant *fiqh* text for madrasahs teaching the Mālikī school of law (Reichmuth 2000, 427). This emphasis on a particular law school and the main books of the school not only connects different madrasahs globally in terms of curriculum, but can provide Muslims with a common identity in the Islamic normative tradition as either Ḥanafī, Shāfiʿī, Mālikī or Ḥanbalī.

A striking characteristic of madrasah education which can fundamentally mediate a common identity amongst Muslims while simultaneously divide Muslims from one another on theological grounds has been the promotion and defence of a particular sectarian tradition or interpretation of Islam. This emphasis on promoting and defending a sectarian tradition can provide and solidify a common identity with textual justifications for Muslims, while setting those Muslims fundamentally apart from Muslims who follow opposing sects and interpretive traditions. The historical Sunnī-Shīʿī, Ashʿarī-Ḥanbalī, Ṣūfī-Salafī and Deobandi-Barelwi divisions and conflicts are important to note in this regard.

There are a number of common texts that madrasahs of the same theological school tend to teach. For example, throughout many Sunnī Ashʿarī West and East African madrasahs, the *Umm al-barāhīn* of Yusuf al-Sanūsī (d.1486) seems to be the standard text for *ʿaqīda* (Reichmuth 2000, 427). While in Sunnī Ashʿarī South Asian and Middle Eastern madrasahs, *Sharḥ al-ʻAqāʼid al-Nasafī* and *ʻAqīda al-ṭaḥāwī* are taught. In addition to teaching particular texts that provide theological interpretations of one particular sectarian tradition in which other sects are critiqued, many madrasahs incorporate the promotion of their sectarian tradition and the critique of the others in their teaching of subjects such as *ḥadīth* and *tafsīr* (Sikand 2005, 134). Furthermore, Sikand points out that madrasahs such as those of Deobandi and Barelwi persuasion have particular debating sessions set aside every week at the madrasah in which students pose as spokespersons of the madrasah's sect and others as those of an opposing sect. These are referred to in Urdu as *munāẓara* (Sikand 2006, 136).

Many madrasahs have also formulated public responses in the form of theological polemics through sermons and pamphlets to what they perceive to be encroachments from other sects and interpretations of Islam in the localities in which these madrasahs have an influence. Metcalf underlines in detail these sectarian activities on the part of the Deoband madrasah against popular Ṣūfī customs and beliefs (Metcalf 1982, 133). Usha Sanyal elaborates on Mawlānā Ahmed Raza Khan's (d.1922) subsequent written defences of popular Ṣūfī customs and beliefs as well as his polemical attacks on Deoband scholars such as Mawlānā Rashid Ahmed Gangohī (d.1905), wherein he declares them to be apostates. Khan made these written declarations from the madrasah Manzare Islam in Barelwi, India (Sanyal 1996, 135). This feature is not limited to South Asia. Shaykh Sulaiman Mbwana, the founder and principal of the Zahrau madrasah in Tanga, Tanzania, delivered a number of public sermons and issued pamphlets in the 1980s against criticisms of popular Ṣūfī practices and beliefs such as the celebration of the Prophet Muḥammad's birth, *mawlīd*, and the belief in the eternal Light of Muḥammad (*nūr muḥammad*). In these sermons and pamphlets, Mbwana condemned the beliefs of the Salafīs and wrote a scholarly defence of the belief in *nūr muḥammad* (Chande 1998, 220).

South African madrasahs

From their inception, the South African madrasahs have followed the core features of madrasah education historically and globally. Their origins and growth, however, cannot be divorced from the position and developments of the Indian communities in the broader apartheid and post-apartheid contexts in which many were established and had developed.

I conducted interviews with the administrative staff at seventeen madrasahs in the Gauteng and Kwazulu-Natal provinces between January 2008 and January 2009. Madrasahs have been run in South Africa from the 1970s onward and continue to be established, especially in these regions.

These madrasahs generally offer six-year courses for the training of scholars in Islamic legal and theological sciences. Courses are offered for both males and females, but they are completely separated. Five of these madrasahs are for female students. The *Dars-e Nizami*, as has been taught at South Asian madrasahs, has made up and continues to make up the core of teaching at most South African madrasahs.

The following is a table providing basic information on each madrasah that I visited, ordered by year of establishment:

Madrasah	**Year of Establishment**	**Orientation**	**Gender**	**Ethnicity**	**Length of Study**	**Region**
Darul Uloom (Newcastle)	1973	Deobandi	Male	Indian	6 years	Kwazulu-Natal
Madrasah Salihaat	1983	Deobandi	Female	Indian	3 years	Kwazulu-Natal
Madrasah Tarbiyat-ul Banaat	1987	Deobandi	Female	Indian	4 years	Gauteng
Jamiah Maseehiah	1987	Deobandi	Male	Indian	6 years	Gauteng
Darul Uloom (Pretoria)	1989	Barelwi	Male	Indian	6 years	Gauteng
Madrasatul Banaat	1990	Deobandi	Female	Indian	3 years	Kwazulu-Natal
Darul Uloom Ashrafiyah	1992	Barelwi	Male	African	3 years	Kwazulu-Natal
Madrasah In'aamiyah	1994	Deobandi	Male	Indian	6 years	Kwazulu-Natal
Darul Uloom Qadria Ghareeb Nawaz	1997	Barelwi	Male	Indian	6 years	Kwazulu-Natal
Madrasah Islahul Muslimaat	1998	Deobandi	Female	Indian	3 years	Kwazulu-Natal
Madrasah Riyad al-Salihaat	1998	Deobandi	Female	Indian	3 years	Gauteng
Markaz al-Da'wa al-Islamia	2001	Salafī	Male	African	7 years	Gauteng
Darul Uloom Nu'maniyah	2001	Deobandi	Male	African	6 years	Kwazulu-Natal
Darul Uloom Samnaniyah	2001	Barelwi	Male	African	2 years	Kwazulu-Natal
Jamiatul Uloom al-Islamia	2001	Deobandi	Male	Indian	6 years	Gauteng
Imamia Hawzah Illmiyah	2007	Shīʿī	Male	African	3 years	Gauteng
Jamiah Imam Ahmed Raza Ahsanul Barakat	2007	Barelwi	Male	Indian	6 years	Kwazulu-Natal

Given their ethnic context, most of the mardasahs conform to either one of the two major sectarian persuasions amongst South African Muslims of Indian origin, Deobandi or Barelwi. I have, however, also conducted interviews at one Salafī and one Shīʿī madrasah. Unlike most of the madrasahs, these two madrasahs have very little connection to the distinct traditions of the South African Indian Muslim communities.

The establishment of the first of these madrasahs, Darul Uloom (Newcastle), introduces the link between madrasah education in South Africa and the development of Indian Muslim communities in a context of racial segregation. It was established in 1973, a period in which Indian Muslims had already been forced to move in segregated areas in terms of the Group Areas Act of 1950. This may have fostered the development of a distinctly Indian Muslim identity. Therefore, an aspect of Indian Islamic reform, namely the madrasah system, became a part of the Indian community's religious landscape.

In its origins, the madrasah had a distinctly Indian character to it. It was founded by Mawlānā Cassim Sema, a South African Indian scholar who grew up and resided in the town of Newcastle. The first directors of the madrasah and those who contributed financially to its establishment were businessmen of Indian origin. The names of Mr. S. I. Vawda and Hajee Ahmed Saloojee are worthy of note in this regard (Akoo 2009). The madrasah's link to South Asian Deobandi learning was and remains a major feature. This was manifested in a variety of respects. Its founder, Mawlānā Cassim Sema graduated at the Deobandi Darul Uloom (Dhabel) in India, and Sema visited the Deoband Madrasah just after the establishment of Darul Uloom (Newcastle) (Akoo 2009).

Whilst on a trip to India and Pakistan, following the establishment of the madrasah, Sema met with one of his former teachers, Mawlānā Muḥammad Yusuf Binnouri (d.1977) and asked him to devise a syllabus for Darul Uloom (Newcastle). Binnouri was the founder and rector of Pakistan's most respected Deobandi madrasah at the time, Darul Uloom (Newtown, Karachi). After a meeting with the teaching staff at Newtown, Binnouri drew up a syllabus for Darul Uloom (Newcastle). The core texts of this syllabus are the texts of the *Dars-e Nizami*. Upon his return to South Africa, Sema implemented this syllabus (Akoo 2009).

For his teaching staff, Sema recruited and employed Mawlānā Mansoorul Haq of Newtown in 1975. Two years later, Mansoorul Haq's brother, Mawlānā Mumtazul Haq was employed (Akoo 2009). As the number of students increased, especially during the 1980s, Sema recruited a number of South African-born Deobandi graduates as teachers. Amongst the earliest and longest-standing of these teachers was Mufti Abdul Kader Hoosen, a Newtown graduate. Others included Mawlānā Feroz Osman, Mawlānā Muneer Fareed Soofie and Mawlānā Suleiman Goga. These teachers were all graduates of Darul Uloom (Deoband). In later years, as students began graduating as *ʿulamāʾ*, a number of graduates began teaching at the madrasah. Having graduated in 1993, the current principal, Mawlānā Ismail Akoo is one such example (Akoo 2009).

The establishment of Darul Uloom (Newcastle) and later madrasahs was indicative of another broader development within Indian Muslim communities during the 1970s and 1980s. Institutionalization of Islam was taking place amongst more settled Indian Muslim communities during the 1970s and 1980s. Indian Muslims began establishing institutions for the practice, transmission and organization of Islam (Vahed & Jeppie 2005, 260).

The establishment of Darul Uloom (Newcastle) was closely related to the running of religious institutions such as mosques and *maktabs*[3] (places for elementary Islamic learning) locally. During the 1970s various *maktabs* and mosques were established. Gradually, these institutions required people with religious authority to be employed within them. The devoted but untrained "apa" could be replaced by a qualified and certified "Mawlānā". This was partly the reason for students, such as Sema himself, travelling to India in order to pursue theological training. As the number of *maktabs* and mosques increased the demand for qualified *ʿulamāʾ* increased. While students were travelling to South Asia to pursue Islamic studies, it was far more viable, logistically and economically, for *ʿulamāʾ* to be trained in South Africa. If we examine some of the letters and sermons delivered by Sema motivating business people to finance a madrasah, we note that his main points were that *maktabs* and mosques required teachers and *imāms* (religious leaders) and that it was not easy to constantly send young men to the subcontinent (Akoo 2007, 67).

The establishment and running of Darul Uloom (Newcastle) precipitated the establishment of other madrasahs amongst Indian Muslims, particularly during the 1980s. In 1982 Madrasah Arabia Islamia was established in Azaadville. Like Newcastle, this madrasah was founded by Deobandi trained *ʿulamāʾ* such as Mawlānā Abdul Hameed Ishaaq (Muhammad 2000, 6). Madrasah Arabia Islamia was founded within the context of an entrenched and closely concentrated Indian Muslim community. It was established at a time of political upheaval in South Africa. Its establishment may be viewed as a part of *ʿulamāʾ* attempts to maintain the religious orthodoxy of the communities in light of the deeply unstable political atmosphere in the country.

The South Asian Deobandi character of the madrasah and its connection to the maintenance and expression of a distinctly Indian Muslim identity is also clear. A world renowned Deobandi scholar from India, Mawlānā Muḥammad Zakariya Khandhalvi (d.1982), was a patron of the madrasah. The first consultation amongst the *ʿulamāʾ* of Natal and Transvaal regarding the establishment of Madrasah Arabia Islamia took place at Zakariya's *khānqa* (Ṣūfī lodge) in Stanger, a coastal town north of Durban. Furthermore, in addition to the *Dars-e Nizami* being taught, classes have always been conducted in the Urdu language (Muhammad 2000, 63).

Other Deobandi madrasahs were also established during this period. One such example is Jamiah Maseehiah, established in 1987 in Lenasia, an Indian residential area of Transvaal. The madrasah is now situated in De Deur, a farming town, south of Johannesburg. This madrasah has a more distinct Indian and Deobandi character than Azaadville and Newcastle. Jamiah Maseehiah was founded by Mufti Hashim Boda, a graduate of the Madrasah Miftahul Uloom in Jalalabad, India. Miftahul Uloom is considered by many of its graduates to be more in ac-

3 In South Africa, *maktabs* are popularly referred to as "madrasahs".

cordance with the teachings of the Deoband founding fathers than Deoband itself (Boda 2008).

Even during the 1990-1994 period of political transition and thereafter, many other madrasahs were established. Both Deobandi and Barelwi persuasions opened their own strongholds. The numbers of students enrolling at the madrasahs established during the 1980s continued to increase after 1994. Certain social, political and economic changes that accompanied the non-racial democracy now contributed to the rapid growth of madrasahs. Muslim communities were exposed to new, "threatening" social trends. The South African constitution is very liberal and the state is secular without the conservative Christian ideas of the Apartheid state. This situation triggered a more emphatic assertion of religious identity with an emphasis on personal piety as opposed to political resurgence, so as to not antagonize the new ANC government. The new South Africa was thought to offer opportunities for the previously excluded Muslim communities and their leadership/s. Madrasahs are popularly viewed as the bastions for the promotion of education stressing personal religious piety.

The new ANC government, of course, did not support an Islamic worldview. A very liberal constitution was adopted that many Muslims, and the *ʿulamāʾ* in particular, viewed as permissive. This was compounded by affirmative action policies, the "African Renaissance" agenda of the ANC, and the impact of globalization. Vahed and Jeppie argue that these changes triggered important behavioural modification among large numbers of Muslims (Vahed and Jeppie 2005). The most striking transformation in their view has been the growth of personal piety. As examples, Vahed and Jeppie point to an increase in the number of women who cover their faces with a veil; greater concern with observing dietary regulations; televisions have been rooted out from many Muslim homes; and a dramatic growth in Muslim schools. They argue that truth has become synonymous with *ʿulamāʾ* and to question the *ʿulamāʾ* means questioning the truth (Vahed & Jeppie 2005, 262).

The promotion of personal piety was part and parcel of the public discourse presented by madrasahs established during and after 1994. Drawing on the example of Azaadville, Mawlānā Abduraheem Khan, principal of Darul Uloom Nu'maniyah in Chatsworth, an Indian township west of Durban, pointed more specifically to the potential and vision for pietistic religious socialization with the establishment of his madrasah in 2001. When I asked him why he established this particular madrasah, Khan responded:

> Generally, my experience is that where there is a Darul Uloom the community around the Darul Uloom is affected spiritually. After a few years in Azaadville I watched people transform themselves … I looked back home in Chatsworth and saw that we have many vices. Many Muslim girls are marrying non-Muslim boys, for example. So I thought that if the madrasah is in Chatsworth, eventually our goal will be achieved (Khan 2008).

Organizational overview

The area in which most large-scale changes have taken place over the years at South African madrasahs has been in their organization. Changes have taken place in the acquisition of funds, recruitment of teachers and students, teaching methods and ideas around job-market education.

A comprehensive array of approaches for the acquisition of funds has and continues to be present in the organization of the madrasahs. Money received through *zakāt* (alms) from Muslims at local mosques and fees paid by students who are able to afford it, have remained a source of funding for all the madrasahs I visited. The madrasahs have also sought assistance through monetary donations from local Indian Muslim businessmen. This was the case with the establishment of the Barelwi madrasah, Darul Uloom Qadria Ghareeb Nawaz, in the town of Ladysmith in the Kwazulu-Natal Midlands. In 1997 the madrasah was established through the help of donations which the founder and principal, Mawlānā Sayyid Muḥammad Aleemuddin, acquired from various South African Indian Muslim businessmen. Since his arrival in South Africa from India in 1991, Aleemuddin built up a network of admirers and well-wishers in South African Barelwi circles. Local businessmen of a Barelwi persuasion in Johannesburg, Pretoria, Port Elizabeth and Cape Town have continued to play a pivotal role as Darul Uloom Qadria's donors (Aleemuddin 2008). While also having tapped into sectarian networks for funding, some of the Deobandi madrasahs have set up specific committees of Muslim businessmen for funding. For example, since the establishment of Madrasatul Banaat in 1990, all members of the board of trustees have provided the funds for the functioning of the madrasah. The incomes acquired from the donations given by the trustees have outweighed the income gained from the annual tuition fees (Amod 2008).

The diversity in organizational methods and the links which the madrasahs have built up, have also affected the recruitment of students. The majority of students have been recruited through word of mouth. This method has, however, been channelled through certain informal networks which the madrasahs have had in place. At all the madrasahs I visited, most students had heard about the madrasahs from friends or family members who were students. In addition to the graduate and student network, many students have come to know about the Deobandi madrasahs in particular through the visits of the local *Tablighi Jamāt*[4] around various parts of South Africa and the world. For example, while most of its Gauteng students have heard about the madrasah from their families and friends, since 1990 the majority of Cape Town students at Azaadville's female madrasah (established in 1987, Tarbiyatul Banaat) gained prospectus information about the madrasah from their male family members who in turn heard about the madrasah from men in the *Tablighi Jamāt* on their visits to mosques in Cape

4 *Tablighi Jamāt* is a proselytizing movement was founded in Delhi, India, in the 1920s and which now has operations worldwide. Founded by Mawlānā Muḥammad Illyas (d.1949), the *Tablighi Jamāt* places major emphasis on strengthening the faith of Muslims. This movement is promoted at most of the Deobandi madrasahs. The movement's first missionaries in India were students and graduates from the madrasah at Deoband. See Moosa, 1993, p. 50

Town. Many of these men are from Azaadville and its surrounding areas. From 1994 onward, students from countries such as Singapore, Thailand, and Malaysia came to hear about Tarbiyatul Banaat from South African *Tablighi Jamāt* members (Ali 2008).

There has also been diversity and change with the recruitment of teaching staff. Certain Deobandi and Barelwi madrasahs initially only recruited teachers from specific madrasahs in India and Pakistan. For example, from its establishment in 1992 up until 2001, Darul Uloom Ashrafiyah has only employed South African graduates of Jamiah Na'eemiyah in Lahore, Pakistan, to teach. Jamiah Na'eemiyah is a respected Barelwi madrasah at which its principal, Mawlānā Farhaad Ebrahim qualified. This particular method of recruitment came to an abrupt end in 2001 due to the events of September 11, after which no South Africans undertook studies in Lahore (Farhaad Ebrahim 2008). At Darul Uloom Qadria all teaching staff since 1997 have been graduates of the renowned Barelwi madrasah, Misbahul Uloom, in Mubarakpour, India. Aleemuddin is a graduate of Misbahul Uloom. Currently all twenty of the teaching staff at Qadria are Mubarakpour graduates (Aleemuddin 2008).

There has been much change in this area. Since their first graduation various madrasahs have begun employing their own graduates as teachers. We recall Darul Uloom (Newcastle) and the case of its current principle, Mawlānā Ismail Akoo. Furthermore, between 1987 and 1990, Tarbiyatul Banaat only had male teachers. But since 1993, as the first students graduated, female graduates began teaching at the madrasah (Ali 2008). Madrasah In'aamiyah, established in 1994 in Camperdown in the Kwazulu-Natal Midlands, also began employing graduates as teachers after its first graduation in 2000 (Desai 2008).

This development of a whole teaching sector is further underlined by the fact that many of the Deobandi madrasahs have consistently supplemented this approach by making vacant teaching posts known at other Deobandi madrasahs in South Africa. At Darul Uloom Nu'maniyah there have been many teachers who had graduated at Madrasah Arabia Islamia in Azaadville as well as from Darul Uloom (Newcastle) (Khan 2008). And at Jamiatul Uloom al-Islamia in the Gauteng province, most of the teaching staff since its establishment in 2001 has consistently been spread over graduates from Azaadville, Camperdown, and Newcastle (Saabir Ebrahim 2008).

A similar pattern is followed at the Salafī madrasah, Markaz al-Da'wa al-Islamia in Pretoria North and the Shī'ī Imamia Hawza Illmiyah in the sprawling black township of Soweto, west of Johannesburg. Since its establishment in 2001, Markaz al-Da'wa has been sending news of vacant teaching posts to the Islamic University of Medina in Saudi Arabia (Jacobs 2008). The founder and principal of Imamia Hawza, Mawlānā Nuru Mohammad, has made information of teaching posts available at various Islamic seminaries in Qom, Iran (Nuru 2008). The sectarian element of the madrasahs is still maintained through these developments in staff recruitment.

In terms of the method used for the teaching of the classical texts, the dictation approach has generally been followed. Minor changes to this have taken place at some madrasahs. These adjustments have, however, not shifted the intellectual engagement with the teaching material in any way. From 2004, Darul Uloom (Pretoria) started screening DVDs for History classes (Hazarvi 2008). At Jamiatul Uloom, PowerPoint presentations of classical *ḥadīth* commentaries such as Ibn Ḥajar's *Fatḥ al-Bārī* were employed from 2005 since Mawlānā Saabir Ebrahim was appointed principal (Saabir Ebrahim 2008).

In line with maintaining the general character of the madrasah, most of the change in the area of teaching methodology, has been focused around language. While some madrasahs have, since their establishment, continued to use Urdu as the medium of instruction, other madrasahs have used English and Arabic. For the first two years of study, English is the language of instruction, after which students are taught through the Arabic medium. The Urdu language is still taught, but through English medium. Jamiatul Uloom in Johannesburg (Gauteng) has changed its method of teaching Arabic and Urdu since 2005 when Saabir Ebrahim was appointed principal. Having previously worked as a secondary school inspector for the Kwazulu-Natal Department of Education, Ebrahim introduced what he refers to as "dynamics of non-native language teaching" to the teaching of Arabic and Urdu. Ebrahim explains that these dynamics include the thematic, communicative, interactive and suggestive pedagogical approaches. In 2005 he also added what he calls "Functional Arabic" and "Functional Urdu" to the traditional emphasis on Arabic and Urdu grammar. According to Ebrahim, the traditional emphasis on grammar equips students to read the Arabic and Urdu texts, while "Functional Arabic" and "Functional Urdu" gears students towards conversing in Arabic and Urdu (Saabir Ebrahim 2008).

Some of the madrasahs have also accommodated, to an extent, some of the change that has taken place in the general landscape of secondary and tertiary education. Since 2000 there seems to have been a shift towards job-market education at schools. At the same time there has been rising unemployment (Kallaway 2000, 18). Through introducing certain programmes to their syllabi, some madrasahs have sought to adapt to this context. Some madrasahs have introduced the teaching of secular subjects on a secondary school level. Students who enrol at the madrasahs without having completed their secondary secular education are expected to do the secular subjects and write the South African National Matric examination. Since 2002 Darul Uloom (Pretoria) employed local school teachers in the evenings to teach Mathematics, English, Afrikaans, Biology and Accounting (Hazarvi 2008). At Nu'maniyah since 2001 and at Ashrafiyah since 2003, students without a secondary education have been sent by the administration to actual secular non-Muslim schools during the day (Farhaad Ebrahim 2008). The administrators of these three madrasahs all indicated to me that these changes were introduced due to the need for students to find jobs outside madrasahs and mosques after graduating.

Jamiatul Uloom (Gauteng) has been more direct in this regard. With a complete primary education and Matriculation Exemption as a prerequisite for admission since its establishment in 2001, the madrasah has had a programme in place that ensures its students pursue secular tertiary degrees whilst at the madrasah. These tertiary studies are meant to ensure that the graduates are able to secure professional jobs in so-called secular fields in addition to qualifying as *ʿulamāʾ*.

Since 2001 students have had to undergo career aptitude tests, after which they would enrol for correspondence degrees at the University of South Africa (UNISA) in fields such as Law, Business Science, Teaching, Engineering and Information Technology (Saabir Ebrahim 2008).

It must be noted that these programmes of study have run parallel and separate to the traditional Islamic sciences. No religious dimension is added to the teaching of the secular subjects or to the choice of career, nor do the secular subjects or career paths have any relation to the Islamic sciences. UNISA is a secular distance learning institution. The historical function of madrasahs as spaces from which to socialize Muslims into the traditions of Islam as interpreted by the revered scholars of the past and sectarian identity formation has not been altered by these changes.

Teaching of Islamic law (*fiqh*)

Through changes in student demographics after 1994, transformation has taken place at many madrasahs in the syllabi from the original Indian Ḥanafī-based *Dars-e Nizami*. The Ḥanafī school of Islamic law is no longer the only one taught.

With the exception of Darul Uloom (Newcastle), Deobandi and Barelwi madrasahs were dominated by Indian students from Gauteng and Kwazulu-Natal prior to 1994. These students came from homes where Ḥanafī *fiqh* was practiced. The madrasahs only taught Ḥanafī texts. The male madrasahs focussed on the *Nizami* texts, *al-Mukhtaṣar* of al-Qudūrī and *Sharḥ al-wiqāya* of Mullah ʿAlī Qārī, while female madrasahs placed an emphasis on an Urdu text, *Beheshti Zewar* of a renowned Deobandi scholar, Ashraf ʿAlī Thanvī (d.1943).

Since 1994, Indian Muslims of Gauteng and Kwazulu-Natal moved away from being as isolated as previously from the "Malay" Muslims of the Cape. There has been an increased sense of religious exchange between *ʿulamāʾ*and Islamic organizations across this ethnic line. As a result, many students from Cape Town have been enrolling at primarily Ḥanafī Deobandi and Barelwi madrasahs in Gauteng and Kwazulu-Natal. The majority of these students are from families which practice Shāfiʿī *fiqh*. In addition to this, the bulk of foreign students from East Africa, Malawi, Mozambique, Malaysia, Indonesia, Philippines, Thailand and Singapore that have enrolled at the madrasahs after 1994 are Shāfiʿīs. As a direct result of this increase and at times dominance of Shāfiʿī students, most madrasahs have, since 1994, incorporated the teaching of Shāfiʿī *fiqh* in their *Dars-e Nizami* syllabi. In the *Nizami* syllabus, only Ḥanafī texts, al-Qudūrī's *al-Mukhtaṣar* and ʿAlī Qārī's *Sharḥ al-wiqāya* were previously taught.

From 2000, when Shāfiʿī students from Malawi enrolled, Darul Uloom Qadria started teaching students basic Shāfiʿī rulings from the Arabic text, *al-Madhāhib al-Arbaʿa*. This particular text covers rulings regarding ritual purity, prayers, fasting, alms and pilgrimage in the four Sunnī schools of law (Aleemuddin 2008). With relatively more numbers of Shāfiʿī students from Cape Town and foreign countries having enrolled since 1994, other Ḥanafī madrasahs accommodated more substantive change with regards to the incorporation of Shāfi'ī *fiqh*. They have introduced classical Shāfi'ī texts to the teaching content, albeit in separate classes for Shāfi'ī students only. At Tarbiyatul Banaat, widely used Shāfi'ī texts, *Bulūgh al-marām* of al-Asqalānī and *Minhāj al-ṭālibīn* of al-Nawawī have been taught since 1995. It was from 1995 that Shāfi'ī students from Cape Town, Malaysia and Thailand began attending the madrasah (Ali 2008). Darul Uloom (Pretoria) began teaching these two texts since the first Shāfi'ī students came to the madrasah from Cape Town in 1990 (Hazarvi 2008).

Compared to other madrasahs, Darul Uloom Nu'maniyah has brought further transformation to the traditional *Dars-e Nizami* emphasis on Ḥanafī *fiqh* through a gradual evolution in the teaching of Shāfi'ī *fiqh*. By 2005 Nu'maniyah began teaching classical Shāfi'ī texts to all its Shāfi'ī and Ḥanafī students alongside the *Nizami* Ḥanafī texts. When the madrasah was established in 2001, only Indian students with Ḥanafī backgrounds from Chatsworth attended the madrasah. So for the first year, only *al-Mukhtaṣar* and *Sharḥ al-wiqāya* formed part of the *fiqh* syllabus. Thereafter, between 2002 and 2004, with many students from Tanzania, Kenya and Cape Town enrolling, *Bulūgh al-marām* and *Minhāj al-ṭālibīn* began to be taught to the Shāfi'ī students. By 2005, the numbers of Shāfi'ī students from Tanzania rose to considerably outnumber the local Ḥanafī students. From 2005 two additional Shāfi'ī classical Arabic texts, *al-Iqnā'* of Shams al-Dīn al-Shirbīnī (d.1569) and *al-Matn ghayāt al-taqrīb* of Abū Shujā' al-Asbahānī (d.1095) were introduced into the syllabus and taught to all students alongside the Ḥanafī texts (Khan 2008).

At Darul Uloom (Newcastle), the accommodation of foreign students after 1994 has even led to the teaching of *fiqh* beyond Ḥanafī and Shāfi'ī texts. In 2007, Mālikī *fiqh* was incorporated in the syllabus for Mālikī students from Algeria. From 2001 Algerian students began enrolling at Newcastle. By 2006, the number of Algerian students had increased to 25. Its principal, Mawlānā Akoo said that in order to "accommodate" these students he appointed a Tunisian Mālikī teacher, Shaykh Faruq, in 2007, to teach the Mālikī *al-Mukhtaṣar* of al-Khalīl (Akoo 2009).

Changing face of sectarianism in South Africa

From the establishment of the first madrasah in South Africa, Darul Uloom (Newcastle) in 1973, a plethora of Deobandi madrasahs was established around the country. The very establishment of some of the madrasahs under study changed the overall landscape of madrasahs to a more diverse one.

Darul Uloom (Pretoria) was the first fully-fledged Barelwi madrasah. It was established in 1989, at a time when the Deobandi-Barelwi conflict in South Africa was at its peak. During the 1980s, Deobandi attacks had heightened against popular Ṣūfī practices such as the visitation to shrines of Ṣūfī saints, the celebration of Muḥammad's birth (*mawlīd*), and against beliefs in the intercession of saints (*tawaṣṣul*). These attacks were followed by the defence of these beliefs and practices as well as condemnations of the Deobandis by their Barelwi counterparts.

The very reasons given by the patron of Darul Uloom (Pretoria), Mawlānā Haseenudin Shah al-Qadri Razavi, for its establishment were directly related to this heightened South Asian sectarian conflict and identities that had been entrenched in the South African Indian Muslim community. According to Haseenudin Shah, there was a great need for a "Sunnī" madrasah that followed the teachings of Ahmed Raza Khan to be established so that the needs of the "Sunnī" Muslims could be served and their religious practices defended against what he referred to as Deobandi "encroachment". Haseenudin Shah is the rector of Ziah al-Uloom, a Barelwi madrasah in Rawalpindi, Pakistan. Mufti Akbar Hazarvi, the current principal of Darul Uloom (Pretoria) is a graduate of Ziah al-Uloom. Akbar Hazarvi was sent to South Africa by Haseenudin Shah for the purpose of running a "Sunnī" madrasah. Ever since its first graduation in 1993, graduates have been sent to Rawalpindi to study for one year (Hazarvi 2008).

The establishment of Darul Uloom Qadria Ghareeb Nawaz eight years later in Ladysmith is in tune with what we see with Darul Uloom (Pretoria). The madrasah is named after two celebrated Ṣūfī saints, Sayyid Abdul Qādir Jilānī (d.1166) who is buried in Baghdad, Iraq, and Khwaja Muʿīnuddīn Ḥassan Chistī (d.1230) who is buried in Ajmer, India. They are affectionately referred to by their South Asian admirers as "Ghous Paak" and "Ghareeb Nawaz" respectively (Aleemuddin 2008). Darul Uloom Qadria was established when Ladysmith was gripped by Deobandi-Barelwi conflict. In 1996, two groups of Barelwis came into conflict with each other because one group had agreed to perform a mass *Eid* prayer with the Deobandis of the town. According to Aleemuddin, the madrasah was established because no Sunnī madrasah that was teaching the complete *Dars-e Nizami* at the time was responding to what he saw as a Deobandi threat to Sunnīsm. He described Sunnī and Sunnīsm as being "*Maslake Ala Hazrat*", the ideas of Ahmed Raza Khan (Aleemuddin 2008).

In line with the sectarian polemics of Darul Uloom (Pretoria) and actually taking this further, in 2006, Darul Uloom Qadria translated into English and published *Jāʾ al-Ḥaq wa Zahaqal Bāṭil*. This is an anti-Deobandi polemic written in Urdu by a renowned Barelwi polemicist of Pakistan, Mufti Ahmad Yaar Khan Naeemi (d.1971). This anti-Deobandi sectarianism has also been illustrated in the syllabus. From the madrasah's establishment in 1997, many of Ahmed Raza Khan's *fatāwa* (legal opinions) in Arabic from his *al-Malfūẓāt* have been taught and promoted. His *fatāwa* provided justification for beliefs and practices which the Deobandis had condemned as well as his declarations of *kufr* (disbelief) on certain Deobandi *ʿulamāʾ* (Aleemuddin 2008).

With the establishment of the Salafī Markaz al-Da'wa al-Islamia in 2001 and the Shīʿī Imamia Hawza Illmiyah in 2007 a different sectarian response to this Deobandi-Barelwi polemic has emerged. There is a possibility that globalization and the development of black Muslim identities have facilitated this. Heralded by an increase in Saudi and Iranian influence in South African Muslim communities after 1994, Salafīsm and Shīʿīsm have become growing sectarian identities amongst Muslims in South Africa, particularly black Muslims. Both groups have been attacked by mainstream established *ʿulamāʾ*.

With its focus on the teaching of core Salafī texts, *Kitāb al-tawḥīd* by Muḥammad ibn ʻAbd al-Wahhāb (d.1791), and *ʿAqīda al-wāṣiṭiya* by ibn Taymiyah (d.1255) instead of *ʿAqīda al-ṭaḥāwī,* inferences can be drawn about Markaz al-Da'wa being a Salafī madrasah. Given the scholars that are revered by the Salafīs, the madrasah can be seen as Ḥanbalī in theology. The principal and founder, Mawlānā Sadiq Jacobs, a graduate of Darul Uloom (Newcastle), summed up this theological self-definition as well as what others may term the madrasah. Jacobs said: "Our *ʿaqīda* (creed) is Ḥanbalī. The Deobandi Darul Ulooms in South Africa label us as Salafī and are opposed to us". Defining what this Salafī or Ḥanbalī approach is opposed to, Jacobs told me that it is the madrasah's aim to "work against *bidʿa* (innovations) in belief, practice and *fiqh*" (Jacobs 2008).

The Salafī trend of de-emphasizing the *taqlīd* (emulation) of the past scholars in matters of *fiqh* is also underlined by the manner in which the *Dars-e Nizami* texts that make up Markaz al-Da'wa's syllabus are approached. Since its establishment, all *Nizami fiqh*, *uṣūl al-fiqh*, *tafsīr*, and *ḥadīth* texts are taught at Markaz al-Da'wa. But these texts have been taught without any accompanying written commentaries by past scholars. Instead, the teachers approach these texts directly. A strong Salafī approach also exists in the comparative study of *fiqh*. Rulings of the Ḥanafīs are mainly targeted for critique. Many Ḥanafī rulings are generally viewed by Salafī scholars as not being derived from *ḥadīth* literature but from *qiyās* (analogical reasoning) (Jacobs 2008).

The student demographics and the reasons given for them attending Markaz al-Da'wa, support the idea that an increasing black critique and frustration towards having to follow an Indian Islam have contributed to the rise of Salafīsm and the strengthening of a Salafī madrasah in South Africa. The madrasah currently has 500 students, all of whom are black. From its establishment the majority of these students have come from various black townships in Pretoria. Some students are from Zimbabwe and Mozambique. The reasons, as claimed by Jacobs, behind many of these students enrolling at the madrasah reflect a frustration with Indian Islam. Most of the students were first enrolled at Deobandi madrasahs in South Africa, but left frustrated and disillusioned. They felt uncomfortable studying Urdu texts, focusing on Indian sectarian debates, and surrounded mainly by Indian students and having to participate in graduation ceremonies of an Indian character. Jacobs believes that it was for this reason that they enrolled at Markaz al-Da'wa. Jacobs said that his madrasah attracts "indigenous people" because students feel that most other madrasahs are "purely based on Indian culture and students can see that this madrasah does not teach them to become Indians" (Jacobs 2008).

The Shīʿī Imamia Hawzah Illmiyah, established in Gauteng's most historic township, Soweto, in 2007 by the Ghanaian-born Qom graduate, Mawlānā Nuru Mohammad, is similar to its Salafī counterpart. The madrasah has only had black students from Soweto, and other areas in Gauteng such as the East Rand. It has also attracted students from the provinces of Limpopo and Mpumalanga. Some of these students initially converted to Islam through Sunnī Muslims, but later adopted Shīʿīsm as its presence as a perceivably non-Indian tradition in the black townships increased. Imamia Hawzah was established and continues to be sustained by black members of Nuru's congregation in Soweto. When the madrasah was established, Ali Kumane, a building contractor originally from Soweto, provided a boarding house for students, paid for their food and gave each student a monthly stipend (Nuru interview). Given the madrasah's establishment in an African township, its purely black student-base, and the feeling of marginalization on the part of many black Muslims from what they often view as an exclusive South African Indian form of Islam, the rise of this Shīʿī madrasah reflects a changing face of sectarianism in a South Africa which is no longer defined solely by the theological contestations originating in South Asia.

With its establishment, Imamia Hawzah had as its central goals the needs of Shīʿī communities, and the defence and propagation of Shīʿīsm in South Africa. According to Nuru, the madrasah was established out of a need to see South African-born Shīʿī *ʿulamāʾ* occupying leadership positions in Shīʿī mosques in the country so as to facilitate heightened propagation work. Pointing directly to the madrasah's sectarian objective, Nuru stated in the interview: "The aim is to produce scholars who are propagators of Shīʿīsm amongst the people of South Africa". Immediately after graduating in Qom, Nuru was sent to South Africa in 2004 by the Iranian government to promote Shīʿīsm, particularly in townships in Gauteng. Nuru was initially employed by the Iranian Embassy in Pretoria for this purpose (Nuru 2008).

Imamia Hawzah has been using the three-year *Maqṭaʿ al-awwal* syllabus. This particular syllabus is used in the Shīʿī seminaries in Qom to prepare students for another three years of advanced sharīʿa studies, *Baḥth al-khārij*. After studies in Arabic grammar for the first year, over their final two years students are taught texts authored in Arabic by contemporary Shīʿī scholars. The following is a breakdown of these texts:

- *Fiqh*: *Maʿrifatul abwāb al-fiqhīyya* by Ayatollah Sayyid Ruhullah Khomeini (d.1989).
- *Uṣūl al-fiqh*: *Kitāb al-uṣūl* by Ayatollah Sayyid Muḥammad Baqir al-Sadr (d.1980).
- *ʿAqīda*: *Durūs fil ʿaqīda* by Ayatollah Shaykh Misbah Yazdi and *ʿAqīda imāmīya by* Ayatollah Shaykh Muḥammad Ridha Muẓaffar.
- *Tafsīr*: *Taʿarruf al-tafāsīr* by Ayatollah Shaykh Hadi Ma'rifat.
- *Tārīkh*: *Tārīkh al-islāmīya* by Dr. Ghulam-Hassan Muharrami.
- *Ḥadīth*: *ʿIlm al-rijāl* by Ayatollah Sayyid Abul Qasim al-Kho'i (d.1992).
- *ʿIrfān* (Mysticism): *Sīrat al-Sulūk* by Ayatollah Shaykh Hassan Zadeh Amuli.
- *Falsafa* (Philosophy): *Bidāyat al-Ḥikma* and *Nihāyat al-Ḥikma* by Ayatollah Sayyid Muḥammad Hussain Ṭabāṭabāʾī (d.1981).[5]

The manner in which the *ḥadīth, tafsīr, ʿaqīda* and *tārīkh* texts are approached underlines the madrasah's awareness of what Nuru sees as "Sunnī threats to the promotion of Shīʿīsm in South Africa". According to Nuru, counter-arguments to

5 The authors, for whom no date of death is provided, are still alive.

Sunnī claims against central Shīʿī beliefs have generally made up the discussions around the texts for these subjects. Nuru claimed that this was due to what he sees as a concerted effort on the part of certain Deobandi *ʿulamāʾ* in Gauteng to attack Shīʿī beliefs (Nuru 2008).

After studying these texts over three years, graduates have the option of completing advanced *sharīʿa* studies at certain Shīʿī seminaries in Qom, Iran and Damascus, Syria, with which Imamia Hawzah has official links. Arrangements are in place for graduates to get funding to pursue further studies at the madrasah run by one of Nuru's former teachers, Ayatollah Sayyid Sādiq Shirāzi in Qom, and at the madrasahs in Sayyidah Zaynab, Damascus, run by Ayatollah Sayyid Muḥammad Taqi Modaressi and Ayatollah Sayyid Murtadhā Shirāzi (Nuru 2008). The educational relationship connects the madrasah in Soweto to the rest of the Shīʿī world and to its leadership. These *ʿulamāʾ* are considered amongst the highest religious authorities (*marājiʿ*) in the Shīʿī world. Furthermore, they have officially sanctioned the establishment of Imamia Hawzah and are patrons of the madrasah. Ayatollah Sayyid ʿAlī Sistānī of Najaf, Iraq, was also consulted by Nuru before the madrasah was established (Nuru 2008).

A change in sectarian focus has also taken place with many Deobandi madrasahs. Change tends to take place when a new sectarian group occupies public religious space in South African Muslim communities. During the 1980s the focus at Jamiah Maseehiah related to critiquing the Barelwis. The critiques were in line with the dominant Deobandi attacks at the time. Then during the early 1990s up until 2002 the focus shifted to detailed critiques of the writings of Muslim "progressive" academics such as Dr. Farid Esack and Dr. Ebrahim Moosa for what Boda refers to as the "unfettered freedom of thought which they promoted". Esack and Moosa's writings on issues of Qur'anic exegesis and Islamic law respectively were focused on. Then from 2006 the sectarian polemics at Maseehiah shifted to the Salafīs. In the teaching of *fiqh* and *ḥadīth*, particular emphasis is placed on conducting critiques of the Salafī's perceived de-emphasis of *taqlīd* (emulation). Boda told me: "We despise the Salafīs de-emphasizing of the schools of law. We train our students in *fiqh* and *ḥadīth* to attack them" (Boda 2008).

This same shift in sectarian concern towards refuting the views of the Salafīs has taken place since 2006 at Tarbiyatul Banaat and the Deobandi girl's madrasahs in Kwazulu-Natal. From 1987 till 1992 the sectarian polemics at Tarbiyatul Banaat was against what Mawlānā Haroon Akbar Ali describes as the "innovations" of the Barelwis. From 1993 until 2005 the sectarian focus shifted to condemning the beliefs of the Shīʿīs. In particular, the Shīʿī criticism of some of Prophet Muhammad's companions and their claim that ʿAlī was Muḥammad's rightful successor was the target of criticism. *Firqa Bāṭila*, an Urdu text authored by Mawlānā Muḥammad Yusuf Ludhianvi, was taught for this purpose (Ali 2008). The text attempts to refute and condemn all the ideological groups which the Deobandis oppose. Most of the text is dedicated to discussing the Shīʿī beliefs though. Madrasah In'aamiyah in Camperdown also focussed its refutations on the Shīʿīs at this stage. From 2006, as with the other Deobandi madrasahs, the focus at Tarbiyatul Banaat and In'aamiyah shifted completely to attacking the Salafī approach to *taqlīd*.

While not emphatically clear, it can be inferred that Jamiatul Uloom (Gauteng) has also begun placing a focus on countering the Salafīs from 2006. When providing me with a detailed breakdown of the syllabus at Jamiatul Uloom, the principal, Mawlānā Saabir Ebrahim told me that since 2006, a group that claims to be part of the "mainstream" Muslims has risen to prominence in the Gauteng province. Ebrahim said that this particular group, which "rejects the authority of the *ʿulamāʾ* and goes straight to the Qur'an and Sunna", poses a major challenge to young Muslims. When I probed him as to the exact identity of this group, Ebrahim had the following to say: "Let us just say that they are an internal Sunnī threat and that this internal Sunnī threat is more dangerous than groups that do not claim to be Sunnīs" (Saabir Ebrahim 2008).

Unlike their Deobandi counterparts, Darul Uloom (Pretoria) and Darul Uloom Qadria (Newcastle) seem not to have focussed much on the Salafīs. From Darul Uloom Pretoria's establishment in 1989 until 2003 the main sectarian focus has been on refuting the Deobandi critiques of popular Ṣūfī beliefs and practices. According to Hazarvi, it was for this reason that sections in Ahmed Raza Khan's *Kanzul Imān* that deal with these beliefs and practices were specifically focused on in *tafsīr* classes (Hazarvi 2008). This has also been the central focus since 1997 at Darul Uloom Qadria in a much more polemical manner. Qadria actually introduced *munāẓara* (debating) since 2006 into the syllabus. Once a week students are divided into groups of debaters. One group of students has to pose as Deobandis and the other as Barelwis. A topic of contention between the Deobandis and Barelwis is debated (Aleemuddin 2008).

Even the newly-established Barelwi madrasah in Newcastle, Jamiah Imam Ahmed Raza Ahsanul Barakat has made defence against perceived Deobandi attack its central focus. Since its establishment in 2007, the anti-Deobandi aspects of Khan's *al-Malfūzāt* have been taught. Furthermore, in January 2008, the madrasah issued a letter to the Kwazulu-Natal Jamiatul *ʿulamāʾ* refuting the contents of one of its pamphlets. During the Islamic lunar month of *Muḥarram*, the Jamiatul *ʿulamāʾ* distributed a pamphlet concerning the commemoration of the murder of Prophet Muhammad's grandson, Ḥusayn, at Karbala, Iraq, in 680. The pamphlet described these commemorations as Shīʿī "innovations" and called on people not to recall and mourn the killing of Ḥusayn. The principal, Mufti Shamsul Haq wrote a detailed letter to the Jamiat attempting to prove the validity of commemorating this event, based on his readings of the Qur'an and certain *ḥadīth* texts (Haq 2008).

Illustrating somewhat of a shift in line with the changing South Africa, from 2003 until 2008 the sectarian focus at Darul Uloom (Pretoria) has moved to Shīʿīsm. Four years ago the madrasah called for a debate with a Johannesburg-based Shīʿī scholar, Mawlānā Sayyid Abdullah Hussayni, in the Jumu'ah mosque in Laudium. Indicating that the rise of Shīʿīsm in South Africa is still a central concern for them, the vice-principal, Hafiz Ismail Hazarvi said: "The Darul Uloom will continue educating people about the Shīʿīs as Shīʿīsm poses a major challenge throughout South Africa. Scholars that we produce must be in a position to counter the spread of Shī'īsm" (Hazarvi 2008).

Conclusion

While the features of religious socialization and sectarian identity formation have generally remained at the South African madrasahs, certain transformations have taken place at madrasahs in South Africa. These changes sustain the function of madrasahs as spaces for religious socialization and sectarian identity formation, but they also reflect broader shifts and developments that have taken place in the South African Muslim communities and in the country. Madrasahs have adapted in a variety of ways to these broader shifts, while remaining voices of orthodoxy and tradition.

The madrasahs have taken on new ethnic dimensions, and there have been developments in teaching methodology, recruitment and adaptations towards job-market education. These reflect broader changes in South Africa and its Muslim communities in particular. In addition to this, there have been shifts in the nature of religious socialization and sectarian identity formation. Changes in teaching of specific Islamic law schools (*fiqh*) and the changing sectarianisms are central in underlining the adaptations on the part of madrasahs.

While the examples cited are indeed reflective of major transformations in the landscape of madrasah education in South Africa, in a broader sense they still fall very much under what I see as the central features of madrasah education, historically and globally. There has been no radical shift, or even a conception thereof, beyond often sectarian religious orthodoxy. Perhaps if this shift were to take place, then madrasahs would eventually cease to function.

References

Ahmed, Mumtaz. 2004. Madrassa Education in Pakistan and Bangladesh. In *Religious Radicalism and Security in South Asia* edited by Satu P. Limaye, Robert G. Wirsing and Mohan Malik, 101-115. Honolulu: Asia Pacific Centre for Security Studies

Akoo, Ismail E. 2007. *Biography of the Founder of Darul Uloom Newcastle: Mawlānā Cassim Mohamed Sema Saheb* Newcastle: Darul Uloom Newcastle.

Chande, Abdin. 1998. *Islam, Ulamaa and Community Development in Tanzania: a Case of Religious Currents in East Africa.* London: Austin and Winfield.

Kallaway, Peter, ed. 2002. Introduction. In *The History of Education Under Apartheid: 1948-1984*, 1-29. Cape Town: Pearson Education South Africa.

Metcalf, Barbara. 1978. The Madrasa at Deoband: A Model for Religious Education in Modern India. *Modern Asian Studies* 12 (1): 111-134.

Metcalf, Barbara. 1982. *Islamic Revival in British India: Deoband, 1860-190.0* Princeton: Princeton University Press.

Moosa, Ebrahim. 1993. Discursive Voices of Diaspora Islam in Southern Africa. *Jurnal Antropologi Dan Sosiologi* 20: 29-60.

Muhammad, Ebrahim. 2000. *Prospectus of Madrasah Arabia Islamia.* Azaadville: Madrasah Arabia Islamia.

Reichmuth, Stefan. 2000. Islamic Education and Scholarship in sub-Saharan Africa. In *The History of Islam in Africa,* ed. by Nehemia Levtzion and Randall L. Pouwels, 419-434. Athens: Ohio University Press.

Sanyal, Usha. 1996. *Devotional Islam and Politics in British India: Ahmad Riza Khan Barelwi and his movement.* Bombay: Oxford University Press.

Sikand, Yoginder. 2006. *Bastions of the Believers: Madrasahs and Islamic Education in India.* New Delhi: Penguin Books.

Talbani, Aziz. 1996. Pedagogy, Power, and Discourse: Transformation of Islamic Education. *Comparative Education Review,* 40 (1): 66-82.

Vahed, Goolam & Jeppie, Shamil. 2005. Multiple communities: Muslims in post-apartheid South Africa. In *State of the Nation: South Africa, 2004-2005,* ed. by John Daniel, Roger Southall and Jessica Lutchman, 252-283. Cape Town: HSRC Press.

Waardenburg, Jacques. 1965. Some Institutional Aspects of Muslim Higher Education and Their Relation to Islam. *Numen,* 12 (2): 96-138.

Interviews

Akoo, Ismail. Interviewed by author, Darul Uloom (Newcastle), Newcastle, January, 27 2009.

Aleemuddin, Sayyid Muḥammad. Interview by author, Darul Uloom Qadria Ghareeb Nawaz, Ladysmith, July, 2 2008.

Ali, Haroon Akbar. Interview by author, Madrasah Tarbiyatul Banaat, Azaadville, February, 11 2008.

Amod, Bashier. Interview by author, Madrasatul Banaat, Stanger, June, 25 2008.

Ashrafi, Mubeen Ahmed. Interview by author, Darul Uloom Samnaniyah, Verulam, July, 3 2008.

Boda, Hashim. Interview by author, Jamiah Maseehiah, De Deur, February, 6 2008.

Chohan, Junaid. Interview by author, Madrasah Islahul Muslimaat, Durban, November, 26 2008.

Desai, Mahmood Madani. Interview by author, Madrasah In'aamiyah, Camperdown, June, 25 2008.

Ebrahim, Farhaad. Interview by author, Darul Uloom Ashrafiyah, Durban, June, 25 2008.

Ebrahim, Saabir. Interview by author, Jamiatul Uloom al-Islamia, Johannesburg, February, 7 2008.

Hashim, Riaz. Interview by author, Madrasah Riyad al-Salihaat, February, 5 2008.

Hazarvi, Ismail. Interview by author, Darul Uloom (Pretoria), Pretoria, January, 31 2008.

al-Haq, Shams. Interview by author, Jamiah Imam Ahmed Raza Ahsanul Barakat, Newcastle, January, 20 2009.

Jacobs, Sadiq. Interview by author, Markaz al-Da'wa al-Islamia, Pretoria North, January, 31 2008.

Khan, Abduraheem. Interview by author, Darul Uloom Nu'maniyah, Durban, June, 26 2008.

Mohammad, Nuru. Interview by author, Imamia Hawzah Illmiyah, Soweto, February, 7 2008.

Moosa Rahim. Interview by author, Ismail. Jamiah Mahmoodia, Springs, February, 5 2008.

Patel, Yunus. Interview by author, Madrasah Salihaat, Durban, June, 30 2008.

Dietrich Reetz

The Tablīghī Madrassas in Lenasia and Azaadville

Local Players in the Global 'Islamic Field'

The Islamic schools in Lenasia and Azaadville in South Africa represent prominent examples of schools that provide religious education in a format which is firmly rooted in traditions and interpretations of Islam originating outside South Africa. Established by the Muslim minority community of the country, the schools follow the Deobandi interpretation of Islam from South Asia. Its tradition goes back to the Islamic seminary Darul Ulum (1866) in the town of Deoband in north India (Metcalf 1982). Its inceptors were promoting a purist form of Islam designed to revive Islamic knowledge, practice and piety in the face of the expanding colonial rule of Britain shaped by its western and Christian traditions.

The Deoband school serves as the spiritual *alma mater* and reference point of hundreds of schools (*madrasas*, *Dārul ʿUlūms*) in South Asia, but also in other regions of the world. These schools have become part of translocal and transnational networks of religious education and activism that have gone global (Reetz 2007, 2010b). They are transcending political and cultural borders. At the same time the schools reflect local requirements and perceptions where they often intersect with social stratification and mobilization, but also with identity politics. As the two localities of Lenasia and Azaadville hosting the schools were reserved for the 'coloured' Indian minority under the Apartheid regime, the schools reflected the evolution of the religious and ethnic politics of South Africa. They thus mediate between the Global and the Local which represent different sides of the same phenomenon. They demonstrate the correspondence between social structures, symbolic labour as a function of religion, and mental dispositions in what Bourdieu called the unfolding of the religious field (Bourdieu 1999). To understand these multiple attachments, the paper will discuss the schools within their competing reference systems, represented by the South African nation state, the Deoband tradition in Islam, the missionary and Sūfī aspects of the schools and their global networking.

Deobandi influence in South Africa

For a long time religious teaching in the Muslim world had been a rather personal affair between a teacher (*shaykh*) and a number of students, at the mosque, or often at home. Although formal madrassas as institutions have been known from various Muslim empires of the middle ages, by the nineteenth century religious teaching in Islam was probably much more private than in Christian or public institutions. The school in Deoband reintroduced a high degree of formality to teaching Islamic knowledge. It featured a regular curriculum with standard course duration, a fixed time-table, salaried teachers and a hostel.

The religious schools in Lenasia and Azaadville are part of a growing number of institutions maintained by Islamic organisations in South Africa. They provide religious education in a structured format as degree courses. They are run like fee-based private schools complete with a fixed teaching programme, permanent teaching and administrative staff. They offer campus-style facilities with separate buildings for administration, teaching, hostels and common kitchen facilities. The most popular courses are aimed at teaching students to become a Ḥāfiẓ or Qāri who memorizes the Qurʾānic verses and recites them during Islamic rituals. More advanced courses of 6 to 7 years teach theology and the classical Islamic literature. Thereafter students become a scholar of Islam, or *ʿālim* (pl. *ʿulamāʾ*). Some of these religious schools also teach secular subjects as part of the so-called national curriculum. Yet, they are distinct from "Muslim schools" that primarily teach secular secondary education in a religious environment with added religious subjects.

In South Africa, the two schools in Lenasia and Azaadville would be primarily viewed as regular Islamic institutions with a conservative slant where the sectarian attachment is not necessarily obvious. But students attending the schools and graduating from them will easily identify them as Deobandi schools. This connection is reflected in the curriculum and the choice of books and subjects, but also in the format of teaching. It is equally evident in the community background of the teachers and the students. Furthermore, the two schools are part of a wider network of religious schools associated with the Organisation of religious scholars of the region (Jamiatul Ulama Transvaal – JUT). This organisation follows the blueprint of similar Deobandi groups in the Southasian subcontinent while it retains local roots in South Africa.

The JUT organisation in South Africa was established in the early twentieth century, in 1923.[1] Its inception was likely influenced by the freedom struggle in colonial British India and the mobilization of Muslims there. In India, the first association of Muslim scholars, the Jamiatul ʿUlamāʾ -e Hind (JUH), had formed in 1919 with a very pronounced political agenda against the British and for the establishment of an Islamic way of life. The JUH particularly helped to shape the up-and-coming Khalīfat movement that became enormously popular in India. It was directed at the preservation and, later, restoration of the Ottoman Caliphate which was being abolished when the Ottoman Empire was dismantled after the end of the First World War in which the Ottomans were on the loosing side.

As Muslims of Indian/South Asian descent formed a large part of the South African Muslim minority, the JUT and other Deobandi organizations found it easy to expand their influence in South Africa. From the 1960s onward their clout visibly strengthened with a reformist campaign against followers of 'traditional' forms of worship associated with Sūfī rituals and the Barelwi school of thought that had previously dominated 'Indian' Muslims in South Africa. Today, the Deobandi-related associations and schools represent probably the most influential segment of orthodox Muslim institutions, although Barelwi schools and institutes have also strengthened their organisations (Vahed 2003; Tayob 1999). In South Africa, the contestation between Deobandis and Barelwis was

1 http://www.jamiat.co.za/profile/history.htm. [29-11-10]

framed as the Tablīghī-Sunnī controversy. The ascent of the Tablīghīs stood for the rise of Deobandi views and practices. Tablīghīs are followers of the Islamic missionary movement of the Tablīghī Jamāʿāt (TJ) founded by the Deobandi scholar, Muḥammad Ilyās (1885-1944) in 1926 in India, which is currently spread all over the world. 'Sunnī' was appropriated as a label by the followers of the Barelwi movement as they maintained to be the only true followers of the Sunna, i.e. the ways of the Prophet and his companions. The Barelwi movement emerged from Bareilly in north India, not far from Deoband town, where it was founded by Aḥmad Raza Khan (1856–1921) around 1900. His followers insisted they were the only true 'Sunnīs' largely in defence against accusations by the Deobandis, that Barelwi practices and rituals, particularly where they related to Sūfī-inspired shrine worship and saint veneration, constituted deviations and impermissible innovations (*bidʿa*).

Since the end of Apartheid the Deobandi religious scholars' association, coming from local and regional pockets of influence, has striven to become more inclusive and national towards different sections of the Muslim community. In 1994, it united its patchwork of branches in a new umbrella group, the United Ulama Council of South Africa. While the association and its functionaries remained strongly orthodox they opened to other Muslim communities, such as the 'Cape Malay' Muslims and the rival Barelwis. The 'Cape Malay' Muslims represent a strong voice on the Muslim Judicial Council (MJC) in Cape Town. The Barelwis are represented by the Sunnī Jamiatul Ulema. Both are now also associated with the JU network (For an overview of the United ʿUlamāʾ Council of South Africa member institutions, see Table 1).

The essence of Deobandi teaching is embodied in the cleansing of existing rituals and beliefs followed by Muslims, in conjunction with what is considered to be the 'true' and correct Islam. These cleansing efforts refer to beliefs and practices of the founding generations of Islam, the pious forebears (*salaf*), which is why sometimes they are considered Salafīs. But the Deobandis cannot be easily merged with other Salafīs who often reject the law schools of Islam which formed later in the middle ages. The Deobandis in contrast strictly follow their own legal tradition and the teachings of their elders in a concept called *taqlīd* (adherence). As is common in South Asia, the Deobandis are Ḥanafīs and therefore particularly attached to the Islamic legal tradition of Abu Ḥanīfa (699-767). But this attachment has never prevented them from providing space for other legal traditions as well, both in South Asia and also in South Africa. 'As early as 1927, the JUT published its first book designed for Shāfiʿī students and adults.'[1] The Deobandi understanding of true Islam is largely based on the study of the Prophetic traditions, the *ḥadīth*, which comprises a large part in their theological curriculum. It is from that understanding and feeling of superiority that they have strongly criticised dissenting readings of Islam. Their critique was originally directed at the Sūfī-related Islam, which then organised through the Barelwi institutions. It was later also directed against followers of the Islamic Party (Jamāʿāt-i Islāmī) of Mawlānā Sayyid Abū ʾl ʿAlā Maudūdi (1903-1979), of the Ahl-i Ḥadīth from South Asia, against Hindus and other Non-Muslims, and in particular against the small group of followers of Mirza Ghulam Aḥmad, the so-called Aḥmadi sect. The Aḥmadis are regarded as heretics and are the subject of fierce hostile rhetoric. In Pakistan they routinely become victims of sectarian violence. The strong ideological slant of Deobandi sectarianism has also inspired *jihādi* groups, notably in Pakistan and Afghanistan, though it is difficult to identify one with the other. The vast majority of Deobandi institutions focus on religious studies and pious character formation.

Table 1: Islamic institutions associated with the United ʿUlamāʾ Council of South Africa

Institution	Website	Founded	Remarks
United Ulama Council of South Africa		1994	Founded after the end of Apartheid to unite different institutions
Jamiatul Ulama Johannesburg (formerly Transvaal)	www.jamiat.co.za	1923	Branches in Laudium, Lenasia, Benoni, Klerksdorp, Middelburg, Azaadville; zonal offices in Vaal, Limpopo, Springs, Delmas, Rustenburg, Bloemfontein (http://www.jamiat.co.za/profile/branches.htm)
Jamiatul Ulama KwaZulu Natal	www.jamiat.org.za	1955	Office: Durban
Muslim Judicial Council	www.mjc.org.za	1945	Office: Darul Arqam, Athlone, near Cape Town
Sunni Jamiatul Ulema KZN	www.sju.co.za	1978	Office: Overport (Barelwi)
Sunni Ulema Council			Office: Crown Mines, Johannesburg
Eastern Cape Islamic Congress			Office: Gelvandale, Port Elizabeth[2]
Northern Cape Ulama Council			Office: Kimberley, Northern Cape
Council of Ulama Eastern Cape	www.councilof ulama .co.za		Office: Port Elizabeth
Al Quds Foundation	www.alquds.za.net		Offices: Cape Town, Gauteng
MJC Halal Trust	www.mjc.org.za	1945	Western Cape Region
National Independent Halal Trust	www.halaal.org.za		

Source: Derived from material received during interview at the JU office in Johannesburg, 22-02-2005, with additional internet research

2 http://www.esinislam.com/African_Muslim_Directories/South_African_Muslim_Directories/South_African_Muslim_Organizations.htm#poverty [29-11-10]

In South Africa, as in general outside South Asia, Deobandi thought is not known to have been linked to militant activism. At the same time it has generated ideological and sectarian polarisation in Muslim communities where it had not existed before. In South Africa it led to the expanding contestation between reformist Islam of the Deobandi variety and Sunnī groups leaning towards the Sūfī-inspired Barelwi interpretation of Islam (Tayob 1999). However, the nature of Deobandi education in South Africa is not as homogeneous and univocal as in South Asia. It is not only a *madrassa* movement of educational institutions, but it is also shaped by the missionary movement of the Tablīghī Jamāʿāt and by Sūfī scholars of Deobandi background. Those influences tend to be more inclusive in nature. Deobandi thought, unlike conventional Salafism, has never cut itself off from mystical Islam and Sufism in particular as long as it is consistent with Islamic law (*sharīʿa*) and the injunctions of the Qurʾān and the Prophetic Traditions (*ḥadīth*).

The two Islamic schools in Azaadville and Lenasia under study here are prime examples of this composite trend. They embody not only the Deobandi tradition, but also intimate connections with the Tablīghīs. They equally demonstrate close affinity with the disciples of the Deobandi scholar and Sūfī Shaykh Muḥammad Zakariyya (1898-1982) who was a co-founder of the Tablīghī Jamāʿāt and a nephew of its inceptor, Muḥammad Ilyās. In this, the schools reflect a more general trend among global Deobandi affiliates: a number of them owe their existence to the impact of Tablīghī activism.[3] In addition, several of the Deobandi key seminaries outside South Asia were inspired by Zakariyya and his disciples.[4] The affinity reflects not only ideological proximity but also logistical convenience: the missionary movement of the Tablīghīs and the Sūfī network of disciples find the expansion by branches across borders around the globe comparatively easy as translocal and transnational networking is the nature of their religious and social operation.

In the expanding religious and Islamic field in South Africa, Deobandi schools, beyond theological qualifications, offer religious and cultural capital in the mold Bourdieu notes, that is seen as beneficial also for social advancement. It is this context that contributes to the continued growth of Deobandi schools offering orthodox Islamic training in a society driven by the goals of advancement and modernisation (see the list of schools in Table 2). The local evolution of the two schools makes those benefits more tangible and concrete.

---

3 This, for instance, applies to the Deobandi schools in Nizamuddin (Delhi, India), Raiwind (Lahore, Pakistan), Kuala Lumpur (Malaysia), Temboro (Indonesia, East Java), Dewsbury (UK), where they are attached to the local centre (*markaz*) of the Tablīghī Jamāʿāt.

4 As far as known currently, this applies to the following schools: Madrasa Saulatiyya, Mecca (f. 1873 by Mawlānā Khalil, the spiritual mentor of Zakariyya); Darul Ulum Bury (Holcombe), UK (1975), Mawlānā Motala; Darul Ulum Dewsbury, UK (1981), Hafiz Muhammad Ishaq Patel – today the Amir of the TJ Europe; Darul Ulum Azadville, South Africa (1982); Darul Ulum Zakariyya, Lenasia, South Africa (1983); Darul Ulum Stanger, South Africa (Mawlānā Yusuf Tatla). In addition, several schools are named in his honour, such as the Jamia-Tul-Imam Muhammad Zakaria in Bradford, UK (cf. Reetz 2007).

Table 2: Islamic seminaries for Boys (Darul Uloom) in South Africa recognised by the 'Ulamā' Council (JU)

Qaasimul Uloom	**First Darul Uloom opened 1998**[5]
Madrassah Ta'leemuddin	Isipingo Beach[6]
Darul Uloom Numaniyyah	Chatsworth, Durban[7]
Darul Uloom Al-Mahmudia	Stanger
Madrassah Inaamiyya	Camperdown
Darul Uloom Newcastle	Lennoxton
Darul Uloom Miftahul Falah	Harding
Jamiah Mahmoodiyah	Springs
Darul Uloom Zakariyya	Lenasia
Darul Uloom Azaadville	Azaadville
Jami'atul Ulum Al-Islamiyyah	Fordsburg – Johannesburg (at JU office)

Source: Derived from material received during interview at the JU office in Johannesburg, 22-02-2005, with additional internet research

The teaching programme at Azaadville and Lenasia

At the core of the schools' attraction is their teaching of the recitation of the Holy Qur'ān (*Ḥifẓul Qur'ān*) – which they do part- and full-time, and the Deobandi curriculum of Islamic theology, which is often also named after the degree it confers on students, the *'Ālim* course. It is the latter which has become their signature degree course as it creates some form of theological equivalent to the bachelor and/or master courses of the secular Anglo-Saxon education system. It is recognised in varying degrees in Pakistan, India, and by individual schools, such as the International Islamic Universities in several countries, which will regard it as equivalent to a bachelor degree in Arabic/Islamic studies. Others, such as the Jamia Millia and Hamdard Universities, or the Aligarh University in India, equate it with secondary education, requiring students to take additional exams in English or other subjects to meet university admission requirements (Reetz 2008, 97). In South Africa, there is no formal recognition of the course. The school functionaries argue defensively: "There were many 'Ulamā' of Deoband who did not even take a certificate after qualifying as this was not their aim" (Muhammad 2000b, 4). For many Deobandi scholars, the education acquired there is supposed to be a value in itself.

5 http://www.islamicmedia.co.za/dev.htm [30-11-10]
6 http://www.eastcoast.co.za/muawiya [30-11-10]
7 South African Muslim Guide and Directory Services – Educational Institutions: Darul Uloom – http://www.islam4u.co.za/ulooms.html [30-11-10].

While Azaadville has become known for its theological *ʿĀlim* course, Lenasia is valued for its Qurʾānic memorization *Ḥāfiẓ* classes.[8] In Azaadville, the theological degree course of the *ʿĀlim* (scholar) or *Fāẓil* (graduate) level will be taken concurrently with classes to become a prayer leader (*imām*), a *madrassa* teacher and elocution classes to pronounce and read the Arabic text of the Qurʾān correctly (*tajwīd, qirāʾāt*). There are also a preparatory class (*iʿdādiyah*) and a legal course (*iftāʾ*) available (Muhammad 2000b, 16).

The Deobandis have formalised and standardised Islamic teaching on the basis of the *Dars-e Nizami*, the traditional curriculum of Islamic teaching current in South Asia. It was conceived in the late seventeenth century–early eighteenth century by two scholars from Lucknow in North India, Mulla Qutb al-Din Sihalwi (d. 1691) and his son Mulla Nizam al-Din of Firangi Mahal (d. 1748) after whom it was named (Robinson 2001, 211). In Deoband, the *ʿĀlim* course is calibrated to be completed in 8 years.[9] The mainstay of the course are studies of the founding texts of Islam, such as the Qurʾān and the Prophetic Traditions (Ḥadīth). The exegesis of the Qurʾān and Qurʾānic commentaries (*tafsīr*) are important; so are Islamic principles of belief (*ʿaqāʾid*), morals (*akhlāq*), mysticism (*taṣawwuf*), jurisprudence (*fiqh*) and history. The main division is into divine (*manqulāt*) and derived rational subjects (*maʿqulāt*), which owe their existence either to the Prophetic revelation or human interpretation. Much space is given to commentaries and glosses of classics of Islamic theology which critics argue often makes the study formulaic, especially as it is largely based on rote learning. The last year is usually called the *Dora-e Ḥadīth*, the year of the study of the traditions, which carries special significance. Often, students go to institutes of higher reputation to complete this final year, along with the degree. The degree is structured around the books being taught, for which a teaching license, or *sanad* is being granted. The junior degree is *Fāẓil* (graduate), awarded after 7 years, completed with *ʿĀlim* (scholar) after the 8th year, and *Kāmil* (master) after a 1-2 year course of post-graduate qualification in Qurʾānic exegesis (*tafsīr*), law (*fiqh*), theology (*kalām*), or Arabic literature.

Outside South Asia, the *ʿĀlim* course has been modified in terms of commentaries used, and also for its duration. At Azaadville and Lenasia the duration is 6 and 7 years, and for girls 4 and 5 years, respectively. The programme has been condensed on the basis of selecting books that cover several subjects. In addition, the Azaadville curriculum pays particular attention to learning Urdu, Arabic and English, historical subjects, including the Prophet's biography (*sīra*), even social welfare (*al-muʿāshara*), and social etiquette in life and for students in particular (Muhammad 2000a, 25-7). The teaching of many subjects in Urdu is justified to "fully maintain the legacy of our past luminaries of the subcontinent" (Muhammad 2000b, 5).[10]

---

8 http://www.sunniforum.com/forum/showthread.php?35704-Darul-Uloom-Azaadville-South-Africa/page4 [30-11-10]

9 http://darululoom-deoband.com/english/sys_of_edu/index.htm [30-11-10]

10 For the curriculum of Darul Uloom Zakariyya in Lenasia, see http://www.sunniforum.com/forum/showthread.php?27235-Madressa-Zakariya-Park-%28Darul-Uloom-Zakariyya%29 [30-11-10]

The orientation of the schools, here as much as in any Deobandi or other *madrassas*, depends highly on the tradition and perspective of the founder of the school. He and his family will guide the school for generations and shape its profile through their cultural roots and doctrinal profile. It is therefore the personality and family network of Mawlānās Abdul Hamid Ishaq and Shabbir Saloojee, who shape the personal atmosphere of the schools in Azaadville and Lenasia, respectively. The function of the principal will often remain in the family, becoming almost hereditary. It is not uncommon that those Darul Ulooms are run like family enterprises. The theological argument given is that the spiritual blessings (*baraka*) can best flow within the family, ideally from father to son.

Both schools, through the personality and orientation of their leaders, are strongly embedded in the Sūfī traditions.[11] The principal of Darul Uloom Zakariyya in Lenasia, Mawlānā Saloojee, is a disciple (*khalīfa*) of Mufti Mehmood al-Hasan, following the Sūfī lineage (*silsila*) of the Chishtiyya Sabriyya Imdadiyya Rasheediyya being the traditional lineage of Deobandi Shaykhs taking pride in being initiated in all the 4 major orders (*ṭarīqa*) common in South Asia. Mawlānā Ishaq following Hamid Akhtar from Karachi (see below) adheres to the Chishtiyya Sabiriyya Imdadiyya Ashrafiyya lineage, that puts special emphasis on the legacy of Muḥammad Ashraf ʿAlī Thanwī (1863-1943).

The teaching of an *ʿĀlima* degree course to girls is in itself a very interesting development that originated in South Asia. It is still being debated whether it leads to the emancipation of girls from conservative and religious families with far-reaching consequences in the religious field, in the Bourdieu sense of acquiring religious/cultural capital, or whether it helps to cement gender separation and the imposition of limitations on the social roles of Muslim girls (Bourdieu 1991). Student activism is integrated into the school course through study circles and wallpaper writing on theological, and also political topics with relevance to Islam. Students also train to hold religious debates preparing them for roles of Imāms and similar functions.

Increasingly, the schools as institutions and the students use new media to project the schools to the wider public and to network among themselves.[12] They thus reflect the compulsions of the religious market space in the sense of Bourdieu sense (Bourdieu 1991). Conversion objectives towards non-Muslims and – often even more importantly – to other Muslims of different traditions, are also well served by the new media. Websites such as YouTube and Facebook have witnessed a new wave of video and media activism of students from Islamic schools testing the limits of social and moral proprieties and standards in Islamic teaching.[13]

---

11 http://www.sunniforum.com/forum/showthread.php?20387-Listing-the-Shuyukh-of-Tasawwuf-in-West/page5 [30-11-10]

12 For the introduction of the Zakariyya school, see http://www.youtube.com/watch?v=cjAFr9NgPTg; for a listing of videos of lectures and ceremonies at the Zakriyya school, see http://www.google.de/#q=darul+uloom+zakariyya&hl=de&tbs=vid:1&ei=1DZkTP_6O8q6jAfFzJ2wCQ&start=10&sa=N&fp=b2ce21fcffd198b6.[30-11-10]

13 See for instance the relaxed communication among students of the Azaadville school at their group page on facebook, http://www.facebook.com/group.php?v=wall&viewas=0&gid=13091542129.

Two South African hamlets of Deobandi learning

Today the two schools present themselves as small walled townships, complete religious settlements, which under modern conditions seek to recreate the pious community of the Islamic forebears. Yet the history of the schools is very much marked by the parameters of Muslim institution-building in South Africa, and as such, displaying a very local history with many common elements. In the process both schools went through similar stages of evolution. Those could be conditionally classified as –

(1) private beginnings;
(2) institutionalisation;
(3) modernisation and expansion; and
(4) ideological and public commitments.

For the two schools, those stages were marked by the following features summarised here:

(1) During the first stage of *private beginnings,* teaching was started as a personal initiative by individual religious scholars. The 1970s and 1980s were the heydays of identity politics in South Africa when not only its black majority, but also its ethnic and religious minorities were searching for its place and role in the country's racially segregated society. "In 1392 A.H. (1972)," as the school's prospectus narrates for Azaadville, "a student desired to become an *Ālim* in Germiston. His lessons started in a humble way – one student and a part-time *ustāẕ* (teacher). Little did we realize that this, however, was the seed for something much more in the future. Yearly students began enrolling for the *Ālim* classes." (Muhammad 2000a, 9) Teaching proceeded in Azaadville under improvised conditions until 1981:

> Lessons carried on in an informal way with classes taking place at the rear end of the *Jamāt Khāna* [prayer hall] while the students lived in the *mu'azzin*'s room [who calls for prayer]. Alhamdulillah, in this humble way, four students graduated as *Ālims* and about twenty as *Hāfizul Qurān*. (Muhammad 2000a)

(2) When the number of students kept growing beyond the expectations of the schools' founders, formal schools were created starting the phase of *institutionalisation.* In Lenasia, a small town to the south-west of Johannesburg, a separate school building opened after a Muslim philanthropist from the area donated twenty acres of land there in 1983. In Azaadville, near Krugersdorp, to the north-west of Johannesburg, a madrassah opened formally in 1982. It was located in a double-story house with eight students doing the *ʿĀlim* course on a full time basis at first (Muhammad 2000a, 7). "Within a month, we were forced to open a *Hifz* class· due to its demand. Within a year, three more *Hifz* classes were established with approximately forty students" (Muhammad 2000b, 6).

The choice of locations for building these institutes was not coincidental. It was connected to another structural process where 'coloured' people of South Asian heritage – similar to others – were forcibly removed from non-segregated areas in Johannesburg. Under Apartheid policies they were resettled to 'Indian group areas' around 1970 (Horrell et al. 1972, 158-9). It was in this context that Azaadville gained prominence as the West Rand Indian group area to the south of Krugersdorp and Lenasia near Johannesburg. The names of the settlements were a testament to the strong sense of cultural and religious belonging with the Muslim traditions of South Asia and their historical and political context. The school in Lenasia was built in Zakariyya Park, named after Muḥammad Zakariyya, the Muslim theologian and co-founder of the missionary movement of the Tablīghī Jamāʿāt from India. He had visited his friends and followers in South Africa in 1981 with great impact and had probably initiated both schools. The township of Azaadville named after the Urdu/Hindustani word *āzād* meaning 'free' was a reminder of the freedom struggle of India and Pakistan from the British. It may have also reminded local citizens of the travails of partition between secular India and the Muslim majority state of Pakistan.

(3) Today the schools in both places encompass huge complexes of modern buildings that speak for the *modern aspirations* of its leaders, but also of its clients and supporters. The schools are financed both through donations and fees. They exude the distinct appearance of settled middle-class institutions – a far cry from the austere and often poor Islamic schools in South Asia which inspired their creation. When this author visited the schools in 2005, they were harbouring far-reaching plans of expansion that would significantly enhance their capacity to take in students, but also further improve their facilities. At Azaadville, the new facilities included modern school buildings, a multi-purpose assembly hall, a large mosque, dormitories, a mess (dining hall) and sports facilities (Muhammad 2000b). Lenasia featured similar institutions such as a large mosque for 2500 attendees; large buildings for *ḥifẓ* and for general classes (east wing); a comprehensive library; two separate hostels, a large dining hall with a well-equipped modern kitchen; a new laundry block and accommodation for teachers and staff members.[14] Extending the existing dorms, the Lenasia school's capacity would increase to 1,000 students. They were also planning to add a separate library for the literature on the curriculum.[15]

Additional services turned the campus-style facilities into self-reliant communities. The Azaadville school is complete with a general store, a book shop, a barber, and public telephones. The school emphasises that these services aid the students, who as a result, do not have to leave the premises of the school as they are fully catered for on its grounds (Muhammad 2000b, 13). Rapid quantitative growth added another common feature of modernisation. The number of students increased manifold since the beginning. Both schools now have more than 600 students and 30-40 teachers each (see Table 3).

14 *Darul Uloom Zakariyya* (n.d.) (Lenasia, Darul Uloom Zakariyya) – 8-page flyer received during a visit to the school on 23 Feb 2005; here: p. 1.

15 Interview at the Lenasia school, 23 February 2005.

Table 3: Particulars of teaching and learning at the Azaadville and Lenasia schools

	Madrassah Arabia Islamia Azaadville 1, Azaad Avenue, Azaadville – Krugersdorp 1750 – Gauteng, South Africa (Principal: Mawlānā Shabir Saloojee)	Darul Uloom Zakariyya Zakariyya Park Lenasia, 1820 – Gauteng, South Africa (Principal: Mawlānā Abdul Hamid Ishaq)
Courses	Theology (ʿĀlim) – 6 years, girls: 4 y. Law (Mufti – Iftā) (Postgraduate – Takhassus) Preparatory (iʿdādiyah) (1 y.) Qurʾānic Recitation (Ḥifẓ) Qurʾānic Cantation (Qirāʾāt) Mosque and Prayer Leader Training Course (Imām Khatīb) (Madrassa) Teacher Training Course (Ustādh)	Theology (ʿĀlim / Fāẓil) – 7 years, girls: 5 y. Qurʾānic Recitation (Ḥifẓ) Qurʾānic Cantation (Qirāʾāt)
Islamic Activities	Teaching and Learning "Nurturing" (appropriate student behaviour) – Tarbiyah Preaching – Tablīgh (Sūfī-way of) Character Building and Self-Reformation – Tazkiyah-e Nafs and Ihsān (Majlis) Additional Ramaḍān Prayer – Tarāwīḥ Overseas Book Donations – Ibn Masood Book Distribution Scheme	Teaching and Learning Student associations – Anjuman Preaching – Tablīgh Commemoration – Dhikr Majlis Additional Ramaḍān Prayer – Tarāwīḥ
Depart-ments	Islamic teaching Office of Islamic Legal Advice – Dārul Iftā Publication Department (222 published books by 2004, posters, pamphlets, quarterly journal *An Nasīhah*, student newsletter *Al Muballigh*, text books)	Islamic teaching Office for Islamic Legal Advice – Dārul Iftā Eickenhof Branch – Teaching *Hifz* Publications – Tasnīf Library Medical aid – Doctor on premise Laundry Secular academics (English, Maths, Computer courses) Computer centre
Girls	Girls' Madrassa "Madrassatul Banaat"	Girls' Madrassa "Mueenul Islam"
Students	638 (ʿĀlim: 359, Ḥifẓ: 150) (2004)	680 (Ḥifẓ: 300) (2007)[16]
Teachers	36 (2004)	~ 40 full-time teachers, ~ 40 staff assistants

Foreign Students	310 students (2004) from the UK (20), US (20), Mozambique (55), Zimbabwe (10), Zambia, Mauritius, Reunion, Comoro, Kenya, Malawi, Madagascar, India, Bangladesh, Tanzania, Barbados, Thailand, Malaysia, Seychelles, Canada (6), Indonesia, Mali, Guinea etc. (breakdown for 2005)	~ 325 (50 %) from 52 countries (2005), incl. Malaysia (70), Mozambique (50), Namibia, Zimbabwe, Botswana, Gambia, Senegal, Somalia, Mali, the US (20), Canada (20), Reunion, China
Fees	Appx. 9,600 SA Rand per year (2008)[17] plus admission fee 10,000	9,000 SA Rand per year + 250 SA Rand for maintenance (2007, Boys)[16] 995 SA Rand (2005) per month (Girls)[18]

Sources: Muḥammad 2000a,b; *24th Annual Report of Madrassah Arabia Islamia Azaadville, South Africa* (10-10-2004) (Azaadville, Madrassah Arabia Islamia); *Darul Uloom Zakariyya* [2004/05] (Lenasia, Darul Uloom Zakariyya); interviews at the schools in Azaadville (24 February) and Lenasia (23 February) in 2005. Data partially patchy, and subject to availability.

It is assumed that the modernising slant of the schools are not least the product of their close connection with the socio-cultural networks of the Gujarati trading castes hailing from South Asia. Several teachers at the schools graduated from Deobandi schools in the Indian state of Gujarat, particularly from Dhabel and Tadkeshwar.[19] The schools were created and supported by many parents who trace their ancestry back to Muslim communities in Gujarat, and who gained considerable economic and social clout in the Muslim communities of South Africa. The modernity of the two schools is thus also a reflection of the newfound prosperity of the South African 'Gujaratis'. It could be inferred from this that graduation from Azaadville and Lenasia thus provides easy entry into the 'opportunity networks' of Gujarati descent.[20]

(4) Along with their modernisation and expansion, the schools took on more visible *ideological and public roles* within the local Muslim communities, the specific religious networks they were serving and for the whole South Africa. The Lenasia school became a centre of sorts and retreat for the Gauteng province activities of the missionary movement of the Tablīghī Jamāʿāt. The traditional weekly Tablīghī meeting, or *ijtimāʾ*, would be held at the local mosque *Masjid-e*

16 http://www.Sunnīforum.com/forum/showthread.php?30431-The-Darul-Uloom-Zakariyya-Thread [30-11-10]

17 http://www.Sunnīforum.com/forum/showthread.php?35704-Darul-Uloom-Azaadville-South-Africa/page5 [30-11-10]

18 http://www.Sunnīforum.com/forum/showthread.php?18606-Madressa-Mueenul-Islam-Information-Thread [30-11-10]

19 My interviews with respondents in February 2005, in particular with Mawlānā Mohammad Ashraf Dockrat who graduated from the Azaadville school.

20 See also the discussion by Thomas Blom Hansen of the ideological and modernist pretensions of Muslim family networks of Gujarati descent (Hansen 2003).

Siddiq on 10 Volta Street across town in Lenasia.[21] In the Lenasia and Azaadville schools, students are expected and possibly required to go out for preaching with the Tablīghīs every weekend and during their holidays.[22]

The Azaadville school also serves the religious needs of the wider Muslim community also by operating an Islamic Legal Advice centre, Darul Iftā, sending out religious decrees (*fatwas*) on inquiries from Muslims near and far, by phone, fax, email or post (Muhammad 2000b, 8).

The Azaadville school was particularly active in becoming a centre for the dissemination of Islamic knowledge by publishing and printing many standard works of scholars with a Deobandi and Tablīghī background. For this purpose it established its own on-premise printing press. In particular, several of its teachers contributed their own efforts to compiling new books or translating well-known classics from Urdu and other oriental languages into English. Their books helped invigorate the Deobandi networking in many countries around the world. Proudly the school proclaims: "The Madrassah has probably become the largest publisher of authentic Islamic books in the Southern Hemisphere. Thus far more than 160 titles have been published while new titles are published every month" (Muhammad 2000b, 10).

Beside the books, the Azaadville school printed posters for Masjid boards and for the public-at-large. It publishes the quarterly journal "An-Nasīhah" (Advice) the student newsletter "Al-Muballigh" (Preacher). Supported by public donations it also dispatched Islamic literature to "brothers overseas who cannot afford to purchase good Islamic books" (Muhammad 2000b, 11).

Thus, from a sociological perspective, the schools, despite their traditional and orthodox image and concepts, climbed a steep path of emancipation and modernisation, where they became influential and independent as well as interdependent players in a growing system of Islamic education and Muslim community service. This visibility and strength not only created space for them, but also exposed them to competing challenges of inter-dependence.

Translocal battles of re-alignment and competition

As the schools were positioned on the crossroads of competing systems of politics, ideology and religion, they arrived at a fusion of those influences shaping their composite character. With the influences and concepts shifting over time, the schools had to make amends with new trends. Politics moved from the era of Apartheid to democracy in South Africa. Theological competition that had started with the polarisation between reformist Deobandi and Sūfī-inclined Barelwi activism moved to new arenas where Salafīs, secularism and human rights NGOs became more prominent players and Sufism acquired new dimensions. The schools and their translocal networks of Tablīghī and Deobandi institutions and activism moved along and readjusted themselves in this configuration.

---

21 http://www.sunniforum.com/forum/showthread.php?27396-Islamic-events-Jo-berg-or-Durban&daysprune=-1 [29-11-10]

22 Interviews at schools in Lenasia, Azaadville on 23/24 Feb 2005.

While the direct impact of Muslim politics in South Africa at the schools is limited, it is mediated by the activist Council of Religious Scholars, Jamiatul Ulama (JU). Due to the connection through the weekly Tablīghī Jamāʿāt meetings in Lenasia, many JU leaders regularly interact with the elders of the schools of Lenasia (Zakariyya) and Azaadville. There are also many personal connections between the JU and the Deobandi madrassas in South Africa in general. Several prominent members are actively involved in running madrassa institutions. And, the programme of Darul Ulums is a major element of JU efforts in religious education.

At a national political level, Deobandi scholars in South Africa had to reconcile the politics and ambitions of the Muslim minority with the emancipatory project of the African National Congress. This was not as straight forward as it might appear today. Conservative Muslim leaders had in fact more or less acquiesced in the racial segregation politics of the Apartheid regime. At a time when political affiliations were suspicious, religious groups used the space provided to them as one of the few permitted outlets of public activity. Under those conditions, the project of re-Islamising South Africa's Muslim minority in the tradition of Deoband had started successfully well before the end of Apartheid. Especially in Transvaal, mosque committees and Deobandi scholars had focused on religious life while they left negotiations with the state to traders and professionals of Muslim background (cf. Tayob 1999, 71-3, 139). As soon as the end of Apartheid neared, the more farsighted scholars of the Deobandi-dominated Council of Theologians (JU) joined the ANC in shaping the constitutional and political space of the free South Africa. Their strong concern was to create legal conditions conducive to the introduction and application of Islamic *sharīʿa* law for South Africa's Muslim minority. The resultant legislative projects faced some difficulty while moving through the various political and state institutions. Currently, several bills on the introduction of Muslim Personal Law in South Africa are under consideration, mainly pertaining to the recognition of Muslim or religious marriages.[23] At the same time, the Deobandi institutions reorganised more successfully and, in cooperation with the Muslim Judicial Council (MJC) from Cape Town, strengthened their own platform with the formation of the United Scholars' Council for South Africa in 1994. Yet today, according to interviews of this author with JU scholars in 2005, the status of the Muslim minority in South Africa, no longer seems to be their only or overriding concern under the new conditions of democratic development. Political conditions in and around South Africa currently confront them with the political and social project of Black and African renaissance. They hope to respond to it by becoming more inclusive towards other Muslim groups and opening up to the Black community which apparently has been a recurrent topic of their leadership discussions. Such opening would also meet more effectively their missionary ambitions of *daʿwa* towards non-Muslims. But it is the social and human conditions of Muslims and other citizens of South

---

23 Cf. Rashida Manjoo, The Recognition of Muslim Personal Laws in South Africa: Implications for Women's Human Rights. Working Paper. Cambridge, MA: Human Rights Program of Harvard Law School, July 2007, at http://www.law.harvard.edu/programs/hrp/documents/Manjoo_RashidaWP.pdf [30-11-10].

Africa that provide the starkest challenge. A recent newsletter of the JU, on the 24th of November 2010, demonstrated the nature of political involvement pursued by the council. It discussed Israeli policies on the West Bank and US responses, and it congratulated a Muslim politician close to the JU, Ismail Vadi, for his appointment "to a Gauteng provincial government position of MEC for Transport." Importantly, the JU functionary Mawlānā Bham highlighted "the importance of public service in an era when community isolationism cannot deliver desired outcomes." A joint message by the JU and the Muslim AIDS Programme was published on the occasion of World AIDS Day. And, students, nearing the end of the academic year, are warned against the habit of 'rowdy' celebrations that usually follow the examinations.[24] These interventions clearly demonstrate the broad spectre of political, social and moral involvement of religious scholars.

At the level of theological doctrine and religious practice, the Deobandis had emerged in direct contestation of public Muslim space with the Sūfī-oriented Barelwi movement. The latter had organised much earlier. The religious activist Soofie Sahib (d. 1910) had been one of the first prominent representatives of this direction (Tayob 1999, 89). Following precedent in the South Asian subcontinent, the Deobandis challenged various practices connected to shrine and saint worship, as well as the expressive veneration of the Prophet through the celebration of his birthday with the *Mawlīd* ritual. Yet, this polarisation was not as clear in South Africa as in South Asia from where it emerged. While Deobandi thinking has also integrated some Sūfī practice and doctrine in the concept of *taṣawwuf*, it was the close association with the legacy of Muḥammad Zakariyya which brought the two schools under study here still closer to Sūfī influences. Zakariyya was not only a Deobandi scholar (*ʿĀlim*), he was also a recognised and widely connected Sūfī teacher (*shaykh*). The missionary movement he helped bring into being, the Tablīghī Jamāʿāt, though transporting a reformist and purist message, made extensive use of Sūfī traditions and practices, including the ritualised commemorative prayers of God, *dhikr* (Reetz 2006b). Still, the main outlook of the two schools in Azaadville and Lenasia was reformist, *iṣlāhī*, with a certain sectarian bent that would regularly criticise all dissenting readings of Islam.

In the late 1990s the ideological alignment among Deobandi schools in South Africa underwent various shifts. The reasons were manifold and diverse: South Africa underwent deep cultural and political changes; a new generation assumed leadership of Deobandi institutions; and the theological and spiritual ties with the South Asian subcontinent weakened and diversified. Previously the schools were connected with particular Deobandi madrassas in South Asia from where many or some of its teachers used to come as graduates. Beside the Darul Ulum Deoband, considered the theological *alma mater* (*madri ilmi*) of all Deobandis, it was the madrassas from Dhabel and Tadkeshwar in the Indian state of Gujarat, and Jalalabad in the state of Uttar Pradesh, not far from Deoband, that played an important role for the Deobandi schools in South Africa. Now an increasing number of teachers were employed from among their own former students. The connection to Zakariyya's spiritual legacy also loosened. After Zakariyya's death in 1982, many senior scholars had switched their Sūfī allegiance to one of Zakariyya's

24 http://www.jamiat.co.za/newsletter/online_newsletter_0547.htm [30-11-10]

most prominent disciples, Mufti Mahmood Hasan Gangohi (1907-1996), the former Chief Mufti of the Darul Ulum Deoband. After the Mufti's death during a trip to Johannesburg in 1996, their spiritual allegiance became more fragmented. According to our information, the founder and principal of the Azaadville school, Mawlānā Abdul Hamid Ishaq, now looked for guidance to Hakim Muḥammad Akhtar from the Sūfī hospice Khanqah-e Akhtari in Karachi. Akhtar had visited South Africa several times and actively courted the allegiance of Deobandi scholars. He ran a school of his own in Karachi that focused on mysticism (*taṣawwuf*) in the reformist (*iṣlaḥi*) tradition. The reorientation was also helped by a personal controversy between Ishaq and local Tablīghī leaders after which he cautiously distanced himself from local Tablīghī activism. He had previously been a regular preacher at Tablīghī events. Now, he took a back seat and also revised the integration of his school with Tablīghī activism. Participation in Tablīghī preaching was no longer compulsory for students whereas the teaching and practice of *taṣawwuf* was demonstrably expanded. Still the school very much supports participation in Tablīghī preaching as an effective form of Islamic character-building (*tarbiyyah*).[25]

From the interviews in South Africa, it also emerged that the Deobandi schools lately feel challenged by the inroads of a new brand of globalised and modernised Salafī teaching. It attracts growing numbers of Muslims seeking religious knowledge and guidance, particularly from among the younger generation no longer so closely attached to the Islamic traditions (*maslaks*) of their parents. Ahl-i Ḥadīth and Salafī scholars from South Asia increasingly target the Deobandis and the Tablīghī Jamāʿāt for their 'un-Islamic' adherence to Sūfī rituals. In this respect, the Azaadville school principal, Mawlānā Ishaq, is also targeted.[26]

Another challenge is seen in secular educational institutions and their competing demands. Deobandi scholars increasingly invest in Muslim educational institutions, teaching the national curriculum in addition to religious knowledge. This reflects the shifting demands and expectations of the community towards knowledge that is recognised in the economy and society, knowledge that is marketable and standardised. One of the prominent scholars of the Council of Theologians (JU), Mufti Zubair Bayat, was the chairman of the South African Association of Muslim schools.[27]

The doctrinal and cultural contestation leaves potential students confused, while it opens space for challenges. Some of those issues troubling potential students can be traced through the related internet forums such as www.sunniforum.com. Several students intending to go to the Azaadville school were looking to have Islamic instruction not in Urdu, as required in Azaadville, but in

25 Based on interviews in South Africa in February 2005.

26 Cf. Sajid A. Kayum, *The Jamaat Tableegh and the Deobandis: A critical Analysis of their Beliefs, Books and Dawah*, Ahya Multi Media, 2001. http://www.ahya.org/tjonline/eng/contents.html [29-11-10] The book makes reference to the work by Mawlānā Abdul Hamid Ishaq, The Reality of Tasawwuf and Ihsaan, Azaadville: Madrasa Arabia Islamia (ibid, Bibliography, 6).

27 See his biography at http://www.direct.za.org/about/profilezb/profilezb.html [30-11-10].

English only.[28] While it was confirmed that Urdu was obligatory, where other schools, such as in Newcastle teach in English only, they in turn were berated by those who disapprove such studies circumventing Arabic as, in their opinion, it would amount to studying from second-hand, i.e. translated sources. Another issue raised was the disapproval of the rector Abdul Hamid of Islamic radio stations, leading to the conclusion the school might have a problem with technology.[29] Members were also debating on *sunniforum* the cultural politics of dress and hair. They were told to wear the Pakistani/Indian-style dress called *kafnie* which is shorter than the Arab-style *thobes* and has slits on the sides. One of the participants by the nick name 'Husain' informed: "The principal views these as closer to the *sunnah*, thus the insistence upon them, as he feels that the Arab-Style ones are a symbol of the Salafīyyah. Most of our country's ʿUlamāʾ don't agree with him on it, but it is the rule, so as a student, you have to obey."[30] The admissibility of cellular phones was another issue raised by list contributors.[31]

The students' concerns mirror the complexity of the cultural, social and theological issues they have to grapple with in order to navigate their academic pursuit of religious knowledge.

Alternate transnational globalities

The contribution of the two schools in Azaadville and Lenasia to servicing their local communities and contesting ideological fault lines, owes much of its effectiveness to their share in global networking. Both of them play a strong role in the regional and global networks of Islamic education and mobilisation beyond the borders of South Africa. Their share of students from outside South Africa is reaching or exceeding 50 percent. This applies to most of the established religious seminaries (*Dārul ʿUlūms*) in South Africa, as was acknowledged by representatives of the Scholars' Council in Johannesburg in 2005. The scholars saw this not only in a positive light in terms of missionary efforts, but also understood it as a potential problem. The high share of foreign students at a time when the local student body is not significantly expanding into the non-Muslim, and black communities, could in their eyes be seen as an impediment to meeting their objectives in South Africa itself. They feel that the organisation is still too much under the impact of the racial segregation of the past. They believe they would have to move beyond the followers of Asian descent and address the needs of the black community more vigorously. The more politically aware scholars feel that the Muslim minority community needs to position itself towards the political trends of the African renaissance which they can neither oppose nor avoid. Re-

28 http://www.sunniforum.com/forum/showthread.php?35704-Darul-Uloom-Azaadville-South-Africa [29-11-10]

29 http://www.sunniforum.com/forum/showthread.php?35704-Darul-Uloom-Azaadville-South-Africa/page2 [29-11-10]

30 http://www.sunniforum.com/forum/showthread.php?35704-Darul-Uloom-Azaadville-South-Africa/page4 [29-11-10]

31 http://www.sunniforum.com/forum/showthread.php?35704-Darul-Uloom-Azaadville-South-Africa/page9 [30-11-10]

phrasing this statement, one could perhaps assume that Muslim activists would prefer to extend their missionary efforts first to the black population in their own country, rather than serving those efforts in the neighbouring countries.

Yet, the schools apparently hold a strong and growing attraction for foreign students. In Azaadville and Lenasia, their numbers have also reached 50 percent, with a strong focus on the African countries located to the immediate and near north of South Africa where movements of Islamic revival gain pace. Mozambique has a particularly large share in this process, apparently also connected to its Muslim minority of South Asian descent (Table 3). The schools are also very popular with South East Asian Muslims, notably from Malaysia, in South Asia, from where the Deoband and Tablīghī traditions emerged, and in the UK, the US and Canada with their own set of Deobandi institutions. It became clear through field research by the author that Deobandi schools in several countries increasingly rely on graduates from Azaadville and Lenasia. The two schools and their graduates are functioning as network multiplicators between Deobandi schools worldwide. The printed publications from Azaadville play an increasing role in this context as well. Especially for teaching the Deobandi curriculum of the degree course to become a religious scholar (*ʿĀlim*) in the English-speaking world, books from Azaadville have become increasingly useful.[32] These connections would also point to a growing economic dimension of Islamic teaching and publishing around the globe.

The religious and doctrinal orientation of the schools make them pivotal points of communication in the worldwide system of Deobandi institutions as well as the related, but not identical, global Tablīghī network, and the personalised networks of Deobandi Shaykhs and their disciples, where the legacy of Mawlānā Zakariyya played a key role, but is currently being overtaken by several other scholars and networks. Teachers, graduates, publications, doctrinal concepts and flows of donations and teaching fees bind the two schools together with similar institutions (Reetz 2007). Closest to them on the international circuit seem to be several Deobandi *Dārul ʿUlūms* in Great Britain, the US, Canada, Pakistan and India. In Britain, the closest affinity is with schools which Mawlānā Zakariyya helped found. First among them is the Darul Uloom Holcombe, Bury.[33] Its rector Sheikh Yusuf Motala published a biography and a listing of the 105 recognised disciples of Zakariyya (Motala 1986). In the US (Chicago, Buffalo, New York), Canada (Toronto) and the UK (Dewsbury, Bury), a new generation is joining the ranks of religious teachers at Deobandi madrassas, where the graduates of Azaadville enjoy a special reputation.[34] They seem to combine the sophistication of religious instruction in the Deoband tradition with a worldly knowledge of English and secular subjects.

For the Tablīghī Jamāʿāt, the two schools are important switchboards for their preaching activities in South Africa, in Africa proper and around the world. The

32 Books from Azaadville can be found at various Islamic internet bookstores, such as *kitaabun*, http://kitaabun.com, *al-Huda*, http://www.alhudabookstore.com, *al-Rashad*, http://www.al-rashad.com, etc. [30-11-10]

33 http://www.inter-islam.org/Pastevents/darululoom.html [30-11-10]

34 My field research in March, May-June 2010.

schools play host to incoming groups and send their students to all destinations near and far. A large international congregation of the movement in 2008 at the school grounds of Darul Uloom Zakariyya bears witness to this trend. Interestingly, its programme captured in the video on YouTube featured Nashid singers Junaid Jamshed from Pakistan, Wahid from South Africa, counselling centres and Muslim drug rehabilitation efforts, thus depicting the whole gamut of the multiple attachments discussed above.[35]

In this way the schools play alternating roles in the regional and global Islamic revival through their foreign students and the Tablīghī Jamāʿāt, in strengthening Islamic education in the Deoband tradition and promoting spiritual devotion in the legacy of Mawlānā Zakariyya and his disciples to the modern world. The schools have thus grown from private study rooms to the status of global players in the religious economy of Islamic instruction and mobilisation. They have demonstrated that Muslims today are not necessarily objects of globalisation if they follow their religious pursuits. On the contrary, they play an active role in the process, forming 'alternate globalities' (Reetz 2010b). As far as the two schools in Azaadville and Lenasia are concerned, their role in shaping these alternate globalities is not only owed to their very visible and growing contribution to Islamic learning, but also to economic linkages of Muslim trading groups, particularly of Gujarati extraction, that operate in the background, as several respondents confirmed. The unique and elevated social, political and legal status of the Muslim minority community in South Africa equally helped the schools to function as global switchboards of Islamic knowledge in the Deoband tradition, of their moral values and experience of interaction with a modern secular society that helped them to obtain and retain particular relevance in the global exchange. It is a cultural economy in line with the thinking of Bourdieu on the relevance of religion as religious and cultural capital (Bourdieu 1991). Through these 'alternate globalities' which strive to pose as contrasting developments to financial and economic globalisation as centred on the west, institutions like these two schools help to unfold a global Islamic field and market where religious and cultural competence is turned into potential social and economic advancement. Bridging the gap between tradition and orthodoxy, on one side, and secular modernity, on the other, they face intense contestation from various angles, doctrinal, political and social. This contestation in itself again help the graduates to precisely play this role of global mediators that by now the two schools have come to be known for in the global communities of Deobandi and Tablīghī followers. It is here where the explanation for their success has to be found, while their efforts for Islamic conversion and re-conversion anxiously watched by western strategists are more a corollary to this moral economy rather than an end in itself.

35 See the video on the congregation on YouTube at http://www.youtube.com/watch?v=JLW7ISzcJTA. [30-11-10]

References

Bourdieu, Pierre. 1991. Genesis and Structure of the Religious Field. *Comparative Social Research* 13: 1-44

Hansen, Thomas Blom, "'We are Arabs from Gujarat!' The Purification of Muslim Identity in Contemporary South Africa," *RAU Sociology Seminar Series* (Edinburgh, February 14, 2003), http://www.ukzn.ac.za/CCS/default.asp?3,28,10,900 (accessed June 24, 2009).

Horrell, Muriel, Dudley Horner, and John Kane-Berman. 1972. *A survey of race relations in South Africa*. Johannesburg: South African Institute of Race Relations.

Metcalf, Barbara D. 1982. *Islamic revival in British India: Deoband, 1860-1900.* Princeton, NJ: Princeton University Press.

Motala, Muhammad Yusuf. 1986. *Maulānā Muḥammad Zakarīya aor un kē Khulafā-e Kirām*. 2 Vols. Bury: Dār al-'Ulūm al-'Arabīya al-Islāmīya.

Muhammad, Moulana Ebrahim. 2000a. *Prospectus of Madrasah Arabia Islamia.* Azaadville, Krugersdoorp: Madrasah Arabia Islamia Publication Department.

-- (2000b) *A Guide to Madrasah Arabia Islamia.* Azaadville, Krugersdoorp: Madrasah Arabia Islamia Publication Department.

Moosa, Ebrahim. 1989. Muslim Conservatism in South Africa. *Journal of Theology for Southern Africa* 69: 73-81.

-- 1997. Worlds 'Apart': The Tablīgh Jamāt under Apartheid 1963-1993. *Journal for Islamic Studies* 17: 28-48.

Reetz, Dietrich. 2006a. *Islam in the Public Sphere: Religious Groups in India, 1900-1947.* Delhi: Oxford: Oxford University Press.

-- 2006b. Sufī spirituality fires reformist zeal: the Tablīghī Jamā'at in today's India and Pakistan. *Archives de Sciences Sociales des Religions* 135: 33-51.

-- 2007. The Deoband Universe: What makes a transcultural and transnational educational movement of Islam? *Comparative Studies of South Asia, Africa and the Middle East* 1: 139-159.

-- 2008. Change and Stagnation in Islamic Education: The Dar al-Ulum of Deoband after the Split in 1982. In *The Madrasa in Asia: Political Activism and Transnational Linkages,* ed. Farish A. Noor, Yoginder Sikand and Martin van Bruinessen, 71-104. Amsterdam: Amsterdam University Press.

-- 2009. Tablighi Jama'at. In *The Oxford Encyclopedia of the Islamic World*, Vol. 5, ed. John L. Esposito, 293-299. New York: Oxford: Oxford University Press.

-- 2010a. From Madrasa to University – the Challenges and Formats of Islamic Education. In *The SAGE Handbook of Islamic Studies*, ed. Akbar Ahmed and Tamara Sonn, 106-139. Thousand Oaks, CA: London: Sage.

-- 2010b. 'Alternate Globalities?' On the Cultures and Formats of Transnational Muslim Networks from South Asia. In *Translocality: The Study of Globalising Processes from a Southern Perspective*, ed. Ulrike Freitag and Achim von Oppen, 293-334. Leiden: Brill.

Rizvi, Sayyid Mahboob. 1980. *History of the Dāru'l-'ulūm*, 2 Vols. Deoband: Idāra-e Ihtimām.

Robinson, Francis. 2001. *The Ulama of Farangi Mahall and Islamic Culture in South Asia*. Delhi: Permanent Black.

Tayob, Abdulkader. 1999. *Islam in South Africa: mosques, imams, and sermons.* Gainesville, FL: University Press of Florida.

Vahed, Goolam. 2003. Contesting ‚Orthodoxy': The Tablighi-Sunnī conflict among South African Muslims in the 1970s and 1980s. *Journal of Muslim Minority Affairs* 23: 313-334.

Zakariyya, Muhammad. 1994. *Faza'il-E-A'maal.* 2 vols. [English edition, with Ihtishamul Hasan Kandhlawi and Ashiq Ilahi] (New Delhi: Idara Ishaat-e-Diniyat).

Lubna Nadvi

What does it Mean to be a Young Muslim in Contemporary South Africa?

Perspectives on Popular Culture, Education, Muslim Public Discourses and Civic and Political Participation

Introduction

This article is an exploratory discussion of Muslim youth identity formation in the eThekwini (Durban) municipality in KwaZulu Natal (KZN) within a contemporary, primarily urban, context. The discussion does not at this early stage of ongoing research, seek to articulate any definitive conclusions based on quantitative data acquired through intensive field work; rather it focuses on some preliminary observations arrived at through sustained interaction and engagement with young Muslims from various race and class backgrounds, of both genders. Based on these interactions, I have formulated some rudimentary and still to be explored thoughts on the way in which this demographic of young Muslims is grappling with and responding to the issues that would impact on them the most, within their age group, viz, i) popular culture, ii) education and Muslim public discourses and, iii) civic and political participation. Some of the arguments presented here though, rely on archival and other sources for the theoretical and analytic framework within which I aim to contextualise my position. For the purposes of this article, Muslim youth are identified as being between the ages of 15 and 30, however the discussion does not necessary exclude insights gleaned from engagement with those who are slightly younger or older. It is important to point out at this stage that the broad demographic sample that this article is attempting to research is constituted mainly of university based middle class youth, as well as urbanised youth, who may already have graduated and entered the working world. There is also a class and geographic (although unintended) dynamic to the study, which by virtue of the location of the sample, will automatically exclude young Muslims who are non-university based, but may include those from rural areas, or from a working class township setting. Hence it is in many senses a rather diverse stratified sample, which facilitates a discussion that includes a layer of multiple factors that shape the identity of these young people.

My interest in attempting to document the perspectives of South African Muslim youth arises from my research focus on Muslim public participation in a post-apartheid context, as well as my daily interaction with young people in a university context, and observing how it is that many are still grappling with concepts of identity, culture and religion, particularly in an evolving socio-political environment. As a lecturer and mentor to young people, I am often privy to the thoughts, views and occasionally personal feelings of the students that I teach and other young people I encounter through my community networks. These engagements often take the form of extra-curricular discussions and debates. While the Muslim student population at the university where I lecture, viz UKZN, is fairly diverse, more so in terms of class, than race, it is also one, where there is, given my observations, a general tendency and preference among Muslim students to identify with their "Muslimness", in various complex and interesting ways, which I will allude to later in this article. This does not however mean that this is necessarily their primary identity, but in some cases, can be one of many that they choose to identify with, in any given circumstance. This Muslimness ultimately also constitutes a community, where although there may be internal differences of opinion on various issues, there is still enough that binds the individuals, to make them collectively stand apart from other youth formations.

My point of departure is to conceptualise Muslim youth from the perspective of the diverse nature of influences that inevitably shape this identity within the broader South African context. It is however important to state though, given that the Islamic faith is the main framework within which I am attempting to unpack the issues which I am raising in this paper, much of the diversity which contributes towards the formation of this particular demographic is understood as being filtered through a particular religious lens. In this respect, Muslim youth in KZN while being a product of their broader environment are also part of a defined religious community, which while being far from homogenous, also creates a common space where these youth can find common cause around a number of issues which are pertinent to their lives.

I must also admit to constructing the discursive analysis in this paper, from within the context of my own ideological framework which leans towards a more progressive interpretation of Islam, its practice and application to daily life (Safi 2003). While the broad notion of what constitutes progressive Islam may be considered as being subjective to some degree and hence open to further debate and discussion, according to various other scholars of Islam, it is used here as a frame of reference that ideologically locates to some degree the ways in which this particular demographic sample of Muslim youth chooses to express its Islamic identity. This in no way suggests that progressive Islam is the ideal or the only frame of reference, rather its application here as an analytic tool provides a theoretical base from which the actions and thoughts of this group of people can be further explored and analysed.

It could be argued that a fair amount of existing sociological research tends to reflect young people, from within any faith community, as being prone to displaying behavioural tendencies that are often rebellious or inclined towards rejecting conservative or traditionalist ideas that their parents or elders sometimes expect them to adopt. It would perhaps be appropriate to point out that many of the conclusions arrived at in this article, suggest that there is indeed a growing trend, at least within this sample group, towards a partial modification if not outright rejection of conservative Islamic values that would include for example, strict rules regarding the mingling of young Muslim males and females, playing and listening to music, reading certain forms of literature etc. What the broad finding seems to point to, is that these mostly urbanised, middle class Muslim youth are not necessarily opting for un-Islamic ways of engaging, rather they are arguing that Islam as a faith can and does actually make provision for a less puritanical and strict application of the *Sharīʿa* prescriptions. In this context, music for example is not un-Islamic per se, rather it is the manner in which the use of a person's melodious voice or skill at playing an instrument can be used to advance the broader project of Islam (through spreading the message of the unity of the Divine for example, or *Tawḥīd*). This theme will be further explored in the latter half of this paper.

Granted that most of the observations I will refer to are primarily within the context of an academic setting, some of these have however also been gleaned through my work as a community activist, engaging with the younger members of various Muslim and non-Muslim groupings in eThekwini such as the Muslim Youth Movement (MYM), Muslim Students Association (MSA), World Assembly of Muslim Youth (WAMY), Islamic Propagation Centre International (IPCI), Taking Islam to the People (TIP), Al-Ansaar Foundation, Institute for Learning and Motivation (ILM-SA), the African Muslim Youth Congress, (AMYC), As Salaam Educational Institute, Social Movements Indaba (SMI), Palestine Support Committee (PSC), People Against War (PAW) and student leagues such as SASCO among others.

It is also important to point out that the Muslim youth of today, as is the case with young people from other faith groups, are part of the globalized world community which renders its own unique challenges, with regards to how one is to locate them within a particular worldview. In the South African context, Muslim youth are primarily located across three provincial centres, viz, the Cape (Western/Eastern), Gauteng and Kwa Zulu Natal (KZN). Given the historical differences of these regions, Muslim youth from KZN would reflect a particular set of ideas and values which would be quite distinct from that of Muslim youth in the other regions, yet in some ways be surprisingly similar, depending on whether they follow the same *madhhab*, or Islamic tradition. Such factors lend themselves to defining a very complex yet fascinating Muslim youth demographic, across the country. However for the purposes of this article, I will focus on Muslim youth in KZN.

Muslim youth identity formation: Influences and factors

In order to elaborate on the three areas that I have identified as being central to this article, it is critical to engage some of the key underpinning influences and factors that appear to be common to Muslim youth identity formation in general. As a starting point, it is useful to contextualise this within some established research already having been conducted on Muslim identity formation in South Africa.

Muslim social scientists such as Abdulkader Tayob, Goolam Vahed and Shamiel Jeppie, have written extensively on Muslim identity and history in South Africa, focusing on both pre and post-apartheid contexts (Tayob 1995, 1999; Vahed 2000a, 2000b, 2000c, 2001a, 2001b; Vahed and Jeppie 2005). This historiography is well known and has become the authoritative account of what the key influences were in shaping Muslim identity in South Africa more broadly. These accounts among others will form the backdrop against which I will attempt to formulate an understanding of contemporary Muslim youth identity in KZN.

It becomes clear from perusing the literature on Muslim identity within the South African context, that apart from Muslims observing the core religious pillars of faith such as the offering of prayers five times a day, fasting, etc, there are also various traditions, rituals, and cultural practices, that are central to the lives of Muslims, in terms of how they express their religious identity more broadly. Included in these varying aspects of traditions and rituals within KZN in particular, are for example, the holding of *Mīlād* gatherings celebrating the birth of the Prophet Muḥammad, the observing of the month of Muḥarram, as well as the frequenting of the Badsha Peer shrine, and offering of prayers (Vahed 2000c).

What also emerges in the literature is a fascinating sociological analysis of the various ethnic and language identity formations, particularly among Indian Muslims, that are a legacy of the arrival of Indian migrants to South Africa, first as indentured labourers in 1860 and later on as the merchant classes, and how it is that these various sub-formations have evolved into particular groupings within a contemporary context (Vahed 2000c). The class and socio-economic distinctions are perhaps the most obvious when unpacking the historiography of the indentured workers and merchant groupings, in particular the influence that the subsequent generations of the first Indian Muslim trader families have had on the development of the practice of the Islamic religion in KZN. Such influences would include for example, the constitution of the board of trustees of some mosques in KZN, which has hardly changed since the original mandates were established to ensure that only members of certain language and ethnic groups would be voted onto these boards, to preserve class interests and ensure a certain degree of hegemony over the functioning of these spaces (Sulliman 1985). I will reflect later on how these dynamics impact to some degree on Muslim youth identity within a specific context.

These language/sub-ethnic groups have also in some respects defined the issue of marriage between South African Muslims as well as other aspects of social life within broader Muslim society. A few decades ago, the practice of a Muslim from one sub-ethnic group for example, Surti, marrying someone from another, such as Memon or Gujerati, was largely frowned upon, despite the fact that both individuals were Muslim and the religion has in principle never objected to two believing Muslims, regardless of their background, entering into a marriage. These social barriers were arguably largely "constructed" by the elders of the community, based largely on financial considerations or a variety of other social prejudices. Fortunately for young Muslims today, many of these prejudices have been done away with except in the most conservative of quarters. While there might be some interpretations regarding Islamic marriages within the realm of Fiqh, (such as the concept of kafa'a in the Ḥanafī tradition) that point to a preference for marriage between a Muslim male and female of equal social standing, it could be argued that the general practice of contracting marriages according to ethnic identities is located within the framework of privileging caste and tribal considerations in a manner that is very instrumentalist. These practices tend to become part of the set of traditional value systems being passed on from one generation to the next, except where they are challenged and questioned. While this article does not seek to explore this particular dynamic in any great depth, it is useful however to reflect it as part of the broader social fabric of the Muslim community in South Africa.

The writing on Muslims in KZN also illustrates the complex racial demographics which comprise the Muslim community as a whole. Tahir Sitoto reflects on how the Zanzibari Muslim community in Chatsworth, the migrant African workers from countries such as Malawi, and the African Muslims in the township of KwaMashu have become a very significant portion of the Muslim demographic in KZN (Sitoto 2003). In particular, the various educational programmes that have been developed to facilitate learning and empowerment among African Muslims have been instrumental in generating a growing sector of Black South Africans from townships in KZN who have been embracing Islam, as well as supporting young African Muslims who have been born into the faith in a number of ways. One of these programmes, the As Salaam Islamic Institute located in Breamar, a rural area of KZN, has been central in advancing the role that young African Muslims are playing in contributing towards articulating a collective Muslim youth identity in KZN, as well as nationally.

The demographic of African, Coloured and White Muslims in KZN is, compared to Indian Muslims much smaller. It is useful to note though that according to the 2001 South African national census, Coloured Muslims in KZN are the second highest demographic followed by African and White Muslims. Their visibility however, in terms of being documented as regards their contribution to Islam in KZN is minimal, and it becomes clear that there is something of a dearth of available information on how this group is impacting on the religious dynamics within Islam in the province. These statistics also serve to confirm the widely held perspective that Islam in KZN has historically been heavily influenced and shaped by Indian values and culture, and it continues to do so.

Table 1: Muslim Demographic in KZN by Race, 2001 National Census Data (Vahed and Jeppie 2005, 260-67)

Province	**African**	**White**	**Indian**	**Coloured**	**Total**
KwaZulu-Natal	2,987	1,036	117,424	6,143	142,460

The tendency by what is commonly referred to as "Indian" Islam, to dominate expressions of Islamic religious belief by other race groups has arguably led to something of a historical social hierarchy among the broader Muslim community. This has also manifested itself among the level of young Muslims in various ways. For example, Muslim youth formations in KZN have for a long time been led primarily by young Indian men (thereby also revealing a gendered dynamic). While this is slowly beginning to change, with the most visible example of this being the recent transformation of the national structure of the Muslim Youth Movement, there are still pockets within some organizational spaces where old conservative practices remain.

Clearly these practices have emerged out of a range of historical contexts, such as the way in which early Islam was established in the former Natal region (now KZN), as well as the somewhat missionary oriented nature of the propagation of Islam when it first arrived in the province. Various institutional spaces such as the Islamic Propagation Centre International (IPCI), Islamic Dawah Movement (IDM) and SA National Zakaah Fund (SANZAF), have played a key role in creating the dynamics which have established the foundations in terms of how knowledge about the religion is disseminated as well as how the welfare component of the faith is managed.

I have in this section, made brief reference to some of the factors that have according to documentary and archival sources, shaped Muslim identity more broadly in KZN, referring in particular to class and race as visible defining factors in articulating particular modalities of Muslimness. While race and class are perhaps the most obvious factors, there are however many others that impact on the formation of what may be referred to as a community of Muslims; however the demographic picture changes quite considerably according to other variables as they are introduced. These would include gender, age, political ideology, affiliation to particular religious schools of thought, such as Ḥanafī, etc and level of education. I will now move on to focusing on how it is that some of these factors and dynamics combined, are giving rise to a particular Muslim youth demographic within KZN, more specifically within an urban context, viz the city of eThekwini (Durban).

Perspectives on popular culture, education and political participation among Muslim youth in eThekwini (Durban)

At the outset of this paper, I indicated that the arguments and conclusions presented in this article are to be seen as based on preliminary observations and a reflection of archival sources, rather than as the outcome of quantitative field work which will be the next phase of this work. I have nevertheless developed some preliminary findings on the formation of Muslim youth identity in KZN, which are reflected below.

Popular culture

Most literature on youth identity formation will inevitably reflect the impact that popular culture has on shaping the ideas and behaviour of young people, regardless of their race, religion, language, gender, etc. It is often the case that Western popular culture has become the dominant influence with regards to the kind of music that most young people listen to, western produced magazines, books, films and television in terms of what most youth read and watch, and certainly western cultural values in terms of behaviour and image/appearance and dress. This is at an observable level also true of Muslim youth in KZN, but more so within the urbanised middle class Muslim community.

Dress is a particularly interesting aspect of Muslim youth identity in the South African context, particularly among Muslim female youth. Many more young women are opting to wear the *ḥijāb* (head covering), while perhaps wearing somewhat western influenced clothing, such as long tops over jeans. The growing trend however, as seems to be the case globally, is the donning of the long black cloak with stylistic variations such as beading, cut, colour, etc, with the option of covering the face, which is generally not considered as being compulsory according to the faith. Some have argued that this trend has actually become more observable after the changing global dynamics post the events of September 11, 2001, and that Muslim women, who may be politically inactive in other respects, have chosen to don more obvious Islamic dress as a largely political response in order to assert a more visable "Muslim" identity within public spaces. Shopping mall, restaurants and public areas have begun to witness an increase in the number of Muslim female patrons who wear either the *hijab*, *nigab* (face-covering) or full length cloaks, when compared to a decade ago. While more empirical research would have to be conducted within the South African context to establish whether young Muslim females have adopted this type of dress for political reasons, religious reasons or a combination of both, it would be safe to argue that it has certainly become part of the broader popular culture of young Muslim women to be seen in public spaces wearing Islamic oriented dress, and often with a great deal of pride. There are also a number of growing events especially in eThekwini, exclusively for young Muslim women, where discussions about Islamic dress and other topics of interest to this group are held regularly. Such gatherings are also held for young Muslim men separately or occasionally for both young males and females, with segregated facilities.

Another innovative trend among, in particular, university attending and urbanised Indian and African Muslim youth over the last few years, is a growing interest in Islamic forms of music, such as Arabic music, the more globalized Nasheed genre, Qawwali, which is largely an influence from the Indo-Pak subcontinent and of course film music from Bollywood films. What is however most interesting within this growing trend, is that apart from listening to internationally produced music in these genres, there is also a desire for developing home grown talent in South Africa, particularly Nasheed music. The successful launch of popular group Waahid, from KZN, who have gone on to acquire both national and international fame is one example of a growing interest among Muslim youth to develop what could best be described as Islamic popular culture for a South African context. Of course some of this music retains some Western influences, but it is arguably a sort of fusion between Western and other musical influences. Waahid also does not use instruments and utilises a technique called beatboxing which is the use of vocal chords to create the illusion of instruments being played. Together with similar musical groups, Waahid are becoming the preferred option for Muslim youth and a greater number of Muslim youth are buying this kind of music, and spending time on the internet finding out more about international Muslim music artists like Sami Yusuf and Zain Bhika among others.

In addition, there seems to also be a growing interest in incorporating multiple languages such as Zulu, Arabic, Urdu and English into locally produced Nasheed music, a reflection perhaps of a more multi-cultural approach to how popular culture is being constructed, within the South African context. This does not necessarily mean that this demographic group is not listening to the more conventional western produced/other forms of music, however the fact that during Muslim radio broadcasts, Muslim youth actively phone or send text messages with their requests through to the station, to play "Islamic" oriented music, or purchase the compact discs of Nasheed artists is an indication that this music is certainly popular among Muslim youth.

The debate about whether playing or listening to music by Muslims is *ḥarām* (forbidden) or *ḥalāl* (permitted), is however constantly at the heart of debates within mosque, and other Muslim social spaces. This article does not seek to enter that space, as it is irrelevant for the purposes of this discussion, which simply aims to document and reflect the popular trends among Muslim youth, without moralising about such trends. It is of course important to mention though that various Islamic religious bodies in the South African context have entered the fray of the debates, with some declaring the presence of music, even if it is Islamic in nature, in Muslim spaces, as un-Islamic. In response, many of the younger generation, have sought to redefine and rearticulate contemporary expressions of Islam to include an appreciation of the visual and musical arts, as being part of the Muslim experience, without violating any boundaries of *Sharīʿa* or Islamic *Fiqh* (Jurisprudence).

Apart from music, there is also a growing interest among young Muslims in popular literature, such as books, magazines and newspapers, which are designed to engage issues which impact on Muslim youth, and which are not purely religious in nature. There seems to be a proliferation of youth oriented publications (more so for Muslim females), that speak about issues such as relationships, romance, *ḥalāl* cooking, and occasionally elements of the faith such as fasting and prayer. Many of these are produced outside of South Africa and are imported, but there are some, such as *The Muslim Woman*, which are locally produced. Additionally there is a growing pool of South African Muslim writers who are writing both fiction and non-fiction for a local Muslim readership (which sometimes target the youth), such as Imraan Coovadia, Rayda Jacobs and Shafinaaz Hassim. While the local Muslim youth readership has not necessarily grown significantly since 1994, there is nevertheless an ever expanding selection of "Islamic oriented" material, both nationally and internationally produced, for them to choose from.

In analysing emerging trends within popular culture, one cannot exclude the way in which young people socialize with each other. In terms of socializing practices among Muslim youth in KZN, especially within the university context, there have also been some intriguing new developments. While historically at the Universities of Natal and Durban –Westville there have always been "Muslim" spaces, where predominantly only Muslim students frequented, whether it was the cafeteria area or elsewhere, a new trend has emerged within the UKZN space, particularly at the Howard College campus, viz, what can loosely be described as the Hookah/Hubbly Bubbly Club. Muslim students, usually of a more middle class background, congregate between lectures or before and after *ṣalāh* prayers in a specific place, to fraternise and smoke the hookah pipe which, while still predominantly smoked by male students, is also becoming very popular among some Muslim female students. Occasionally non-Muslim students showing an interest in the practice are invited to sample the hookah pipe, thereby creating a more multi-cultural group, however it appears that it is still very much an "Indian Muslim" phenomenon and has yet to catch on among Muslims of other race groups. There is also perhaps a class dynamic to this practice, given that it is usually young people from more affluent backgrounds who are often seen congregating together within the 'Hookah' club. This is also a practice which happens to a lesser degree in middle class Muslim homes, outside of the university context. It is however, certainly not something that would be commonly observed among Muslim township youth in Kwa-Mashu, or even among those young people from the township who attend university. The practice of hookah smoking should however be viewed within a specific context, viz the congregation of predominantly Muslim students for a specific social ritual. This does not mean however that these same students do not socialise with students from other religious/class backgrounds or participate in other social activities, such as sports; rather it points to the emergence of a specific set of behaviours that occur only within a given social context, which can be seen as an extension of their Muslim identity.

There is also a class dynamic to this practice. It is unlike the traditional smoking of cigarettes, and hence there is a cost factor which includes being able to regularly purchase the tobacco and coal used in the preparation of the hookah, including having the hookah pipe itself, which can be costly. Hence it is often a social practice more visible among the more affluent Muslim youth.

Perhaps the most visibly evident trend among Muslim youth with regards to popular culture is the phenomenal use of what are commonly referred to as social networking sites, such as e-Blogs, Facebook, My Space, Twitter and instant messaging software, on the internet, to communicate with each other. While the cell phone medium remains an ever popular tool for verbal communication, it has also become a mobile source for using social networking services, which do not require access to a desktop or even a laptop computer. Facebook appears to be the most popular online space to propagate Muslim identity issues, and there are numerous pages which have themes that make reference to religious practices and various other aspects of the Islamic faith, such as South African Muslims. In particular it has become a common space for Muslim youth to mobilise around global political issues such as Palestine, Iraq and Afghanistan, which might otherwise not have been quite as appealing without the existence of the social networking component, and its many applications. In addition, "blogging" has become a revolutionary new way for many people, both young and old, to share their thoughts on various issues, and post a variety of online material for general consumption. The broad collection of available technologies have effectively enabled young Muslims in particular, to display a more keen interest in sharing information about various activities, both Islamic and non-Islamic or secular with their fellow Muslims and other online users. This is in itself arguably a very revolutionary development, as it creates a platform for both practicing Muslims and those who may want to know more about the religion to be drawn to these spaces, via the medium of technology. It also enables greater social understanding among youth of different backgrounds and faiths. In KZN, Muslim organisations, such as the Institute for Learning and Motivation (ILM-SA) which organises and hosts Islamic events for all age groups are able to promote their activities more effectively via these online spaces, and rely quite heavily on their younger fans and members to "spread the word".

Hence, online social networking has in the contemporary era, come to shape young Muslims in a way that perhaps technologies in previous eras have not been able to do. This is evident more so in the way in which language, especially English, has been adapted for communication, into what is commonly known as SMS language, as well as the speed and complexity with which communication takes place. This is arguably manifesting in various new dynamics that are impacting on the issue of how contemporary social values are evolving and the ever expanding spaces where young people can now interact.

In previous generations, open and unhindered social fraternising between young Muslim males and females was usually frowned upon by parents and older members of the community, for a variety of reasons. With the onset of the information revolution, the internet, e-mail, digital and mobile technology and now social networking, young Muslims of all backgrounds are able to communicate with each other instantly and form "virtual" relationships, even without meeting. While the concept of expanding online communication across various social, national, racial, ethnic and class divides can be considered as desirable at one level, the boundaries of what may constitute "appropriate" Islamic ethics among Muslim youth, according to some spaces, such as Muslim religious bodies, are arguably constantly shifting.

While the purpose of this article is not to engage in any moralising discourses around what is according to Islam appropriate or inappropriate, with regards to the various forms of popular culture and social communication among Muslim youth, it is however useful to make the point that the nature of social interaction has certainly evolved in new and dynamic ways. The observable trends reflect the fact that interest in the Islamic faith and its diverse practices has certainly grown among Muslim youth in KZN and nationally, albeit as a consequence of the effects of a post September 11, 2001 world, or simply as a natural extension of the technological revolution, which makes exploring different aspects of the faith more interesting.

Education and Muslim public discourses

The contemporary views of Muslim youth within KZN as regards education and public discourses more broadly, are quite illuminating. There has over the last few years been greater efforts made by young Muslims nationally and globally in seeking out alternative sources of information and intellectual material to read and engage with, as opposed to accepting what is available within the mainstream and conservative spaces. This is arguably a consequence of the events of September 11, 2001 and the subsequent oppression being felt by Muslims globally, and is therefore perhaps not a uniquely South African phenomenon. However within the KZN context, what is certainly noteworthy are the growing engagements between young Muslims around the need to create spaces for more intellectual progressive discussion on Islam. This discourse is a growing one within spaces such as MYM, WAMY, TIP and the MSA chapters, where young Muslims while still pre-occupied to some degree with Eurocentric paradigms, are also attempting to break out of these. The proliferation of "Islamic" oriented courses and seminars being offered in both the private and public sectors, such as those by the Al-Kauthar institute, ILM SA and others, and the significantly high attendance by Muslim youth at these events, is an indication of the desire by both university students and the general youth community to also engage with Islamic ideas, quite apart from the conventional academic curriculum to which they are exposed, at university.

The popularity of Islamic intellectuals such as Tariq Ramadan, and more mainstream intellectuals such as Mahmood Mamdani among Muslim youth, suggests that there is a growing intellectualism among Muslim youth who are eager for a more progressive engagement around various issues. The nature of this intellectualism is perhaps far more nuanced than the kind of youth activism of the 1970s, 80s and 90s, advanced by predominantly members of the MYM, and suggests that the challenges faced by contemporary Muslim youth have forced a new kind of thinking among young Muslims, particularly in KZN, where there are huge socio-economic challenges which are driving this intellectual, yet more community oriented agenda.

While the Muslim seminary spaces such as the various Darul Ulooms in South Africa continue to produce a particular kind of mindset among their young graduates, which may often reject a more intellectual set of discourses, there are also some observable changes. Where previously the seminary spaces may have rejected a certain set of practices, such as voting in elections, they are now in some cases moving towards reform and adopting more progressive approaches towards how Muslims should engage within broader society.

A common theme of discussion in Muslim public spaces such as Mosques and the print and electronic media, especially during election time, is whether Muslims should engage in public/political participation and general civic activism as a minority community. It is arguably to the credit of the younger generation of South African Muslims, that one now sees greater active participation by Muslims in the national, political and civic life of the country. The work being done by various youth groups with regard to encouraging young Muslims to engage with their immediate community on issues such as poverty, HIV Aids, gender based violence among other issues, is certainly admirable.

Muslim Newspapers such as *Al-Qalam*, *Muslim Views* and *Al-Ummah*, are also a medium through which the desire by Muslim youth for greater intellectual engagement becomes more evident. There is a growing pool of young Muslims entering the fields of journalism, print and electronic media where they are combining their interest in reflecting a sophisticated Islamic worldview, which is erudite, with an ever expanding thirst for professionalising what has up to now been a largely community oriented and ad-hoc approach to Muslim media.

While the push for a more intellectual agenda exists predominantly within the middle class Muslim youth sector, with progressive leanings, one can observe the beginning of greater engagement across race and class divides among Muslim youth at both the university and community level. Albeit that these engagements may be taking place within a predominantly religious context, such as Islamic functions, and not necessarily over more social gatherings, it is nevertheless happening in pockets. WAMY, MSA and MYM in KZN are also very active in terms of advancing interaction between rural, urban and township Muslim youth and encouraging more intellectual engagement, through for example *Tarbiyyah* programmes, seminars and community outreach initiatives.

When one peruses the broad expanse of the field of Islamic education in the South African context, it becomes clear that it is a very diverse space, which has a number of components that one can speak of. I have made reference to aspects of education which are generally pursued by Muslim youth largely of their own free volition, as part of their post school intellectual development, in the form of a variety of Islamic courses on offer, scholarship by leading intellectuals as well as the information available within the space of print and electronic media. It is useful however to make brief mention here of Islamic schools which cater for young Muslims as part of their primary and secondary educational development. Many more Muslim parents are opting to send their children to "Islamic" schools where the conventional secular educational curriculum is offered together with Islamic options, within the framework of an Islamic environment which includes the availability of prayer facilities, etc. This formal education is clearly an important and central stage of a young Muslim's development where formative ideas are imparted and imbibed, and where the basic practice of the Islamic faith is reinforced through various ways. This space clearly also has an impact on how popular culture is understood and consumed by young Muslims.

The transition between school based education and a post-school context, which may include tertiary education, is no doubt a significant period in a young person's life. This articles delves largely into the broader influences that are shaping Muslim youth in South Africa, that are not necessarily always located within the context of formal primary and high school education as alluded to above, however the formal context cannot be ignored as being central to how other influences are embraced. As indicated at the beginning of this article, further empirical data gathering needs to be conducted in order to get a more accurate picture of how these various dynamics, such as the interface between early and tertiary education, are impacting on the evolution of Muslim youth identity and how this in turn is shaping the development of a particular kind of popular culture which is specific to the South African context.

Civic / political participation

It is important to locate Muslim responses to political developments in apartheid South Africa, which unfolded from 1948 onwards, within a broad framework of what Tayob refers to as Islamic resurgence (Tayob 1995). In many ways the period of Islamic resurgence is what has ideologically shaped the general participation of South African Muslims and Muslim youth, in a contemporary and post-apartheid context. This resurgence focused primarily on ensuring that Muslim religious interests were incorporated into broader civic life, through the establishment of various Islamic oriented civic organizations, in the various regions where Muslims were located in significant numbers, such as the Cape, Natal and the

Transvaal (as these regions were referred to at the time). While Tayob contends that resurgent organizations came into existence predominantly after the Second World War, there were according to him, traces of a "new approach" to Islam present at the end of the 19th century, particularly in the Cape (Tayob 1995, 78). The resurgence was driven primarily by a class of educated Muslim elites, who began to establish a variety of Islamic schools and civil society organizations that would service Muslim religious needs and interests such as burial associations and mosque boards and trusts (Tayob 1995, 80–1). It was the establishment of these various bodies, that arguably sowed the initial seeds of what became the institutionalised framework within which Muslim politics, and other aspects of Muslim life in South Africa unfolded, and continues to do so well into the contemporary period.

In Natal, now Kwa-Zulu Natal, anti-apartheid activities among Muslims were organized predominantly through the work of the Natal Indian Congress (NIC), until the formation of the Muslim Youth Movement in 1970 (Tayob 1995, 106). The NIC effectively represented the political interests and aspirations of Natal Indians, both Hindu and Muslim (Bhana 1997). Many Muslims were prominent in the NIC fold. They included, I.C. Meer, Fatima Meer, Dawood Seedat, Cassim Amra, A.K.M. Docrat, Jerry Coovadia and Farouk Meer. The political legacy created by these figures (among others) has in many ways been the broad inspiration for the generation that followed them, to engage in politics. However the post 1994 generation has not really seen a replication of the kind of political work done by these Muslim activists, and the reasons for this are varied and complex. In more recent times there has been a public debate about whether the NIC or a similar political structure should be revived to represent the contemporary interests of Indians either in the region or nationally. However the idea of reviving an NIC like structure has not had much purchase as many have considered this to be racially divisive in an era where political activism should ideally not be engaged according to racial blocs, but rather inclusive non-racial ones.

Muslim youth in KZN within the urbanised context are very often confronted by the realities of class and race dynamics, where there is usually a hegemonizing of political spaces by specific ethnic and class groupings within the Muslim community. There is of course a historical and generational context to how this has evolved and there certainly has been much debate within South African Muslim society around the need for a transformative agenda to ensure greater representation of Muslims from all walks of life across the socio-economic spectrum, in various political spaces. This should ideally include participation by women, different race groups, the working classes, the disabled and nationals of other African countries. Sadly though, the reality on the ground is very different. While there are significant numbers of for example African Muslims within service oriented spaces like *Da'wah* and relief/humanitarian organisations, there are virtually none in leadership positions within political parties and very few occupying religious leadership positions on Muslim boards and trusts.

Muslim identity formations according to class and race both pre and post 1994, as alluded to in the previous section, is certainly a more relevant dynamic when observing Muslim youth in relation to political participation. I have written more extensively elsewhere on the subject of Muslim political participation more generally, however here I wish to focus on trends among the youth in KZN (Nadvi 2008). Today's South African youth are generally less socio-economically and politically conscientized than perhaps previous generations and this is certainly the case among urbanised middle class Muslim youth, who are generally more pre-occupied with commercialized popular trends (as a consequence of class divisions). While there are certainly young Muslims from all class and race backgrounds who are activist oriented and want to make a difference politically, they often tend to gravitate towards "secular" spaces where religious identity constructions are irrelevant, such as social movement spaces like the Social Movements Indaba or Treatment Action Campaign, and occasionally political youth league formations such as SASCO. There are of course also spaces where political engagement assumes a religious face, and young Muslims are recruited on the basis that they are fulfilling a religious duty such as for example engaging in political solidarity with Palestine, in order to protect the Al-Aqsa Mosque.

While I have in the previous sections of this article, argued that a fair amount of credit goes to progressively minded young Muslims for encouraging greater participation in national and civic activities and reform within the Muslim community more broadly, it is important to qualify this, with a note that acknowledges that such progressive spaces are small and often struggle to have their voices heard against those conservative ones, who often with the might of historical bases of power, and class privilege, wish to maintain the status quo. One such progressive group in KZN, which has formed very recently is Taking Islam to the People (TIP), which has a membership of primarily young Muslims, who wish to be able to observe their faith in ways that are transparent, easily accessible to other people who may want to learn more about it, as well as being humane and embracing a diverse approach to the practice of the religion.

TIP members have also engaged a variety of issues of faith within a political context, quite apart from the conventional issues of voting and serving in public office. One such key issue is that of the as yet unresolved question of the application of Muslim Personal Law which has remained controversial in the South African national space for various reasons, which will not be elaborated upon here. It is however a matter of critical import for a largely younger generation of Muslims for whom the issue of being able to observe matters of personal law according to Islamic requirements is central to both their religious identity as well as their constitutional rights to practise customary forms of law. This remains a political cause which has to some degree engaged both young Muslims as well as Muslims in general. It is an ideal example of the kind of complex "religio-political" dilemma facing an emerging younger generation of practising Muslims, who must make difficult decisions, and often are forced into political spaces, to engage the state and its various structures.

Conclusion

This article has attempted to reflect on some aspects of Muslim youth identity formation within KZN, largely within an urban context. These reflections constitute at this stage some rudimentary ideas around how young Muslims in KZN are engaging with in particular, the issues of popular culture, education/public discourses and civic/political participation from within the framework of their "Muslimness". These ideas by no means constitute an exhaustive picture of Muslim youth within a specific context, but rather begin to scratch the surface, alluding to the necessity of pursuing further research into this fascinating area of identity construction.

The fact that there is, for example, growing interest among young Muslims to develop Islamic expressions of popular culture is an indication that there is a deeper connection with religious identities than one might have otherwise assumed. There seems to be a similar trend with regard to education and Muslim public discourses and developing more progressive intellectual paradigms, which challenge the dominant status quo. With regards to civic and political participation, there seems to be a gap in terms of active and sustained participation, by the youth, across the social spectrum, partly because of historical factors and partly due to apathy among the youth sector. This is a state of affairs that clearly needs to be addressed very urgently.

The implications of not advancing a transformative agenda within Muslim society more broadly are clearly quite grave. This would mean that today's Muslim youth who are excluded in various ways from participating in political spaces where Muslim leadership is required, will continue to be marginalised in future through the perpetuation of certain practices that are sustained via class and sometimes race privilege. Clearly such a situation is untenable and requires that more Muslim youth become pro-active in challenging exclusionary practices and ensuring that there is greater transparency within the broader society moving forward.

It is important to note that given the diversity evident among the broader South African Muslim community, it would be misleading to assume that the Muslim youth are a mirror reflection of their parents or the older generation. If anything, what seems to be emerging is a fascinating blend of contemporary influences and historical factors which reveal complex layers of identity formation and certainly also points to a critical engagement taking place at various levels. It is this blend that merits further study.

References

Bhana, Surendra. 1997. *Gandhi's Legacy: The Natal Indian Congress, 1894-1994.* Pietermaritzburg: University of Natal Press.

Nadvi, Lubna. 2008. South African Muslims and Political Engagement in a Globalising Context. *South African Historical Journal*, 60 (4): 618–36.

Safi, Omid. 2003. *Progressive Muslims: On Justice, Gender and Pluralism.* Oxford: Oneworld.

Sitoto, Tahir. 2002. Imam Essa Al-Seppe and 'the emerging and unorganised African Muslim sector': A contextual analysis. *Annual Review of Islam in South Africa,* 5: 43-7

Sulliman, Ebrahim. 1985. *A Historical Study of the largest Mosque in the Southern Hemisphere, namely the Juma Musjid.* University of Durban Westville: unpublished BA thesis.

Tayob Abdulkader. 1995. *Islamic Resurgence in South Africa. The Muslim Youth Movement.* Cape Town: University of Cape Town Press.

Tayob Abdulkader. 1999. *Islam in South Africa. Mosques, Imams, and Sermons.* Gainesville: University of Florida Press.

Vahed, Goolam. 2000a. Changing Islamic Traditions and Emerging Identities in South Africa. *Journal of Muslim Minority Affairs*, 20 (1): 43-73.

-- 2000b. Indian Islam and the meaning of South African Citizenship – A Question of Identities. *Transformation*, 43: 25-51.

-- 2000c. Indian Muslims in South Africa: Continuity, Change and Disjuncture, 1860 – 2000. *Alternation*, 2: 67-98.

-- 2001a. Uprooting, Rerooting: Culture, Religion and Community Amongst Indentured Muslim Migrants in Colonial Natal, 1860–1911. *South African Historical Journal*, 45: 191–222.

-- 2001b. Mosques, Mawlana's and Muharram: Establishing Indian Islam in Colonial Natal, 1860–1910. *Journal of Religion in Africa,* 31: 3–29.

Vahed, Goolam and Shamiel Jeppie. 2005. Multiple Communities: Muslims in post-apartheid South Africa. In *State of the Nation: South Africa, 2004-2005,* ed. by John Daniel, Roger Southall and Jessica Lutchman, 252-283. Cape Town: HSRC Press.

Wolfram Weisse

Muslim Religious Instruction or 'Religious Education for All'?

Models and Experiences in the European Context

Introduction

The religious and public expressions of Islam are as manifold as the opinions others hold of them and its adherents. The public perception of Muslims is located between two poles: whereas on the one side Muslims are regarded as strict and even extremist, we can on the other hand observe a growing understanding of Islam and respect for the role Muslims play in society. In such an ambiguous situation, much work remains to be done in both the public arena as well as in the academic field, in order to contribute to a reduction of resentments and allow an open and equal interaction of the various religious groups in society.

For this aim we can refer to prominent voices. As an example in the academic arena Paul Ricœur has long been an advocate for mutual understanding. With reference to Muslims in the Catholic dominated society of France, he publicly insisted on a perspective shift. Instead of admonishing Muslims to integrate into the majority French society, he emphasised the potential of Muslims to contribute 'communitarian' values to that society. These values, strongly represented in Muslim families, could serve as a resource for societal cohesion in France as a whole, where growing disintegration at the family and group level is observable (Ricœur 1995, 202). Furthermore, Ricœur argued against seeing the "grid of secularisation" (*grille de secularisation*) in France as the only standard by which to judge Islam in the political sphere. On the contrary, he viewed the public expression of religion by Muslims as a contribution towards questioning the dominance of the deteriorating laical system in France. And Ricœur specifically criticised the mainstream position opposing the wearing of headscarves – which in France is even forbidden to pupils at school – by formulating the provocative statement: "I cannot help but feel that there is something silly in the fact that a Christian girl may expose her buttocks in school while a Muslim does not have the right to cover her head."[1]

Our considerations in this matter must be placed in a broader social, religious and philosophical context if we want to get anywhere. The current transformations we can observe in all societies around the globe require new answers to turn diversity into a resource for peaceful coexistence, not a cause of misunderstanding, division and hostility. To this end it is not enough merely to tolerate sharing one's space with people of a different language, origin and religion. Rather, it is more important than ever to move towards respect for the Other, as for

1 Je ne peux pas m'empêcher de penser qu'il y a quelque chose de bouffon dans le fait qu'une fille chrétienne puisse à l'école montrer ses fesses tandis qu'une fille musulmane n'a pas le droit de cacher sa tête (Ricœur 1995, 204).

example Paul Ricœur stresses. He regards as central both, to acknowledge the 'Other' in his or her otherness, but also to recognise oneself as an active and responsible subject to achieve a secure, stable identity in a spirit of mutual recognition (Ricœur 2006). He pleads for a process of identity formation that is not located in a protected space separate from the 'Other', but in immediate engagement with it. The repercussions of this approach at the social and individual level are considerable. Not least, in that it also directs our attention to the question of religious plurality. If recognition and respect for the 'Other' is a necessary precondition for the realisation of the self and recognition in social interaction, a plurality of religious positions offers the opportunity to practice this.

This is all the more necessary since we now understand that religion and religiosity are not moving to the margins of public and private life through a gradual process of secularisation, as was long assumed in Europe. Rather, we observe the opposite development as religions are playing an increasingly important role in Europe's societies – for the dialogue between people from different religious backgrounds, but also as a factor of social tension and conflict.

The renowned German thinker Jürgen Habermas, who for decades had ignored religion in the frame of his philosophical approaches, has since changed his position. Recently he referred to the new role of religions in Europe and the need to acknowledge the presence of religious minorities, including Islam, in the public arena of contemporary democratic societies. With reference to different contexts he stresses the political relevance of including minority groups like the Muslims in a democratic society as the central question.[2] He views their inclusion as a necessary step towards a fully multicultural citizenship rather than as an act of integration into the majority system. He warns against a segmentation of population groups with different cultures and religions, and underlines that "an equal coexistence must not mean a separate existence. It depends on the integration of all citizens – fully cognizant of their subcultural affiliation – into a shared political culture."[3]

Thus the discussion on the role of religions and interreligious dialogue has transcended the traditional borderlines of theology and has been taken up by quite different disciplines like philosophy, sociology, political science, etc. Similar developments can be traced in the public discussion.

---

2 "Integrating religious minorities into the commonwealth serves to increase our sensibilities for the legitimate claims of other minority groups. The recognition of religious groups is well placed to take on this exemplary function because it can tangibly demonstrate and create broader awareness of the claim that minorities have to inclusion (own translation of the following original sentences: "*Die Einbeziehung religiöser Minderheiten ins politische Gemeinwesen weckt und fördert die Sensibilität für die Ansprüche anderer diskriminierter Gruppen. Die Anerkennung des religiösen Pluralismus kann diese Vorbildfunktion übernehmen, weil sie auf exemplarische Weise den Anspruch von Minderheiten auf Inklusion zu Bewußtein bringt")* (Habermas 2005, 274).

3 „Die gleichberechtigte Koexistenz verschiedener Lebensformen darf nicht zu einer Segmentierung führen. Sie erfordert die Integration der Staatsbürger – und die gegenseitige Anerkennung ihrer subkulturellen Mitgliedschaften – im Rahmen einer geteilten politischen Kultur" (Habermas 2005, 278).

As a new trend even international organisations are dealing with the relevance of Islam and other world religions as resources for the core values of a society. This concerns in particular respect and tolerance of people with different cultural and religious backgrounds. For example: the governments of the 47 member states of the Council of Europe in May 2008 emphasised the great importance and relevance of intercultural and interreligious dialogue in a „White Paper on Intercultural Dialogue" in which is stated: „Interreligious dialogue can contribute to a broader consensus in a society on the solutions of social problems." (Council of Europe 2008, 13). It seems thus more necessary than ever to analyse current developments in our societies. Research in this field presents a challenging task for academics, who empirically address the question of whether and how the aims expressed by the aforementioned philosophers or the Council of Europe can be realised.

One of the major fields of research is the whole area of education. During the past few years there has been a broad discussion on the question of whether there is a need for special Islamic education or an overall educational system, where Islam and other religions provide fields of learning and where pupils of different religious and cultural backgrounds are taught together. As an example of this debate I would like to draw attention to a special case, namely the discussion on religious education in Germany, and in particular to the Hamburg Model of an integrative Religious Education (RE) for all pupils.

In the following, I will start with some general remarks on the German context of RE and the special approach in Hamburg. I will then focus on our specific case, the new initiative of a dialogical approach at university level in Hamburg – the Academy of World Religions – to explain our understanding of religion and the underlying rationale for a dialogical RE. This analysis will be embedded in a broader European context: I will refer to the results of the European REDCo project, give some insights into its general aims, and focus on empirical research results on young people's attitudes towards religious diversity. In this chapter I will also refer to the findings specific to dialogical religious education in Hamburg. Finally, I wish to stress the importance of paying greater attention to Islam and to Muslim students at school, not as a group separate from others, but in a space where all are free to learn about different religions and to enter into a learning process based on dialogue and contributing to respect and genuine interreligious learning at school.

Religious Education in Germany: Apart or together?

For several years now, the debate on whether Islamic religious education is needed in Germany, on how it should be taught and administratively integrated into the school system has been ongoing (Bukow&Yildiz 2003, Behr 2005, Biener 2006, Bilgin 2007, Graf 2007, Mohr&Kiefer 2009, Ucar et al 2010). Many contributions to this leave it unclear whether they are based more on anecdotal evidence or well-supported data. It is clear, though, that the advocates of Islamic RE in German public schools are motivated by very different considerations (Malik 2009, 7). To name just two examples: proposing Islamic Religious Education (RE) in public schools as a means of drawing attendees away from (possibly fundamentalist) madrassas is a very different argument than advocating the same, in the interest of equality between Islam and Christianity, which already has established forms of religious education.

Among the many arguments put forward in favour of establishing Islamic RE, one is considered to be of particular significance; it is stressed over and over that Islamic religious education needs to be introduced to help integrate the Muslim population. But is there any basis for this assumption? I would like to offer two brief observations:

- It certainly serves the purpose of equality – and therefore also of the integration of Muslims – to establish an additional Islamic Education in contexts, where religious education is offered separately for Protestant and Catholic pupils. Here it could be seen as an element of societal justice that Muslims are given the same rights as Christians. Moreover it is most relevant to introduce Islamic theology along with Protestant and Catholic theologies as a subject of study and research at our universities. Islamic theology, which as a subject must offer the same academic and critical potential as comparable fields do in Germany, can offer support to an interpretation of Islam more specific to Western societies. If we wish to train competent Islamic religious education teachers, this is a basic prerequisite.

- It is less certain, though, whether the introduction of an additional, segregated form of religious education in public schools serves the purpose of integration at all. Initially, it would instead further the separation of the student body into Catholic, Protestant, Islamic and other religious groups. That societal integration is supported by scholastic segregation is hardly intuitive. At the very least, we need to evaluate more fully the opportunities and dangers of introducing an Islamic RE. (Kiefer 2009)

Between equality and separation; those are the poles – placed on entirely different levels – that must be taken into account in any answer to the question whether a separate Islamic education degree with its own separate form of religious education classes is preferable, or whether a unitary form of RE based on an interreligious dialogical qualification is the better option.

Alongside several, in some cases very different approaches to providing a separate Islamic religious education, such as those in North-Rhine Westphalia, Berlin or Lower Saxony, there are also entirely different options (Reichmuth et al 2006). In the federal state of Hamburg a dialogical religious education is practised in public schools. It does not separate students by religious affiliation or philosophical belief. With only a few exceptions, public schools offer a dialogical 'religious education for all' (*Religionsunterricht für alle*). This type of RE cannot serve as instruction in a specific religion, nor is it designed to do so. The underlying pedagogical assumption is rather, that bringing up children in a faith is the task of the family and religious community. The function of the public school, by contrast, is to offer an introduction to religious issues that allows the students to relate the traditions of different faiths to their own experience. The goal is not an introduction to one specific religion, but to a number of religions coexisting in our city, the 'neighbour religions'. These are defined as the religions of our neighbours in the classroom, the city, and society as a whole.

Dialogical "Religious Education for All": Case study of Hamburg

Context Hamburg: In the multicultural city of Hamburg (which is also one of the federal states in Germany) with almost 2 million inhabitants there is a great variety of different cultures and religions: more than a hundred languages and religions or denominations are represented (Grünberg et al 1994). Eight percent of the population are Muslims. Hamburg always defined itself as a liberal city, where differences of belief did not matter and where people from around the world live together. But at the same time, there is now a trend towards rising xenophobia and distrust of "fundamentalist" Muslims, especially since 11 September 2001. Therefore, all initiatives and forces working towards a better understanding between different communities are both more necessary as well as more difficult now. It is in this context that we see the task of our educational work. While religious education elsewhere in Germany is taught separately for Catholic, Protestant and in very few cases Muslim children, this practice has been different in Hamburg for roughly the last 50 years. Religious education classes have not been divided according to different denominations or religions of students, but there has been *one* religious education class in which all children with their religious or cultural backgrounds participate. This model enjoys the support of representatives at the broader societal level (Neumann 2000) and of various religious communities in Hamburg, including the Islamic Shura council. The local Shura rejected the offer by mayor Ole von Beust to introduce a separate Islamic RE in 2006 and voiced its support for a continuing religious education for all to prevent a separation of the subject.

Dialogical Religious Education: We call our form of religious education a *dialogical* religious education (see Weisse 1999, Weisse 2008). Dialogue is central in our approach, both theoretically and practically. A dialogical RE is marked by the following elements: it relates both to the experiences of the students and to the stimuli of religious traditions. It is contextual and intercultural; and it is based on approaches of ecumenical theology and interreligious learning.

Our approach refers to an experience-oriented understanding of dialogue, which will be explained in greater detail later. By this understanding, dialogue in the classroom takes on greater importance: A dialogue in which pupils can participate with their different and differential religious and ideological backgrounds and in which they can develop their own views and positions. Questions as to the meaning of life and death, as well as ethical questions about justice, peace and the integrity of creation are covered in these lessons. In this spectrum there are many similarities between the religions, but dialogue in religious education is also designed to demonstrate the differences between religious traditions. Individual positions should not be compromised by mixing different viewpoints, but developed by contrasting them with others. Religious education should enable a classroom dialogue that allows the participants to refer to their different religious backgrounds, but does not require those, in order to succeed. Dialogue in the classroom fosters respect for other religious commitments and refers its participants to the possibility of gaining reassurance or making their own religious commitment while critically monitoring it at the same time. This form of religious education must be understood in the context of an educational approach that does not mirror the separation and social division of the population, let alone increase it, but aims at a reciprocal understanding which treats differences with respect.

Neighbour religion: Within the Hamburg model of RE, religion is understood as an orientation in process. It encompasses Christianity and its denominations, and is open to other religions. It relates to the so-called world religions, but is not restricted to them. The whole variety of religions and religious patterns, the reasoning about the origins and purposes of life, the striving for justice and peace is incorporated in the definition of religion as it is used here. My proposal is to use the term "neighbour religions" instead of "world-religions". The expression "neighbour religion" understands a different religion as what my neighbour in the classroom, in my village or town, and in the global village believes. Neighbour here is used in the sense that Immanuel Levinas uses "l'autrui/prochain" (Levinas 1993, 156) and the person, not a certain belief-system, lies at the core of the concept. "Neighbour-religion" refers to ordinary people in the neighbourhood, not to key representatives of religious organisations. In the dialogue with neighbours, the wisdom of religious traditions should be used. It can provide stimuli and input, but should not be a hindrance for dealing with fundamental questions arising in the context of daily life dialogue. Dialogue in the context of neighbour-religions does not come from above, but from below. It is focused on the relevant questions of the participants, namely those of the students at school. The prerequisite for a productive dialogue of this kind at classroom level is the opportunity to take advantage of a variety of different cultural and religious backgrounds among the students and not to separate them along homogenous lines – an approach that in itself is at least ambivalent if not inadvisable, in addition to being almost impossible in practice.

Interreligious groups for a dialogical religious education: The initial reason for the founding of an interreligious discussion group for religious education was the development of a syllabus for religious education in primary school. It became clear that the sporadic contact with members of religions other than Christianity was inadequate for developing a curriculum. A religiously mixed group was founded with representatives of Christianity, Judaism, Islam and Buddhism. Additionally, members from the University, schools, and the teacher training institute were part of this group. It was constituted about 12 years ago and meets regularly –a unique group in Germany in which trust has been built up to an enormous extent. The idea that pupils should all participate in religious education without regard to their different religious and ideological backgrounds – with all the pros and cons discussed exhaustively – was approved and developed in this group.

This is clearly documented in a unanimous statement by this interreligious group for dialogical religious education in Hamburg – called the GIR (Gesprächskreis Interreligiöser Religionsunterricht) – on 11 February 1997. They advocate a "religious education for all" that is not divided along religious or ideological lines. Against the fear of some parents that their children would be alienated to the religion lived at home if they learn in a religiously heterogeneous class, they argue that such an approach is necessary in order to prepare them for life in a multicultural society: Such classes should enable young people "to find their own position in a diversity of religious beliefs and communities and to develop a happiness in the common ground of the diversity. The meeting and debate with the foreign and the possible change of perspective helps the process of development and (re-)discovery of oneself and supports the development of an identity "(Doedens & Weisse 1997, 37). The statement further specifies the tasks of religious education in school and emphasizes the difference from religious education at home and in a community. In summary, it says that pupils should develop their own positions on the meaning and claims of religions in dialogue with their fellow students and contribute their own opinions.

The members of the interreligious discussion group have distanced themselves from any form of religious – and political – fundamentalism. This was clearly formulated in a statement of November 1998 (Weisse 1999, 294-96).

This conference rejected the offer of a separate Islamic RE with the same decisiveness as the Shura council when it was debated for Hamburg. In a resolution passed unanimously by representatives of seven religious communities on 12 December 2006, the body emphasised that religious education for all should continue. The resolution, enjoying the full support of the members of the Hamburg Shura council, states:

> In our plural society, it appears indispensible to us to thematise religions in their diversity. This reflects the real-life experiences of children and youths and helps them understand the specific nature of religions and respect them without creating distance or developing prejudice. It appears more important than ever today to perceive the Other not as a threatening stranger, but as a human and neighbour who can help us expand our own horizons. This will be made more difficult if students are separated by religion and confession in RE instead of teaching them together, as was previously the case... We reject a separation of religious education along religious or confessional lines both on grounds of religious pedagogy and integration policy. (Weisse 2008, 234-235)

The resolution supports academically supervised experimental study in school environments and demands the provision of resources for teacher training in religious education for Muslims, Jews, Buddhists and others. Establishing an 'Academy of World Religions' is regarded as necessary for this purpose.

Interreligious dialogue at university: The Academy of World Religions

In order to make the Hamburg approach viable, the various religions represented in our society need to be given greater attention in teacher training and provision must be made in law and administrative structures to allow religious education to be provided by teachers not just of the Christian, but also of Jewish, Muslim, Buddhist and other faiths. We are considering these aspects and consulting expert opinion at all levels. However, introducing a separate Islamic religious education would represent a regression for Hamburg in terms of integration. Rather, we need additional academic resources to train teachers towards an integrative model of RE. In pursuit of this goal, we have been working for many years to establish an 'Academy of World Religions' at Hamburg University and succeeded in opening it in June 2010.

The "Academy of World Religions" focuses on religious and cultural plurality (Weisse 2009). The approach includes establishing a chair of Islamic Theology from 2011 onwards, but goes beyond similar activities at other universities. It offers the institutional framework within which to establish the theologies of world religions at Hamburg University. Resources for the study and teaching of Islam, Judaism, Alevism, Hinduism and Buddhism alongside Christian theology will be provided here. The religions represented at the Academy are not established separately, but relate to each other dialogically. Their respective theological concepts are connected with those of others to thematise their differences and commonalities.

The Academy of World Religions pursues the following main aims:

- It embraces and develops theological approaches and concepts within all world religions that focus on dialogue as a central feature. These approaches should relate to contemporary plural society and actively address their context.
- Empirical research is conducted into the lives and situations of people of different religions in our society – focusing on Hamburg and other large urban areas in Europe and worldwide – that significantly add to extent data and can help us to productively relate theological approaches to the reality of living religious practice.
- Contributions to two academic curricula are offered: On the one hand, the Academy is actively involved in the development of training for religious education teachers. The Hamburg model of offering inclusive religious education for pupils of all religious beliefs and confessions also requires a religious pluralisation of the teaching body. This requires academically viable, university-level theological studies in the world religions we address. We also intend to offer a Master's Degree to provide competencies in the area of religion and dialogue to students from a wide variety of fields. These competencies are increasingly important in an ever-growing number of professions, not least in multinational companies.

The Academy of World Religions focuses on interdisciplinary and transdisciplinary research in an international setting. A particular focus of research and teaching is on reform-oriented approaches, and on actual religious practice, with a strong emphasis on the centrality of dialogue. Within Hamburg University, the Academy of World Religions has established cooperation with a wide variety of academic disciplines, among them education, sociology, political studies, economics, Protestant theology, Islamic and Buddhist studies. This breadth is necessary to adequately analyse the complex field of religions, education and social practice. Co-operations outside the scope of local institutions with academics at universities throughout Europe, in Africa, the Middle East, the United States and China are equally fundamental to our work.

Thus, the Academy of World Religions provides a focus for an international and interdisciplinary academic approach towards addressing modern society's cultural and religious plurality within the structure of the university.

Interreligious dialogue is increasingly drawing attention worldwide as a foundation for productive and civilised coexistence in times of growing pluralism. The dialogical approach of the Academy of World Religions contributes to broadening the horizon of society at large. It addresses questions of interreligious dialogue not only in their fundamental dimensions, but also in their relevance for current social issues, in order to make a tangible contribution towards peaceful coexistence in our multireligious and multicultural society.

Dialogical Religious Education in the European context – The REDCo project

Finally, a few words on global perspectives: Throughout the world, interest in religion and religious education is increasing. A number of innovative research projects have been addressing this question. As an example the REDCo project will be sketched in the following section. The project headed by the author of this contribution is titled REDCo: „Religion in Education. A Contribution to Dialogue or a Factor of Conflict in changing societies of European countries."

REDCo – an overview: Religion in Education is the thematic background of the REDCo project. REDCo is the acronym for "Religion in Education. A Contribution to Dialogue or a Factor of Conflict in Transforming Societies of European Countries." (Weisse 2007) This project was funded by the research department of the European Commission over a period of three years from March 2006 onwards with a total of 1,188,000 Euros. Nine projects from eight different European countries participated: Estonia and Russia to Norway, Germany, The Netherlands, England, France and Spain. The author of this article is the overall coordinator of REDCo. The main aim was to analyse how religion can be integrated into the educational systems of different European countries in such a way as to create a net gain in mutual understanding rather than separation.

Despite a wide range of societal and pedagogical backgrounds (Jackson et al 2007), the research group held a common conviction: religion must be included in schools, as it is too important a factor in the social life and the coexistence of people with different cultural and religious backgrounds throughout Europe.

All our projects looked at religious education for school students in the 14-16-year age group in various countries. We combined analyses of concepts of RE with the concrete views of pupils: We observed them, we interviewed them, we asked for written answers in questionnaires, and we analysed their interaction. Through this combination, we could capture both the perspective from above and the perspective from below.

The views of pupils in Hamburg: RE for all or separation in a confessional RE?

In the context of the REDCo project, we asked pupils in Hamburg, whether they would prefer to continue in RE for all – where students of different religious and cultural backgrounds share the same classroom – or whether they would prefer an RE separated along the lines of different confessions and religions. All of the pupils were in the 14 to 16 age group.

Few pupils favoured separate religious education. They mainly cite three aspects in support of their choice: In RE separated by religion, the competence of the teacher, belonging to the same faith as the pupils, is thought to be higher. In a religiously mixed group problems and difficulties might arise. Religions other than the own could be boring (Knauth 2008, 240-241). However, the majority of the pupils in Hamburg are in favour of an integrated RE. Here are some of their arguments.

The first refers to the didactic setting: religious education at school becomes interesting through a dialogue with students from other backgrounds, and it should not mirror religious instruction in a religious community. A Muslim girl wrote:

> I personally think it is better if pupils from different religions are taught together. By this you can much better find out what others think than by just reading it in a book. It is much better to get to know people from other religions who are able to say something about their own religions. If for example in my religion class there would only be Muslims we would all have the same opinion and would not really be able to, well not be able to discuss things at all or learn something new. Then you only learn what you learn at the mosque. I go to the mosque in order to learn that! It would not be very interesting for me if I would have to repeat in school everything I have learned. It would be boring (Knauth 2008, 238).

The second concerns social ethics: Getting to know "the other" contributes to reducing hate. A girl with no formal religious background wrote:

> I would not find it to be so good if they were taught separately. This way one can more easily learn about other religions. Besides I think that by this the hatred of people who do not belong to one's own or a specific religion would more easily be reduced. Besides the people belonging to a particu-

> lar religion can explain certain things in their religion. I think if one would separate the pupils who belong to different religions it makes it seem as if they were different (as if you would teach foreigners and non-foreigners or Blacks and Whites separately) (Knauth 2008, 238).

The third argument refers to theology: Separation is considered a sin. The following quotation comes from a Muslim girl:

> Yes and in religious education pupils of different religions and ideologies should be taught together. What is the use of separating the pupils according to their religion in religious education? Also the separation of humanity can be considered as a sin. It is said: "Love all people since they have all been created by God, if you do not love them then do not hate them either! (Knauth 2008, 239).

The last refers to the need to deal with difference: Professional competence is the argument of a Christian girl:

> No I think we should not be separated. Few (or none at all) have got a problem with us having different religions. And even if you have something against it, you have to get used to it. Later in professional life you will not be able to choose with whom you want to work together. (Knauth 2008, 239).

As the quotations show, students themselves have solid convictions as to why RE should be taught at school and what aims could be envisaged for an integrated RE in public schools. And if you would care to pay special attention to the Muslim students: their arguments should not be forgotten when it comes to decisions on how to structure religious education in public schools.

Glimpse of the overall results of the REDCo project

The results of our qualitative study underline the importance of including religion in education at an international level.

Apart from the differences shown by the answers to the qualitative written questionnaires (this is hardly surprising when you remember the variety of countries from Estonia and Russia on the one hand, to France and Spain on the other) the following findings apply in all these countries:

- Religious pluralism is not only accepted, but welcomed by the pupils.
- Pupils expressed criticism of truth claims that exclude people of other religions or worldviews.
- Prejudices have been mainly directed against Islam "which was depicted as a harsh religion projecting violence to the outside and oppressing its adherents" (Bertram-Troost et al 2008, p. 407).
- Despite the awareness of the conflicts caused by religions and the difficulties arising from religious plurality, the majority of young people in the European countries we studied "appeared to share a vision of peaceful coexistence in a religiously plural society. The realisation of this vision was often presented as

> contingent on the existence of attitudes of tolerance, open-mindedness and respect, and on the exercise of key dialogue skills: learning about each other's belief; listening to each other; getting to know a variety of views" (Bertram-Troost et al 2008, p. 408).

Without going into a thorough interpretation of what we are able to analyse on the basis of our qualitative written questionnaires, the relevance of the school as an institution of instruction on religions and a venue for interreligious dialogue at classroom level (Avest et al 2009) becomes quite clear. Many of the pupils are prejudiced towards the religions of others, but at the same time are prepared to enter into dialogue with others whom they regard as interesting. The school provides a unique forum for them (Jozsa, Knauth & Weisse 2009).

Yet: no effort to understand the possibilities and approaches to foster dialogue between people of different faith can afford to underestimate the potential for conflict inherent in religions. José Casanova's expression of surprise about, „how widespread the belief that religion is intolerant and a source of conflict is in Europe", only serves to emphasise that point (Casanova 2007, 344-5). His analysis referred to adults in Europe. Fortunately, it turns out that this is not the case among most young Europeans. We were pleasantly surprised to find during the course of our surveys, that the majority of respondents in all countries studied showed themselves open and accepting of religious and cultural heterogeneity and stated that peaceful coexistence between people of different religious backgrounds was easily achievable (Knauth et al 2008; Valk et al 2009).

The desire of many pupils in these countries to learn more about religions and interreligious dialogue presents a great chance for interreligious understanding in European schools. How would or could this be possible in a structure of RE that separates the pupils according to their different religions?

Special attention might be directed to a quantitative study we have conducted in all our REDCo-countries (see Valk et al 2009). I can only indicate one result. We asked for the experiences pupils in Europe have had with religion in school and how they evaluate school in dealing with religion. It turned out that they mostly agree with the statement that "Learning about different religions at school helps us to live together." Out of ten items this one achieved the highest approval overall so that obviously, Religious Education is believed to support a peaceful co-existence of people with different religious backgrounds and is accepted and appreciated especially in its social dimension.

Conclusion

The inclusion of Islam in the curricula of RE is a first and very important step, but care must be taken from the beginning to ensure other religions and belief systems are considered as well. Otherwise, it may well amount to no more than welcoming another religion into the privileged 'in-group', while continuing to discriminate against the rest. In this respect, it appears especially important to consider that not all aspects of religious education are properly the purview of the public school system. This is true for Muslim religious education as much as any other: The basic task of public schools and the division of labour with Muslim instruction in families and mosques are extremely important issues.

Regardless of the fact that within Germany as much as within Europe, different ways may lead to the same goal of integrating world religions other than Christianity into school RE, I would consider the following to be of vital importance: We need far more research and evaluation to make informed decisions along this road. Yet we must also state that in the context of religious education for all in Hamburg, more efforts are required to integrate and address Islam and students from a Muslim background. For this purpose, we need an academically established teacher training curriculum that pays the required attention to other world religions such as Islam. As an example of the challenges of the future, I would again point to efforts to establish an Academy of World Religions at Hamburg University, as outlined above.

Furthermore, we need a dialogue in religious education classes that does not merely talk about others, but to others; that offers a didactic environment for daily and normal encounters with the other; and that neither hides differences nor uses them to discriminate. There is a tension of demands, which could be sketched in the following way:

- We need forms of religious education that represent Islam as well as the traditions of other faiths in their plurality and differentiation and address the realities of people living in our society so as to interweave knowledge, values and ethics. It is quite evident that the introduction of an Islamic RE is more complex than anticipated and that it could lead to different confessional forms of Islamic RE (Kiefer 2009). And
- We need a religious education in public schools that does not divide students by religion, but allows them to learn with and from each other. This serves the goal of individual religious education as much as social education in the classroom and society as a whole. Religious differences can thus aid the perception of plurality without fear and discrimination and become a building block for a future integrated society.

Much research has to be done to evaluate existing forms and conditions of religious education, whether it be special forms of Islamic or other confessional schools, or integrated forms of religious education in public schools. On this basis perspectives can be founded, in order to establish viable forms of religious education according to the preconditions and demands of different contexts, but: with the aim of creating space in public education that takes account of the resources of religions as well as of the dangers of instrumentalization of religion. In the educational sphere it seems to be more important than ever to pave the way for an adequate understanding of the dynamics, of the roots, and the perspectives of religions, both with their special traditions and with their commonalities. Such a basis is not a guarantee for peacefully living together, but it could serve the aim for a better understanding between people (Weisse 2003), irrespective of their differences, even: seeing the differences not as factors of irritation, but as rich resources for explanations of life.

References

Avest, Ina ter, Dan-Paul Jozsa, Thorsten Knauth, Javier Rosón & Geir Skeie eds. 2009. *Dialogue and Conflict on Religion. Studies of classroom interaction in European countries*, Muenster: Waxmann.

Behr, Harry. 2005. *Curriculum Islamunterricht. Analyse von Lehrplanentwürfen für islamischen Religionsunterricht in der Grundschule. Ein Beitrag zur Lehrplantheorie des Islamunterrichts im Kontext der praxeologischen Dimension islamisch-theologischen Denkens.* Dissertation, Universität Bayreuth, Kulturwissenschaftliche Fakultät.

Bertram-Troost. G., Ipgrave, J., Jozsa, D.-P. & Knauth, T. 2008. European Comparison. Dialogue and conflict. In *Encountering Religious Pluralism in School and Society – A Qualitative Study of Teenage Perspectives in Europe*, eds. Thorsten Knauth, Dan-Paul Jozsa, Gerdien Bertram-Troost, G. & Julia Ipgrave, 405-411. Muenster, Waxmann.

Biener, Hansjörg. 2006. *Herausforderungen zu einer multiperspektivischen Didaktik: eine Problemdarstellung anhand einer Lehrplananalyse zur Berücksichtigung des Islam im Religions-, Ethik- und Geschichtsunterricht.* Schenefeld: EB-Verl.

Bilgin, Beyza. 2007. *Islam und islamische Religionspädagogik in einer modernen Gesellschaft* . Mit einer Einf. von Johannes Lähnemann. Berlin [et al.]: Lit-Verl.

Bukow, Wolf-Dietrich & Erol Yildiz, eds. 2003. *Islam und Bildung*, Opladen: Leske und Budrich.

Casanova, Jose. 2007. Die religiöse Lage in Europa. In *Säkularisierung und die Weltreligionen*, eds. Hans Joas & Klaus Wiegandt, 322-57. Frankfurt am Main: Fischer Taschenbuch Verlag.

Council of Europe. Ministers of Foreign Affairs. 2008. *White Paper on Intercultural Dialogue "Living Together as Equals in Dignity"*. 118th Ministerial Session. Strasbourg: Council of Europe.

Doedens, Folkert. & Wolfram Weisse, eds. 1997. *Religionsunterricht für alle. Hamburger Perspektiven zur Religionsdidaktik.* Muenster: Waxmann.

Graf, Peter. ed. 2007. *„Islamische Religionspädagogik" – Etablierung eines neuen Faches.* Bildungs- und kulturpolitische Initiativen des Landes Niedersachsen. Göttingen: V&R Unipress.

Grünberg, Wolfgang, Dennis Slabaugh & Ralf Meister-Karanikas. 1994. *Lexikon der Hamburger Religionsgemeinschaften. Religionsvielfalt in der Stadt von A-Z.* Hamburg: Dölling und Galitz.

Habermas, Jürgen. 2005. *Zwischen Naturalismus und Religion. Philosophische Aufsätze.* Frankfurt am Main: Suhrkamp.

Jackson, Robert, Siebren Miedema, Wolfram Weisse, & Jean-Paul Willlaime, eds. 2007. *Religion and Education in Europe: Developments, Contexts and Debates.* Muenster: Waxmann.

Jozsa, Dan-Paul, Thorsten Knauth & Wolfram Weisse, eds. 2009. *Religionsunterricht, Dialog und Konflikt. Analysen im Kontext Europa.*, Muenster: Waxmann.

Kiefer, Michael. 2009. Islamische Religionspädagogik und -didaktik. Offene Fragen zu den Gegenständen einer neuen wissenschaftlichen, Fachrichtung. In *Islamunterricht, islamischer Religionsunterricht, Islamkunde. Viele Titel – ein Fach?* eds. Irka-Christin Mohr & Michael Kiefer, 19-58. Bielefeld: transcript.

Knauth, Thorsten. 2008. "Better together than apart": Religion in School and Lifeworld of Students in Hamburg. In *Encountering Religious Pluralism in School and Society – A Qualitative Study of Teenage Perspectives in Europe,* eds. Thorsten Knauth, Dan-Paul Jozsa, Gerdien Bertram-Troost & Julia Ipgrave, 207-45. Muenster, Waxmann.

Knauth, Thorsten Dan-Paul Jozsa, Gerdien Bertram-Troost, G. & Julia Ipgrave, eds. 2008. *Encountering Religious Pluralism in School and Society – A Qualitative Study of Teenage Perspectives in Europe*. Muenster: Waxmann.

Levinas, Emmanuel. 1993. 'Penser Dieu à partir de L'Éthique'. In *Dieu, la Mort et le Temps*, Emmanuel Levinas, 155-8. Paris: Bernard Grasset.

Malik, Jamal. 2009. Vorwort. In *Islamunterricht, islamischer Religionsunterricht, Islamkunde. Viele Titel – ein Fach?* eds. Irka-Christin Mohr & Michael Kiefer, 7-8. Bielefeld: transcript.

Mohr, Irka-Christin. & Michael Kiefer, eds. 2009. *Islamunterricht, islamischer Religionsunterricht, Islamkunde. Viele Titel – ein Fach?* Bielefeld: transcript.

Neumann, Ursula. 2000. Religionsunterricht im Gespräch mit W. Beuß, C. Goetsch, E.Woisin, D. Budack und R. Lehberger. In *Religiöses Lernen in einer pluralen Welt. Religionspädagogische Ansätze in Hamburg*, eds. Wolfram Weisse & Folkert Doedens, 111-26. Muenster: Waxmann.

Reichmuth, Stefan, Mark Bodenstein, Michael Kiefer & Birgit Väth, eds. 2006. *Staatlicher Islamunterricht in Deutschland. Die Modelle in NRW und Niedersachsen im Vergleich*, Berlin: LIT-Verlag.

Ricœur, Paul. 1995. *La critique et la conviction: Entretien avec Francois Azouvi et Marc de Launay*. Paris: Hachette.

Ricœur, Paul. 2006. *Wege der Anerkennung. Erkennen, Wiedererkennen, Anerkanntsein.* Frankfurt am Main: Suhrkamp.

Ucar, Bülent, Martina Blasberg-Kunke & Arnulf von Scheliha, eds. 2010. *Religionen in der Schule und die Bedeutung des islamischen Religionsunterrichts*. Osnabrück: Universitätsverlag.

Valk, Pille, Gerdien Bertram-Troost, Markus Friederici, & Céline Béraud, eds. 2009. *Teenagers' perspectives on the Role of Religion in their lives, Schools and Societies. A European Quantitative Study*. Muenster: Waxmann.

Weisse, Wolfram. 2003. Difference without discrimination: religious education as a field of learning for social understanding? In *International Perspectives on Citizenship, Education and Religious Diversity*, ed. Robert Jackson, 191-208. London: RoutledgeFalmer.

--. 2007. The European Research Project on Religion and Education 'REDCo'. An Introduction. In *Religion and Education in Europe: Developments, Contexts and Debates*, eds. Robert Jackson, Siebren Miedema, Wolfram Weisse, & Jean-Paul Willlaime, 9-25. Muenster: Waxmann.

Weisse, Wolfram, ed. 1999. *Vom Monolog zum Dialog. Ansätze einer dialogischen Religionspädagogik*, 2nd ed. Muenster/New York: Waxmann.

--, ed. 2008. *Dialogischer Religionsunterricht in Hamburg. Positionen, Analysen und Perspektiven im Kontext Europas*. Muenster: Waxmann.

--, ed. 2009. *Theologie im Plural. Eine akademische Herausforderung*. Muenster: Waxmann.

Andreas Hieronymus

Muslim Identity Formations and Learning Environments

Introduction

This article sets out to present a substantial description of the learning environment of Muslims living in the district of Hamburg-Mitte, with a particular focus on identity formation and how this can promote or hinder learning in a highly selective education system.[1] In contrast to other recently published studies (Rieger 2008; Beck & Perry 2007; Brettfeld and Wetzels 2007), on migrants and Muslims, the OSI-study looks into aspects of Muslims urban everyday life in Hamburg-Mitte, a district which has undergone fundamental change and is home to the majority of Muslims in Hamburg.[2] Education is said to be crucial to integration[3] in Germany and highly valued by the Muslim respondents in the study. The experiences and concerns of Muslims towards the education sector suggest obstacles stemming from real and perceived discrimination which are hampering academic achievement directly related to their experiences as Muslims and their ethnic group. Alongside reported questionable quality and selection processes within the educational sector, the impact includes low educational attainment levels amongst Muslim pupils, the effects of racism on self-esteem and aspirations, and the role that a lack of recognition of a person's faith can play in ensuring that an individual can fully participate in society. The failure of public and social policy to acknowledge and respect important aspects of a person's identity and sense of self can hinder integration (Malik 2005). There is also a growing recognition of the importance of meaningful contact and interaction between people of different ethnic and cultural groups in creating social cohesion, as this helps overcome prejudice and challenge stereotypes in the education system as well.

---

1 The article is based on the data of the "At Home in Europe" Project of the Open Society Institute (OSI) and reflects findings of the report on Hamburg. See: Andreas Hieronymus 2010.

2 A study that places its focus on Muslims as a group faces the challenge that Muslims are not a fixed group with defined boundaries, but rather a diverse set of individuals with different religious practices, ethnic attachments and linguistic and cultural backgrounds, who are currently defined and marked as such mainly from the outside. It can include those who adhere to the religion of Islam as well as those who, because of their cultural or ethnic background, are perceived as Muslims by others in society, even if they are, in fact, adherents of other religions or non-believers. In the context of this study the identification of a person as '*Muslim*' has been left to the self-perception of the interviewee and has not been associated with any prefixed religious or cultural definition.

3 Integration in this article is understood as a two way process that requires both engagement by individuals as well as opportunities for participation provided by the society.

Methodological approach to identity formations and education

The article presents findings based on a study done in 2008 in three areas of the district of Hamburg-Mitte.[4] The study is part of the "At Home in Europe" project of the Open Society Institute (OSI), which studied the life of Muslims in 10 other European cities.[5] The study comprised a survey in all cities with a uniform questionnaire to 100 Muslims and 100 non-Muslims, each group including 50 males and 50 females in each category, as well as different social and religious backgrounds. The questionnaires were supplemented by six focus group discussions, with approximately 50 Muslims of a variety of backgrounds, one focusing on education in depth. There were a further range of in-depth interviews with stakeholders including local politicians, members of non-governmental organizations (NGOs), Muslim community leaders and representatives in addition to other relevant actors. At a round table in Hamburg about 50 participants, representing a diversity of organizations (Muslim organizations, civil society, city administration), discussed the results of the study and its recommendations in detail.[6]

The 200 interviews were based on a sample-frame that identified characteristics of the sample in terms of age, gender, and ethnic group. The ethnic origin of respondents was obtained through questions on nationality, place of birth and self identification on ethnic and/or cultural background. The study shows the diverse and varying identities amongst Muslim respondents in Hamburg-Mitte.

Muslim and non-Muslim identities in Hamburg

The concept of a "*Muslim identity*" is very polarizing (Hieronymus 2010, 29). A Muslim participant in a focus group described the situation as follows:

> Look, there are 3.5 million Muslims, that makes four percent of the population. We know from experience, that not more than 25 percent are really practising people. 'Practising' means, that they go to Friday prayers. That means, that approximately one percent of the population lives Islamically. Let's take 70 million Germans and leave those 10 million people with migration background aside, 70 million are afraid of one percent of the population. (Hieronymus 2010, 29)

The above quotation can be seen as quite commonplace in terms of identity and its construction in Germany. The ethnic German population is pitted against the ethnic "other" – in its majority "Turks" – who in turn are seen predominantly as Muslims. Ethnicity, nationality and religious identity merge to create a dichotomizing construct of "German" and "non-German" identities, which are lived

4 Area 1 included the city centre and surrounding areas such as parts of Altona, St. Pauli and St. Georg. Area 2 included the southern part of the district, Veddel and Wilhelmsburg. Area 3 included the eastern part of the district, like Hamm, Horn and Billstedt.

5 http://www.soros.org/initiatives/home, accessed 1.2.2010.

6 The full data of the questionnaires as well as the full length transcriptions of the Focus Groups are with the authors and originators of the research.

in everyday life. Available data often still reflect only this uniform "German" – "Foreigner" dichotomy. Two opposing forms, a positive and a negative form of cultural identity, are described in the Hamburg Action Plan on Integration (HHAP 2007[7]), the central document for the integration of the migrant population in the city: the culture of origin, which is positively valued and maintained as an aspect of identity that is publicly presented to enrich the cultural life of Hamburg, although many migrants are born in Hamburg and have no or little experience with "their" culture of origin. This "cultural perspective" bears the danger of "orientalising" certain parts of the Hamburg population as the "exotic other", adding "flavour" to an otherwise mono-cultural society, instead of reassessing the underlying assumptions about culture itself. It is seen as negative, when there is a withdrawal into the culture of origin on the one side, and if the cultural institutions of the host country do not adapt to the needs of a diverse society (Hieronymus 2010, 38). These are the effects of closed or narrow cultural concepts, which are reproduced by certain social groups in an act of resistance to the ascribed cultural concepts. On the other side religious identities are positively valued in Hamburg. Around 100 different religious communities exist in Hamburg, but a trend towards secularization in all religious groups is reported: 40 percent of the pupils in Hamburg do not belong to any religious community (Hieronymus 2010, 39).

In the OSI research, 141 of the 200 interviewees (70.5 percent) had a German passport, while 47 (23.5 percent) hold a Turkish passport. This roughly matches the proportion of "German" and "foreigner" residents in Hamburg. But among Muslims, more than half (56 percent) of the interviewees hold a German passport and among non-Muslims 85 percent have one, while 29 percent of Muslims hold a Turkish passport. Looking at the place of birth, 31 percent of Muslims with German citizenship and 37 percent of all Muslims were born in Germany. Eighteen percent of Muslims with German citizenship and 46 percent of all Muslims were born in Turkey and 6 percent in Afghanistan.[8] These numbers show that there is a considerable German-born Muslim population with German passports, who can be considered "German Muslims", even if the same individual might self-identify as Turkish.

The data show that there is a strong sense of belonging among Muslims (68 percent) and non-Muslims (69 percent) in Hamburg, most strongly tied to personal experience, as being someone from the neighbourhood of Wilhelmsburg or St. Pauli. The majority of both groups agreed that their local area is a place where people from different backgrounds get along well. A regional belonging, like being eastern, southern or northern German has only been articulated by non-Muslims. It is clear from the data for all eleven cities that for Muslims, local and city-level belonging is stronger than national belonging. For non-Muslims, the levels of national belonging are greater than, or about the same as, city or local belonging. The three exceptions to this are Berlin, Hamburg and Stockholm

7 Freie und Hansestadt Hamburg Behörde für Soziales, Familie, Gesundheit und Verbraucherschutz refered to as HHAP.

8 The vast majority of non-Muslims (76 percent) were born in Germany and 75 percent of them have German citizenship. 10 percent of non-Muslim Germans were born outside of Germany (Argentina, Eritrea, Finland, Guyana, Kazakhstan, Poland, Russia, Switzerland, Trinidad and Tobago).

(Emerson 2011).[9] In the case of Hamburg, a greater sense of national belonging was found among Muslim respondents (52 percent) than non-Muslim respondents (36 percent). But when it comes to self-perception as German, there is a very significant difference between Muslims and non-Muslims. 63 percent of non-Muslims see themselves as Germans, but only 22 percent of Muslims do, although 56 percent have a German passport. In comparison to the 10 other cities, this differs substantially. In Leicester (82 percent), London (72 percent), Amsterdam (59 percent), Marseille (58 percent) and Antwerp (55 percent) the majority of Muslim respondents saw themselves as nationals included. Hamburg rated lowest in a cluster of cities where only a minority of Muslims saw themselves as nationals, followed by Berlin (25 percent), Copenhagen (40 percent), Paris (41 percent), Stockholm (41 percent) and Rotterdam (43 percent). At the same time, in the cases of Hamburg and Berlin, the gap between the respondents' sense of cultural identification and how they anticipated others seeing them is among the narrowest (Hieronymus 2010, 74). In the European comparison, the country of birth correlates with a sense of national identification: just over two-thirds of European-born Muslims felt a sense of national identification, compared with less than 40 percent of those born abroad. In most cities, a majority of Muslims born in the country expressed a sense of national cultural identification. This was not true for Hamburg and Berlin. In Berlin, only 35 percent of German-born Muslims identified themselves as German; in Hamburg, this figure was 46 percent. By contrast, 94 percent of Leicester's UK-born Muslims said they saw themselves as British. Although the majority of Muslim respondents did not believe others saw them as British, Muslims born in the EU states were 2.2 times more likely to respond positively in comparison with those born elsewhere (Hieronymus 2010, 75).

Responses to the question on how interviewees would describe their ethnicity can be clustered around three types of identity formations, which often overlap:

Ethno-national identities

44 percent of Muslims said they have a Turkish or mixed Turkish identity[10] and fourteen percent of Muslims indicated other national identities. Four percent of non-Muslims described themselves as Serbian (1 percent), Indonesian (1 percent), Italian-Spanish (1 percent) and Franco-Senegalese (1 percent). Muslim respondents of this cluster indicated that they do not want to deny or lose their identity. "Everybody else should know that I am a Turk" (Hieronymus 2010, 22). Others reported disliking German culture or having a greater sense of belonging to Bosnian culture than to the culture of Germany (Hieronymus 2010, 22). These respondents sought to be seen as a genuine Moroccan, some described themselves as Kurd originating from Turkey, while others expressed pride at being a

9 For a detailed comparison between Hamburg and Berlin see: Mühe, Nina and Andreas Hieronymus (2011): Has Multiculturalism Completely Failed in Germany? In: Michael Emerson (ed.) Interculturalism: Emerging Societal Models for Europe and its Muslims (forthcoming 2011).

10 Mixed Turkish identities are e.g. Turkish-German or Turkish-Portuguese.

Turk (Hieronymus 2010, 22). Interviewees were seeking acceptance and indicated readiness to conform to majority society, because they perceived it as the appropriate approach, but they also rejected dissembling.

Those ethno-national identities must be seen in the context of the German identity formation, which also historically perceived itself as an ethno-national identity. Among non-Muslims the ethno-national identification seems to be less important, although these respondents have lived in Germany for a long time and acknowledge that they have become a mixture, they remain proud to have their roots in their country of origin. Some non-Muslims mentioned that people cannot choose their own birthplace and do not want to be defined on the basis of their nationality. A feeling of wanting to be seen as equal not as similar was also articulated.

German, European and other identities were articulated as well, such as being German or mixed German[11], "*Bildungsbürger*"[12], supranational identities[13], European[14], belonging to subcultures[15], do not belong to any culture[16], social groups, local identity[17], humanist identity[18] or having no culture (Hieronymus 2010, 33).

European or supranational identities

European or supranational identity formations have been articulated by non-Muslim interviewees. These take regional forms, like belonging to Central, Western or Northern Europe. Similarly, some Muslim interviewees indicated that they belong to the Turkish-Ottoman culture and explicitly stated that they do not identify with the secular, Kemalist culture. The reference to the Ottoman Empire, as a supranational unit resembles in some respect the Muslim counterpart of a Christian Europe (Inalcik 2006). Some Muslims reported seeing themselves as Turkish-Kurdish, referring to a regional and ethnic belonging. While the ethno-national identities were often proudly presented by non-Germans, Germans were more reluctant to define themselves along this line. Interviewees explained that to be perceived as German carries the stigma of the Nazi era, and furthermore, Germans are seen as humourless and bureaucratic. This historical stigma is most noticeable

11 German (12%), German (south) (1%), German (white) (1%), German (without religion, belonging felt to other ethnic groups) (1%), German-"Bildungsbürger" (1%), German-Bosnian (1%), German-East (1%), German-Latino (2%), German-north (2%), German-Portugese (1%), German-Russian (2%).

12 Describes an idealised self-perception of the German middle-class.

13 Non-Muslims: African (1%), African (because of children) (1%), Latino (2%), Mediterranean-Slavian (1%), Multi-ethnic (1%), World Citizen (5%).

14 European (5%), European (white, middle) (1%), European-East (1%), European-middle (2%), European-northern (1%), European-West (5%).

15 Subculture (anti-globalisation) (2%), Alternative Culture (3%), artist (1%), Leftist (3%), libertarian communist (1%), social movement (1%), Alternative Culture (3%), Class (lower-middle) (1%), Working Class (2%).

16 no culture (7%), no culture (carribean) (1%), (neither German nor Eritrean) (1%), (not defining along national identity) (3%), (Polynesian) (1%)

17 Non-Muslims: Hamburger (1%), St. Paulian (1%).

18 Human (5%), Human, women, Bavarian (1%), Humanist-German (northern European) (1%).

when travelling in European countries, where Germans are edged into a political corner because of their past, without reference to the actual political opinion of the person (Hieronymus 2010, 33). Among this group of interviewees, an ethno-national identity was rejected, while an identity as a European or world citizen was often preferred. This identity can be found among non-Muslims with migrant backgrounds as well. They identified themselves as EU-citizens or Afro-European and hoped for a world without frontiers and nationalities (Hieronymus 2010, 33).

Non-Muslim interviewees frequently responded that belonging to Germany is not important. They did not want to be identified by their German nationality, but as individuals. For them other identities, such as gender, regional belonging or political attitude were considered more important. Differences between migrants and Germans were also perceived on the local level as differences between rich and poor and the different levels of education.

Ethno-religious identities

Another set of identity constructions were centred on religion, and often merged with ethnic or cultural differences, and differences in lifestyle. A religious or ethno-religious identity was expressed by nineteen percent of Muslims and six percent of non-Muslims.[19] Muslim interviewees summarized their identities as differences in lifestyle, religion and physical appearance. It is the skin colour and Islamic appearance that convey this identity, which signals difference to the majority community (Hieronymus 2010, 33). But for some, appearance on its own is not the indicator, but a combination of originating in Turkey, along with following Turkish traditions, customs and religious practices, which is perceived as clashing with majority culture. Ethno-religious identities are often viewed in opposition to German identity (Hieronymus 2010, 33). As long as there is this cultural and religious difference, one is not accepted as German, interviewees said. But those articulated cultural differences do not necessarily mark a withdrawal from German society, on the contrary, those expressing their identity in this way may seek acceptance (Hieronymus 2010, 33). Such oppositional sentiments are widely expressed by responding Muslims. Statements such as "I'm Muslim. I am Turkish by birth, and it's not good to deny one's own ethnic origin" (Hieronymus 2010, 34) articulating a specific ethno-religious belonging can be contrasted against those such as one Muslim interviewee's argument that "everybody should self determinate, if they see themselves as Germans or not. I would say, that I am in fact a German" (Hieronymus 2010, 34).

The European comparison indicates that the views of non-Muslim respondents born abroad are closer to those of Muslim respondents. Among Muslim respondents, the perception of ethnicity as a barrier to national cultural identification differs by gender and country of birth. Men and those born in Europe, are more likely to see ethnicity as a barrier to inclusion, and almost a third (32 per-

19 6% of non-Muslims defined themselves as Christian (1%), Christian (social) (1%), Christian-German (2%), Christian-German (northern European) (1%), Christian-Protestant (1%).

cent) of European-born Muslim men feel that "ethnicity/not being white" is the main barrier to being seen as nationals. Very few non-Muslims (1 percent) and Muslims (6 percent) in the eleven cities which the study covered, think that not being Christian is a barrier to national belonging (OSI 2010, 9). This is consistent with the analysis of the European Social Survey, which suggests that alongside education and employment, language and cultural values are important symbolic boundaries for national belonging in Europe:

> As second generations of non-white and non-Christian immigrants come of age, racial and religious distinctions may not only become less conspicuous but also less politically tenable. While public discourse necessarily shifts from the accommodation to the integration of immigrant populations, natives may become more concerned about the longevity of their linguistic and cultural identity. Or, natives may realize that language and culture guarantee the privileges of group status that were previously "protected" by race or religion. (Bail 2008)

Learning as an important Muslim value

Among the Muslims participating in the OSI study, 53 percent were displaying visible signs of religiosity,[20] and 83 percent said they were actively practising. Those numbers are in line with findings of the Religion Monitor 2008, which states:

> Muslims in Germany are characterized by high religiousness. 90 percent of Muslims in Germany above the age of 18 are religious; including 41 percent highly religious. For comparison: for the German society as a whole, the Religion Monitor 2008 revealed that 70 percent of the German-speaking population is religious, including 18 percent highly religious. (Rieger 2008, 7)

These findings contradict those of the 2007 study of migrant milieus, which only refers to religion and religiosity in the context of an "archaic tradition": which is identified as a parallel culture, has traditional values and religious (often Islamic) dogmas, a patriarchal worldview, outdated family values and forced norms, a rigidly conventional lifestyle, strict morals, living in cultural enclaves and no willingness to integrate (Beck & Perry 2007). Only two Muslims participating in the OSI survey fit these criteria, suggesting that such a characterization does not correspond with the general way Muslims experience their religion and interact with their environment in Hamburg.

Those Muslims who were actively practising demonstrated a diversity of practices in three specific fields. The *five pillars of Islam*, including praying five times a day (*shahāda, ṣalāh*), fasting (*ṣawm*), eating halal food and not drinking alcohol, welfare (*zakāh*), following the Islamic dress code, pilgrimage (*ḥajj*) or going to the mosques. The Religion Monitor 2008 reports 86 percent of Muslims strict-

20 Such as head-scarf or a beard.

ly complying with the prohibition on eating pork, and 58 percent claiming never to drink alcohol (Rieger 2008, 8). Closely related to this is the *individual behaviour* of Muslims, maintaining a good character, being peaceful and tolerant, believing, practising and respecting the law or being responsible for oneself and avoiding evil.

The third cluster of answers to the question of how they actively practice, was related to *learning*. The reading of the Qur'an or of books in general and religious education was mentioned most often. Childhood education or working with Muslim youth was mentioned as well as discussing religious questions with others or imparting general knowledge to others, going to Islamic events and meetings, educating the self and being intellectually religious[21]. The Arab concept of "*adāb*" describes this field as "education" and a "cultivated self-presentation". Especially among Islamic mystics and in the tradition of Sūfīsm, the term is used to describe the relation between pupil (*dervish*) and his teacher (*sheik*) (Hefner & Zaman 2005).[22] In the Religious Monitor 2008, education is said to be a core aspect in the lives of 94 percent of Muslims in Germany as well (Rieger 2008, 8). This importance of learning within Muslim culture however, contradicts the general achievements of Muslim students. Saeeda Shah claims in her study of multiethnic schools in the U.K, that the motivation of Muslim students is undermined by discrimination (Sha 2006, 34; 215). To understand Muslim learners, one has to know their expectations, develop a diversity-friendly teacher-learner relation and one needs to understand that religion and culture cannot be separated (Sha 2006, 217).

Appearing of a "non-German" Germanness

While in our sample most Muslims and non-Muslims alike identify as a big barrier to being German, the fact that one does not speak the national language, only Muslims perceived adherence to religion as an obstacle to being accepted as Germans. In the eyes of non-Muslims, this is perceived as an attitude where "Muslims hold on too much to their beliefs" (Hieronymus 2010, 35), as one interviewee said, while for Muslims, such preconceived notions about people from Muslim countries or what people think about Islam more generally, are considered as barriers to acceptance.

While Muslims are often overtly visible in public, non-Muslim religions are in general invisible in the public sphere and in day-to-day interaction, reinforcing the view that religion does not play a significant role in public and private practices. Nevertheless, nineteen percent of Muslims consider not being Christian as the main barrier to be German: cultural life is perceived as being dominated by Christianity, along with historical hostility against Muslims, such as the Crusades, the Reconquista of Andalusia, colonialism and imperialism (Hieronymus

21 Somebody is considered as intellectual religious, when he or she is able to refer to a broad range of religious arguments.

22 http://www.adab.com/en/modules.php?name=Content&pa=showpage&pid=18, accessed 15.02.2010

2010, 35). In this view, Christianity is merged with Western expansion to form a mentality that is still dominant. This long historical memory, which enshrines more than 1,400 years of history of Muslim culture, shapes a different perspective in the ordinary Muslim towards historical events. This differs significantly to the historical perspective of ordinary non-Muslims, who often do not even consider contemporary history.

Many interviewees emphasized the difference between "*our*" values and "*theirs*" and relied on stereotypes. Muslims and non-Muslims alike failed to see common values and expressed concerns that their own values were not respected (Hieronymus 2010, 35). Alleged differences in values go hand in hand with an experience related to their own appearance as not being considered German. This experience, of not being considered as German based on outward appearance, is shared by non-Muslims of migrant background (Hieronymus 2010, 35). Muslim and non-Muslim migrants consider the way Germans interact and deal with others and themselves, as mirroring another mentality. In fact, even some non-Muslims of German background disassociated themselves from a certain type of Germanness, which is described as "German values and virtue" (Hieronymus 2010, 35). This attitude is characterized by little tolerance and respectful contact among each other and many do not identify themselves with this mentality, which accords status to achievements through formal qualification as its core and is said to be important for Germans (Hieronymus 2010, 35).

Looking at the ranking in each group, to the question of what the most important values are, it appears that for the majority of Muslims, respect for law and faith, and the freedom from discrimination are most important. This result is supported by the Religion Monitor 2008 as well, where a high level of tolerance towards other creeds is found: "86 percent think one should be open to all religions. This value is the same for all examined groups, no matter which gender, age, confession or origin. (Rieger 2008, 8)"

While 51 percent of Muslims think religion says the most about who they are, it does not play any role for non-Muslims, who instead rank family, their interests, the level of education or the kind of work they are doing as most important.

Language identities: Ways of living the German language

Speaking the national language was regarded as one of the important values by Muslims and non-Muslims alike. Language in general and communication skills in particular, are seen as essentially important for the local, city and national arena. A desire for a common language (German or another language) was articulated especially by older interviewees and recent immigrants. Some Muslims highlighted the need to speak the national language to get in contact with others (Hieronymus 2010, 38). Non-Muslims also consider knowledge of the national language as the most important prerequisite for self-confident participation in society. A support of multilingualism, combined with early childhood language support not only in German, but in the languages of the migrants as well, accompanied by language courses for mothers in schools and kindergartens, is regarded as helpful by Muslims and non-Muslims. But the acquisition of German is only one aspect of how language functions in society. The interviewees reported multi-layered problems, which cannot be solely solved through language and integration courses.

Non-Muslims emphasized the fact that even speaking German fluently but with an accent is often an obstacle: "I look different and speak German with a Spanish accent." (Hieronymus 2010, 38). Language and appearance are believed to be a barrier to perception as a Hamburger, even for native German non-Muslims: "Because the way I look and my accent people tell me that I am not a Hamburger" (Hieronymus 2010, 38).

The lack of communication skills is sometimes described as a fear of communication: foreigners are afraid to approach people, because they do not know how they will be treated, whereas Germans perceive foreigners as not opening themselves up to interaction. This is regarded as a continuous stalemate on both sides. The capacity of language to exclude people and make power relations visible was recognized, as some Muslims in the focus groups explained:

> We met on a train at an excursion with twenty children. When we then spoke Turkish, we all were Turkish; somebody came and asked why do you speak Turkish. One parent who fluently spoke German started a discussion with him and said, that we can talk the way we like. (Hieronymus 2010, 38)

Another described a situation in the schoolyard: when pupils were speaking amongst each other; a teacher came and warned them not to speak Turkish. Young people may not differentiate between German and Turkish as two languages when they speak, but to outsiders it appears as if they are speaking false German or Turkish (Hieronymus 2000). This further highlights a lacking in awareness of how to teach German in a multilingual environment, where German is neither a second language nor a single mother-tongue. To address this problem the HHAP suggests a novel perspective by promoting a multilingual approach for the education system.

The German gaze: Perceptions, appearance and lifestyles

The OSI-research suggests that integration, which is understood as a two-way process and needs openness, tolerance and dialogue from all sides[23], is not always practised in this way. The dynamic of being perceived as a foreigner in the eyes of society and by the natives, reinforces the feeling of being foreign. This is frequently reported by the interviewees. A Muslim said "I live here 20 years and still have the feeling, that they see me as foreigner" (Hieronymus 2010, 39). People do not feel welcome here, because physical appearance is valued very highly. Muslims expressed that they are perceived differently, and that it is not accepted that there are German Muslims. A native German young female Muslim noted that Muslims must get away from the immigration discourse, they are a part

23 HHAP 2007, p. 9.

of the society and have themselves integrated; now it is time they are incorporated into society by the majority (Hieronymus 2010, 39).

This dynamic of being perceived in the gaze of others, and the emotional resonance it has for self-perception and the self-image, is illuminated by the fact that 75 percent of non-Muslims interviewees think that they are seen as Germans by other people, but only 44 percent of them actually want to be seen as Germans. Among Muslims, this is exactly the other way around, only 13 percent think that they are seen as Germans by other people, but 31 percent want to be seen as Germans. Additionally, the majority of Muslims have a very or fairly strong sense of belonging to Germany, while among non-Muslims this is weaker. Muslims want to live as they are and want to be seen as such, expressing a high degree of individuality.

Examining the experiences of those who are perceived as Germans, but do not define themselves as such, gives a specific image of a German: "I am not a German, I just look like one of them for the Germans, because I am fair and large and I dress in a modern style" (Hieronymus 2010, 40) a young Muslim girl said. The counter-image of a German is described as wearing a headscarf or having dark eyes or hair. Being German is limited to physical appearance: "even if I had ten German passports, they would not see me as a German" (Hieronymus 2010, 40). This affects even Muslim women, who are native German, but not seen as German, because they wear a headscarf. Skin colour also marks this difference, as a black Muslim man reports: "It doesn't matter, where I come from. As long as I am black I am an African" (Hieronymus 2010, 40). Visible signs like the dark skin, the black hair, Islamic dress or headscarves function as markers of difference. Many non-Muslims read these markers as signs that do not belong to Germany. Those markers are not only related to appearance, but to lifestyle as well: "I am living differently than the Germans do. I have a totally different idea of how to enjoy life, for example. For the Germans in my environment, having fun means to party every weekend, this is nothing that I can do" (Hieronymus 2010, 40) a young Muslim girl reported. On the other side there are prejudices against Germans, you are thought to be either fussy or a racist, a German non-Muslim said (Hieronymus 2010, 40). Although there is a big difference between somebody who is stereotyped by a member of the dominant group, and a member of a subordinate group stereotyping a member of the dominant group, we can speak of a mutual production of stereotyped images.

A different outlook on Germanness was articulated in the focus groups by some Muslims. It is a quest for citizenship: "Each human has the same rights, it doesn't matter where he comes from. Being German means ethnicity, that's why I can't be German, but I can be a German citizen" (Hieronymus 2010, 40). This positive definition of Germanness is often undermined by exclusionary experiences: "I felt German, until I felt exclusion in all phases of life" (Hieronymus 2010, 40). Those stereotyped perceptions of ethnic Germans produce outsiders, aliens not coming from this country.

Although a strong sense of belonging to the neighbourhoods is articulated in the questionnaire, Hamburg is not experienced as home by everybody. This is even felt by Muslims who are born in Hamburg. It was said that native Germans hardly accept that parents come from another country, but their children who are born here see themselves as German. Migrant Muslims and non-Muslims perceived the "*W-Questions*" (Where do you come from? What do you do here? When do you leave?) as irritating, and they feel treated as though they just arrived from a foreign country. Things which are normal for a German, they have to explain, a Muslim said (Hieronymus 2010, 40).

Interviewees reported growth of rivalries and jealousy especially among young '*Potatoes*' (Germans) and '*Kanacken*' (migrants) and among Alevis, Sunnis, Turks and Kurds. People do not show readiness to get along with other people in the St. Pauli area, especially youth in public spaces, who are at the centre of local ethnic rivalries. Older people feel that young people misbehave in the public space and that a bad social climate has been created. Young people do not get along with each other, they are at an age in which things heat up very fast and they get quickly frustrated. Some interviewees expressed the feeling that there is no respect, especially not for women and for people with other origins and culture.

Interviewees perceived a demonstration of ethnic superiority among all ethnic groups. For some, Germans are bad people and they feel discrimination from Germans. This stalemate on the different sides seems to be the effect of an alienation which transforms social conflicts into mutual ethno-religious rivalries where youth of other ethnic groups insult German youth and think they have the better religion, as reported by one non-Muslim (Hieronymus 2010, 42). On the one side the German ethnic group becomes one of many ethnic groups and represents the ethnic diversity of the area, on the other side German ethnicity is hegemonic and represent a massive differential in terms of power relation among the diversity of ethnic groups. Even if there is an attempt to communicate, there is always a point where people say he is only Albanian, Kurd, etc., a young non-Muslim pointed out (Hieronymus 2010, 35). Some see parents as partly responsible for stirring up prejudices.

Turning points for the feeling of belonging

For the majority of Muslim women (40 percent), discrimination based on religion is their main experience, whereas discrimination based on gender is the major experience for the majority of non-Muslim women (35 percent). The headscarf issue combines different aspects of gender, ethnic and religious discrimination. This is highlighted by the Human Rights Watch Report on Germany (HRW 2009).[24] 175 interviewees (87.5 percent) feel there is a lot, or a fair amount of

24 Eight Federal states (Baden-Württemberg, Bayern, Berlin, Bremen, Hessen, Niedersachsen, Nordrhein-Westfalen and Saarland) have laws or regulations which ban wearing visible religious clothes or symbols for teachers in public schools. In two Federal states (Hessen and Berlin) this ban is valid as well for a range of other public servants. The majority of Federal states banning religious symbols allow exceptions for "Christian-occidental" traditions. Eight Federal states have no special laws banning religious clothes and symbol, among them Hamburg. Three Federal states (Brandenburg, Rheinland-Pfalz and Schleswig-Holstein) considered introducing a ban,

prejudice in Germany. Among Muslims there is a feeling that the situation has worsened in the last five years.

Discrimination against Muslims has become increasingly acceptable, especially where visible expressions of religious affiliation are concerned like women's headscarves (Hieronymus 2010, 122). The author was approached by several Muslim women after the murder of the pregnant, 31 year old Egyptian pharmacist Marwa El-Sherbini on the 1st of July 2009 in a court room in Dresden after she took legal action against a Russian-German man who had insulted her at a playground. The three women were looking for means to express their fears and anger about their own experiences of Islamophobia publicly. The fact that it took almost a week until this attack was reported in the mainstream media as a minor event was a sign for them, that discrimination against Muslims has become socially acceptable[25].

Turning points are described in the questionnaires and the focus groups as the period before 9/11 and the unification of Germany. Two older Muslims in a focus group were discussing the reunification of Germany in negative terms:

> One shouldn't have taken up the citizens, if you cannot keep them. That's how my rights are taken away. We are 5 million foreigners, we did not get anything of the money going to the GDR in return. With the GDR 20 million new citizens were taken in. That shouldn't have been done. They let me work and they get the money. (Hieronymus 2010, 44)

While unification brought in the whole population of one state into the Federal Republic of Germany on an ethnic basis, ethnicity moved into the focus of identities (Cil 2009, 40-6). One of the stakeholders put it as follows:

> We have lived through several integration eras. At the beginning there were the 'guest workers', then the 'foreigner problem', a couple of years later it was a 'Turk problem' and nowadays it is a 'Muslim problem'. (Hieronymus 2010:44)

The racist and discriminatory attitude remained the same, the enemy was just defined differently because things get mixed up, explained by and reduced to being Islamic. (Hieronymus 2010:44)

11 September 2001, is frequently mentioned in the data as the other turning point. Even young Muslims in the OSI focus groups remembered that day vividly. One girl described the change of atmosphere: people were reacting more aggressively on the one side and on the other they were more fearful (Hieronymus

---

but did not. According to Human Rights Watch these regulations discriminate against Muslim women wearing headscarves, because they get excluded from teaching and public service because of their religion. Those Federal states banning the headscarves, but allowing Christian symbols discriminate as well on grounds of religion and in a practical way they discriminate on the basis of gender. Women are forced to decide whether to work or to express their religion, and that violates the right to equal treatment, the report concludes (Human Rights Watch Report (2009).

25 TAZ, 06.07.2009, http://www.taz.de/nc/1/politik/deutschland/artikel/1/mord-mit-islam feindlichem-hintergrund , access 17.08.2009. See as well comments: http://www.taz.de/1/politik/deutschland/artikel/kommentarseite/1/mord-mit-islamfeindlichem-hintergrund/kommentare/1/1/, accessed 17.08.2009.

2010:44). Another young Muslim man described a bus trip with his mother at that time.

> I took out my Qur'an to study a bit. The bus was already driving for 45 minutes, it was an ordinary public service bus. Suddenly a German frantically leaves. The bus continues and stops again and the bus driver approaches us. I was wondering, what is happening now. The bus driver said to us: 'calm down, don't panic if a police unit is coming. This man, who just left said that you and your mother are planning a terrorist attack.' My mother doesn't even wear a headscarf, just because I took out my Qur'an. (Hieronymus 2010:44)

But Muslims reported not only fear and aggression, but also the fact that since 9/11 a lot of people engaged with Islam and the rate of converts increased. People started asking questions on their own, about what Islam is and about the background of the terrorism. At present Muslims have more opportunities to speak out and articulate what Islam really is, one Muslim girl reported (Hieronymus 2010:44). Another Muslim explained that the more talk there was against Muslims, the stronger the solidarity and the communication within the Muslim community became, with the side effect of sealing-off the rest of society (Hieronymus 2010:44). Although some of the mainly younger interviewees drew a dull picture about some aspects of their local area and the hardening of ethnic identity borders, the interaction between different ethnic and religious groups is quite active, non-Muslims showing a higher rate of inter-religious and inter-ethnic interaction at home than Muslims. Both groups interact more on a weekly than on a daily basis.

Certain entertainment places, like discos, bars or clubs, are often seen as places where strange or rich people meet and exclude others, especially dark-skinned people, as one Muslim reported (Hieronymus 2010, 44). If young Muslims decide to socialize in bars and clubs, they may have difficulties in accessing those locations. In 2008 the *Hamburg Abendblatt* conducted a test with two young high school students of Ethiopian and Iranian descent. In eight out of nine bars and discos they were stopped by bouncers and denied entrance.[26] The conclusion of a round-table organized by the head of the district to discuss the issue was that it is difficult to talk about discrimination, because the majority of the bouncers were of Turkish origin, which was understood to mean they could not discriminate themselves.[27] This episode makes clear that there is a lack of understanding as to what discrimination represents, what the regulations of the General Equal Treatment Act (AGG) are, and how it affects victims.

---

26 Hamburger Abendblatt, 08.09.2008: Die Toleranz endet beim Türsteher, http://www.abendblatt.de/hamburg/article937604/Die-Toleranz-endet-beim-Tuersteher.html, accessed 23.7.09

27 Hamburger Abendblatt, 28.10.2008: Türsteher: Die Debatte geht weiter, http://www.abendblatt.de/hamburg/article571813/Tuersteher-Die-Debatte-geht-weiter.html, accessed 23.7.09

Learning in a selective education system

Education is highly controversial in Germany. The controversy is related to two main questions: How long should children stay at home under their mothers' care, and is the existing three track school-system still adequate? Since the OECD Pisa[28] studies in 2000, where the achievements of schools were internationally compared for the first time, it became obvious that the education system in Germany is inefficient and highly selective.[29]

There is a variety of school types in Hamburg-Mitte.[30] The differences between these schools can be difficult for an immigrant to understand, as one Muslim women articulated

> When we came at that time we didn't know the school systems. We thought it is like in Turkey. We didn't know what a 'Realschule' and what a 'Gymnasium' is. Although my oldest daughter was really intelligent and her teachers insisted that she should go to the 'Gymnasium', I thought like in Turkey, that she will be working anyway and sent her to 'Realschule'. (...) she is now working for 15-20 years as a clerk with AOK (Health Insurance). (Hieronymus 2010, 52)

Another Muslim girl told a story about her Algerian neighbour:

> He was an only child and he was not that good in school and they told the parents that he needed to go to a 'special school' (Sonderschule). The parents understood unfortunately that it was a really special school and were happy and pleased. Somebody must have recognized that they misunderstood something. No parent is happy when his child goes to 'special school'. I got really angry because nobody really explained anything to them. (Hieronymus 2010, 52)

There is data on the number of foreign students in each of the school forms, which indicates that the lower the profile of the school the higher the number of foreign students who enrol.[31] This trend continues in the numbers of school dropouts, students who leave school without a "*Hauptschul*" certificate[32]. Muslim parents may be overstrained by the complexity of the German school system and some children take advantage of their parents' ignorance for their own purposes, as a focus group participant reported: "I know a lot of students, who tell their

---

28 PISA = Programme for International Student Assessment, www.pisa.oecd.org, accessed 13.3.09.

29 It is efficient in the sense that the education system fulfills its function to select for a society based on industrial production, but it is inefficient in providing young students with competencies necessary for a knowledge based society.

30 Freie und Hansestadt Hamburg, Behörde für Bildung und Sport 2007/2008

31 Freie und Hansestadt Hamburg, Behörde für Bildung und Sport 2007/2008

32 The German education system knows three basic school-leaving certificates, "Hauptschule" after 9 years, "Realschule" (qualifies for e.g. technical universities) after 10 years and "Gymnasium" (Abitur, comparible to an A-level, qualifies for university) after 12 years. Because of changes on the labour-market, which requires higher school-leaving certificates for most jobs, the "Hauptschule" leaving certificate has been dequalified.

parents, that they are going to have an A-level (Abitur), although they even do not have a 'Hauptschul' certificate"(Hieronymus 2010, 52).

A Muslim participant of one focus group further emphasized that,

> The level of education of the parents plays a big role. That already starts with parents' involvement in school. Fathers and mothers barely speak German, because they a working hard and therefore have no time to develop themselves. They don't come to such gatherings. The teacher then gets the impression, that they are not at all interested in school. This has the effect of a less good relation between teachers and students. (Hieronymus 2010, 52)

Another Muslim interviewee highlighted an additional difficulty of some Muslim parents:

> They cannot check homework that well, because they do not have the level of education of the German parents. (...) Then immediately comes up the question of private lessons for 10€ per hour, the average is around 20€. This is really expensive. Especially for those people who live of Hartz IV (social welfare), they do not have the money and do not get the necessary support of the state. (Hieronymus 2010, 52)

Advice for parents and students is clearly needed: 47 percent of Muslims in the OSI study indicated they needed advice in relation to education, and likewise 55 percent of non-Muslims are in need of advice in this area. The research data support the general view of other studies, that Muslims have a lower level of education. But the outcome of the education process is mainly an effect of the German education system itself. Although education and learning is central to Muslim culture it does not affect the performance of Muslim students in the German education system. At the round table workshop on education, it was stressed that the participation of Muslim parents is low, and that religious active parents along with teachers play a key role for learning. They can bridge the gap between teachers and students. It was said that barriers, like the high formalization of the parents' representation, too little dialogue with Muslim parents or the social gap between teachers and families need to be identified; and new forms of working with parents to increase their participation needed to be found (Hieronymus 2010, 54). Best practices like the training of parents as mediators or translators are a step in the right direction according to the participants.[33] Often teachers do not know anything about the parents' backgrounds and schools lack social workers who can work with the parents. It was also stressed that Muslim and migrant parents in the current structures can hardly enforce their demands or get their rights.

33 http://www.bqm-handbuch.de/site/html/cms.php?cont=144, accessed 18.8.2009.

Muslims perspective on performance of students and teachers

The HHAP sees poor skills in speaking and reading German as the main barrier for the integration of students with migrant backgrounds. Migrants are behind their fellow students of German origin when it comes to learning performances (*Lernrückstand*). From a Muslim perspective, being left behind is experienced as more of a systematic downgrading of migrants by the educational system and was widely reported in different focus groups. One participant reported that teachers have sent children without disabilities to the special school (*Sonderschule*) where they were tested and found to be highly intelligent. The teacher then asked "Are our teachers supposed to be unemployed?" implying that migrant students are there to guarantee the jobs of special school teachers. Another young Muslim wondered why a friend, who, at that time was 13 years old, was sent to a special school, but was able to learn the Qur'an by heart in 45 days. An older Muslim father talked about his experiences:

> When my child was [in Germany], they said that he is not doing well in school. They said he is mentally not capable. We then brought him to Turkey and there they took him into the 3rd grade. Now he has finished university. He went right from the first to third grade. (Hieronymus 2010, 55)

These experiences suggest that Muslim children may be placed in special schools (*Sonderschule*) and the *Hauptschule* not necessarily because of disabilities. Some research has posited that this is a result of a downward dynamic of the education system, which has not yet adapted to dealing with diversity and the needs of a diverse learning environment (Gomolla 2000). The standard way of dealing with difference in the existing education system is to single out differences and transfer them to the next lower level. The school system is viewed by Muslims and non-Muslims alike as highly selective and not good, although 29 percent of Muslims and 22 percent of non-Muslims are satisfied with the local primary school. Complaints about primary schools are related to the reproduction of spatial segregation (ghettos) in the class, because children attend neighbourhood schools. The school climate was criticized as aggressive and the pre-school services were considered inadequate. Non-Muslims expressed concern about a lack of attention towards improving social competencies. An interviewee reported that underprivileged, non-German children are being excluded from their neighbourhood school as the area gentrifies. Local primary schools, but other schools as well, demand too little from the children in the eyes of Muslims. The education level is too low and interviewees expressed concerns that Muslim children do not get support, and xenophobia is prevailing. In overcrowded classes, children only learn what is most necessary. There are perceptions that a large number of migrants reduce the quality of education offered. A Muslim complained about the low standard of his school, because there are too many migrants. Another Muslim reported that all foreigners are usually put into one class with the effect that the level of education is not desirable. A non-Muslim explained that education policies in the schools cannot integrate existing cultural differences or organize an exchange among each other. It is felt that there are too few schools like *Gesamtschule*, which integrate those differences.

The interviewees reported discontent with the way resources are allocated and how it affects the quality of teaching. For some Muslims, there are not enough local schools, those that do exist are bad, too small or do not teach basic knowledge. One interviewee reported in the area where he is living there is neither a *Realschule* nor a *Gymnasium* anymore, because they were closed down. Another parent complained that there is a lack of educational materials despite school fees.

It was further suggested that courses are dropped and an atmosphere of violence and ignorance exists due to a lack of teachers. Some Muslims indicated that schools need more human resources and an open space; others say that there must be more policing, surveillance and more human resources to improve security in schools. Because there are too many pupils, sometimes up to 30 students in one class were reported, students do not get enough support. In particular, a non-Muslim observed there are increasing numbers of children with psychological problems but insufficient resources.

The situation of teachers

Muslims and non-Muslims are aware of the fact that teachers are overextended. One Muslim saw the new working time model, introduced in one of the many reforms in Hamburg, as having negative effects on the quality of teaching. Some non-Muslims described teachers as overwhelmed by the social problems of the students, unmotivated, lackadaisical and resigned (Hieronymus 2010, 57). In primary schools, a Muslim said, teachers are not trained to teach foreign students.[34] Another Muslim indicated that in primary schools in other districts, the teachers take better care of their students, like in the grammar school (Gymnasium) in Kirchdorf-Wilhelmsburg.

A shortage of teachers was cited as a serious problem in Hamburg. This shadows a national problem of shortage of teachers as an overview about the prognosis on the supply of teachers in all federal states shows.[35] A study commissioned by the Trade Union of Education and Science (GEW) sees the reasons for the shortage in Hamburg until 2020 in a decline in the number of pupils which is lower than expected, a high average age of teachers in Hamburg (55 years), which leads consequently to a need to employ new teachers, but current numbers of newly employed teachers are too small to compensate the retirements. Because of the general lack of trained teachers nationwide, teachers cannot be recruited from other federal states.[36] Additionally the current school reforms require even more teachers and the former changes in the teachers working time model have

34 In this construction of students as "foreign" by a Muslim, although most of the students have a German passport or are born in Germany, the notion of not belonging is again reinforced.

35 http://www.bildungsserver.de/zeigen.html?seite=5530, accessed 5.8.2009.

36 GEW press release from 17.6.2009: http://www.gew-hamburg.de/Binaries/Binary2034/Klemm-Gutachten%20GEW%20Hamburg%20Spezifika.pdf, accessed 6.8.09.

led to the highest working hours of teachers in Hamburg compared to teachers in other federal states, which makes Hamburg less attractive.[37]

Both Muslims and non-Muslims perceive the educational system as flawed and based on incorrect premises, with a lot of theory and little practice. According to interviewees, the prevailing teacher-centered lecture style does not respond to the needs of individual students and the school administration does not help teachers develop themselves or support them in modernizing their approach. The lack of investment in education was regarded as the problem.[38]

One Muslim raised the topic of lacking discipline and complained that students have too much freedom and the teachers do not emphasize discipline; there are too many holidays and, for example, girls attend school wearing too much makeup and too little clothing, which distracts from learning.[39]

Teachers are the centre of interaction between Muslim students and the school system and face significant criticism. Teachers bring their personal opinions, often framed by stereotypes and prejudices, too much into the foreground and improperly influence the students, a Muslim reported (Hieronymus 2010, 58). In secondary school, according to a young Muslim,

> They have an opinion of you and you can't change it, you can do what you want. The teacher doesn't treat everybody the same. For the same offense like drinking alcohol at a school outing, the students get punished differently. I have the feeling that there are a lot of right wing teachers, e.g. they make jokes about foreigners. (Hieronymus 2010, 58)

A variety of such discriminatory incidents were reported in the survey and in the focus groups. The classifications of those incidents as discriminatory reflect the perspective of Muslims, their perception and interpretation of the situations where those incidents happened. Muslims described situations like being put into a corner for not knowing the language or being the subject of unfair grading (Hieronymus 2010, 58). Some Muslims reported that teachers systematically give bad grades to Muslim students (Hieronymus 2010, 58). Muslims observed a degrading of Islam by teachers, who ridicule Islam through ironic questions, and laugh about Muslim customs, like fasting in the month of Ramadan (Hieronymus 2010, 58). Muslim students reported being offended by hate speech, teasing and devaluation. Non-Muslims were concerned about a lack of basic knowledge of other religions, while noting some improvements like teachers trying to explain commonalities and differences of other religions. Schools are seen as a mixture of different religions and teachers have started in the last few years to learn and to understand what it means to believe in another religion and how to teach this to students, according to interviewees. But Muslims also reported intolerant teachers, who do not accept students of other cultures. Other non-Muslims took the view that the attitude of teachers depends on their generation: younger teachers are seen to be more open than older ones. A non-Muslim noted that

---

37 Ibidem
38 Ibidem
39 Ibidem

there are rarely teachers with a migration background and that the recruited personnel are drawn mainly from the majority society.

Prejudices in school

A non-Muslim emphasized that unsubstantiated prejudices against people from Turkey or students with headscarves are common in schools. Muslim students experience such prejudices in school buses: „They don‘t sit next to us in the buses; they would rather stand up, even though there is room to sit next to a Muslim“ (Hieronymus 2010, 59). It was indicated that there is no acceptance or respect and students have to justify themselves because of their religion. "They pretend that they respect different religious customs, but they make us upset by expressing some insulting comments and prejudices. I know this from my four children who go to school" a Muslim mother reported (Hieronymus 2010, 59). Another Muslim agreed that children are not treated equally; there are prejudices against Afghans and Muslims, despite respect for other religious customs. Several interviewees, both Muslim and non-Muslim, suggested that the principle of non-discrimination needs to be better implemented in schools, particularly regarding the conduct of children themselves. The problem of discrimination within schools is not yet openly articulated in the HHAP or other policy documents, and the importance of the teachers´ attitudes towards minority children and to their educational success needs to be addressed. Participants of the working group on education at the round table stressed that they see a correlation between language competencies and ethnicity as problematic, reinforcing prejudices and called for more studies on discrimination and language. The workshop also recommended a check-list for schools to be developed by the institute for teacher education (LI), which shows them how far along they are in terms of succeeding in opening up and achieving an inter-cultural environment (Hieronymus 2010, 59).

A recurring theme emerging in several cities is the impact of teachers' expectations, which can be mediated by factors such as ethnicity. Differing expectations manifest themselves in many subtle ways, from the kind and amount of feedback a student receives, to the encouragement and opportunities for participation in class. Participants of the OSI focus group in Hamburg cited instances where the teacher's poor assessment of a pupil's ability was proved incorrect after being challenged by parents. In Berlin, over half of the focus group participants reported severe examples of discouragement. Interviews with other stakeholders and focus group participants in Marseille revealed how individuals had to struggle at various moments of their education careers against unfavourable assignments imposed by the schools. Few took short cuts to arrive where they are. Many others felt that they had to struggle against the unconscious desire of teachers to keep them in their place ((Hieronymus 2010, 100).

Other Muslim parents were more optimistic, remarking that intolerance is the exception and everybody learns to handle religious questions better over time (Hieronymus 2010, 60). Few major conflicts were reported, and a non-Muslim parent noted that many foreign children go on to finish school and have successful careers (Hieronymus 2010, 60).

Religion in school

A large majority of Muslims expressed the opinion that schools respect the religious customs of the people belonging to different religion insufficiently, while the majority of non-Muslims found the level of respect appropriate. Nevertheless, many Muslims interviewed had positive experiences to report from the schools. Those positive experiences stem from the schools' respectful approach to the religion of their students. Muslim students are allowed to pray and fast in school and when Ramaḍān starts, teachers treat the children carefully, ask how they feel and if they are tired. Classmates are told to treat fasting children carefully during that time, Muslims reported (Hieronymus 2010, 60). A non-Muslim indicated that schools have become more open towards other religions and their customs, due to the high number of foreigners in Germany (Hieronymus 2010, 60).

There seems to be no uniform approach to the use of headscarves in the schools of Hamburg-Mitte. Muslims and non-Muslims report of schools where the headscarf is allowed and respected, and others report of schools where there is hostility against veiling and Muslim children have been harassed in school and hassled by teachers (Hieronymus 2010, 60). There is also a wide range of practices on how to deal with religious holidays. Some schools have no problems in giving leave of absence on religious holidays, others celebrate together and the teachers offer congratulations on Muslim holidays or at Chinese New Year, a non-Muslim reported. But both groups report that there are schools where rites are ignored (Hieronymus 2010, 60). Some schools provide prayer rooms for students. If there are no separate rooms available, dressing rooms are provided by some schools for prayers. A non-Muslim sees this as a reaction of German politics, media and population, which has enhanced the role of religion in school (Hieronymus 2010, 60). Other schools do not provide praying rooms. Some Muslims still pray in the common rooms without the school management's awareness. Areas where interviewees expressed concern included swimming classes and class outings. Some Muslims took the view that students should not be forced to attend swimming courses, while others considered that gender separation in sports was a good thing. Non-Muslims reported that on class outings the wishes of the parents are respected, and that solutions can be found for other issues, like girls' swimming classes. Often the Islamic Education and Science Institute are asked for advice on religious matters (Hieronymus 2010, 60).

The Hamburg model of religious education

The Federal Minister of the Interior recently decided at the Third Islam conference to introduce Islamic religious classes in German. There is religious education in all federal states in different forms and Islamic religious classes already existed in some federal states.[40]

In 1994, a joint commission of schools and churches was established, which worked on the pluralization/integration of the Hamburg religious education in a "*school for all*" in which all pupils with their different cultural and religious backgrounds are taught together.[41] This model is accepted by the Muslim community as a "third way" beyond denominational religious education and ethics. The Muslim community was involved at an early stage in this discussion through their participation in the forum "inter-religious education", which was established in 1995. In 1999 the "*inter religious forum Hamburg*", closely following the British model of inter-faith dialogue was established.[42] A detailed description of the Hamburg model can be found in the chapter on Muslim religious instruction in the European context by Wolfram Weisse (see his contribution in this book).

There is little agreement about the role of religion in schools among those interviewed. While some non-Muslims see the school's role as a neutral place where children learn about the similarities and differences between religions, some Muslims found this approach pushes religion into the background and does not promote acceptance (Hieronymus 2010, 61). Daily customs and obligations that must be practised during school hours do not receive enough attention, according to some Muslims (Hieronymus 2010, 61). They would welcome Islam classes in German for their children, and complained about the lack of Muslim teaching (Hieronymus 2010, 61).

Other Muslims indicated they would accept an alternative to religious classes, when the existing lectures are extended to different other religions. This reflects the Hamburg model for religious education. The majority of Muslims in the research did not reflect on religious classes in schools, but the OSI data suggest a high rate of interreligious and inter-ethnic contacts in school.

New impulses for a pluralization in research and teaching at University level have been worked out since 1999. This resulted in an interdisciplinary centre, World Religions in Dialogue, which has been transformed into the "Academy of World Religions" in 2010, supported by the head of the University and the government of Hamburg. The guiding idea is to support an academic approach allowing a redefinition of Islam and other religions in the context of Europe. There

---

40 Most commonly, this takes the form of denominational education, where each denomination is responsible for its own religious education. The other model, focusing on ethics and religion, only plays a minor role. See http://www.jurblog.de/2008/03/16/umfrage-islamkonferenz-beschliesst-islamunterricht-an-deutschen-schulen/, accessed 27.08.08.

41 "School for all" was promoted mainly by the Green Party and is suppose to replace the old model of the three strands school system. It is part of the conservative-green coalition agreement. In what way it is implemented is currently debated within the coalition.

42 Özdil: Gesprächskreis interreligiöser Religionsunterricht.

should be Muslims in academic positions who are socialized, educated and qualified in Germany and understand the way of life. It is believed that they can better work in the communities in the sense of integration (Hieronymus 2010, 62).

Conclusion

The OSI research suggests that religious discrimination against Muslims remains a critical barrier to full and equal participation in society, not only in Hamburg, but in all eleven cities surveyed (OSI 2010, 23). The findings of the Hamburg and the European report are consistent with other research and suggest that levels of religious discrimination directed towards Muslims are widespread and have increased over the past five years. The persistence of discrimination and prejudice affects their sense of national belonging. Despite this reality, Muslims living in the cities of the OSI study emphasized the need to put prejudices aside and build up empathy. There is a high awareness that Muslims should not discriminate against others, and reciprocally, Muslims do not want to be discriminated against by others either. The freedom from discrimination was one of the four most important values among Muslims and non-Muslims alike; at the same time, discrimination was seen as a reason for the ethno-religious closing up of local communities. In Hamburg, discrimination is not publicly articulated and the majority see barriers and bad performance of Muslims and migrants, as individualized failures, rather than as forms of structural discrimination.

Across all the cities of the OSI study, there is increasing recognition of the importance of pre-school education in ensuring that pupils from minority and other disadvantaged backgrounds do not start formal schooling under prepared. There is also growing evidence that education systems which place pupils into different education streams too early are disadvantaging young people from minority groups, who need more time to develop the linguistic skills to excel in education. But the sole reduction of integration to a language problem in Germany is a problem in the eyes of Muslims in Hamburg. Language itself becomes an instrument of and in exclusion. Speaking "correct" or "proper" German does not prevent discrimination, if the accent is not "correct" either. Muslim pupils are confronted by low expectations from teachers. There is still a need for schools to work on themselves, the teachers, the general atmosphere and also a need to confront issues and deal with Muslim parents and their integration into the school life (Fürstenau 2009).

Overwhelmingly, the OSI data portray the needs and priorities of Hamburg's Muslim communities as similar to those of other residents. This is similar to all the other cities of the OSI study. Like their neighbours, Muslims in Hamburg, and all the other cities, are concerned about the quality of education in schools, the safety and cleanliness of their streets and the availability and cost of health care. The Muslims participating in the OSI survey indicated both a developed sense of belonging to Hamburg and a high degree of religious observance; nevertheless, they reported that there is little recognition of a German, Muslim identity in the mainstream. This result separates the two German cities Hamburg and Berlin from the rest of the cities in the OSI study. In the other cities surveyed, there exists a strong sense of belonging to the nation and recognition of Muslim identity, which does not necessarily diminish discrimination. The OSI research indicates widespread perceptions of discrimination not only in Hamburg, but in all cities of the OSI study. There is evidence of a high level of discrimination experiences among Muslims, especially in the field of education, but in other fields as well, on the grounds of their – perceived – religious affiliation, which adds to pre-existing ethnic discrimination of "*Turks*" in the German context. The impact of discrimination on self-esteem means that it has an even greater impact when it takes place in education. The HHAP also does not adequately address the role of discrimination as an obstacle to integration. Instead, it is centered on language acquisition as a means to foster full access to society. The effects of exclusionary processes need to be clearly recognized to put in place measures to address these barriers appropriately. Rising Islamophobic attitudes within society have added another strike against people whose origins are in a country with a Muslim majority. Whereas racist discrimination against foreigners had been – and still is – widely perceived to take place on the fringes of the German society[43] and is considered a problem of right wing extremism, discrimination against Muslims has to a certain extent become socially acceptable, especially where visible expressions of religious affiliation are concerned such as women's headscarves, prayers at public places like schools or the building of mosques.

With the non-segregated Hamburg model of religious education for all, the city has created a new possibility to include Muslims in the education sector. It has established a best practice example, which can function as an alternative model to the Netherlands, where there is an official curriculum on Islam or to Belgium, where public schools are required to provide religious courses on Islam (Open Society Institute 2010, 105), but still share the premises of segregated religious education.

References

Bail, Christopher. 2008. The Configuration of Symbolic Boundaries against Immigrants in Europe. *American Sociological Review* 73 (1): 37-59 .

Beck, Sebastian and Thomas Perry. 2007. Migranten-Milieus. Erste Erkenntnisse über Lebenswelten und wohnungsmarktspezifische Präferenzen von Personen mit Migrationshintergrund in Deutschland. *VHW FW* 4: 187-195.

Brettfeld, Kathrin and Peter Wetzels. 2007. *Muslime in Deutschland. Integration, Integrationsbarrieren, Religion und Einstellungen zu Demokratie, Rechtsstaat und politisch-religiös motivierter Gewalt.* Hamburg: Publikationsversand der Bundesregierung.

Cil, Nevim. 2009. Türkische Migranten und der Mauerfall. *Aus Politik und Zeitgeschichte*, 21-22: 40-46.

Freie und Hansestadt Hamburg Behörde für Soziales, Familie, Gesundheit und Verbraucherschutz. 2007. Hamburger Handlungskonzept zur Integration von Zuwanderern: http://www.hamburg.de/contentblob/128792/data/konzept.pdf, accessed 24.07.2009.

---

43 Several recent national and international publications are challenging this perception by locating racist attitudes in all parts and institutions of the German society.

Freie und Hansestadt Hamburg, Behörde für Bildung und Sport. 2007. Hamburg Schulstatistik im Überblick: Schulen, Klassen, Schülerinnen und Schüler in Hamburg.

Fürstenau, Sara and Mechtild Gomolla, eds. 2009. *Migration und schulischer Wandel: Elternbeteiligung*. Wiesbaden: VS Verlag für Sozialwissenschaften.

Gomolla, Mechthild. 2000. Ethnisch-kulturelle Zuschreibungen und Mechanismen institutionalisierter Diskriminierung in der Schule. In *Alltag und Lebenswelten von Migrantenjugendlichen*, eds. Iman Attia and Helga Marburger, 97-112. Frankfurt am Main: IKO-Verlag.

Hefner, Robert W. and Muhammad Qasim Zaman, eds. 2005. *Schooling Islam: The Culture and Politics of Modern Muslim Education*. Princeton: Princeton University Press.

Hieronymus, Andreas. 2000. *Ibo lan, das ist der Kral! Bei uns nur Deutsch. Sus lan! Qualitativ-heuristische Explorationen in urbane Lebenswelten vielsprachiger Jugendlicher in Sankt Pauli und Altona*. Dissertation. University of Hamburg: www.sub.uni-hamburg.de/disse/228.

Hieronymus, Andreas. 2010. At Home in Europe, Muslims in Hamburg, Open Society Institute, New York-London-Budapest.

Human Rights Watch. 2009. "Diskriminerung im Namen der Neutralität – Kopftuchverbote für Lehrkräfte und Beamte in Deutschland". 26 February 2009. http://www.hrw.org/node/80861.

Inalcik, Halil. 2006. *Turkey and Europe in History*. Istanbul: Eren.

Malik, Maleiha. 2005. Equality and Discrimination. In *Muslims in the UK: policies for Engaged Citizen*, ed. by Tufyal Choudhury, 46-99. Budapest: Open Society Institute.

Mühe, Nina and Andreas Hieronymus. 2011. Has Multiculturalism Completely Failed in Germany? In *Interculturalism: Emerging Societal Models for Europe and its Muslims*, ed. by Michael Emerson. (forthcoming 2011).

Open Society Institute. 2010. *At Home in Europe: Muslims in Europe. A report on 11 EU Cities*. New York/ London/ Budapest: Open Society Institute.

Rieger, Martin. 2008. The Religion Monitor. In *Muslim Religiousness in Germany. Overview of Religious Attitudes and Practices*, 8-12. Gütersloh: Bertelsmann Stiftung.

Shah, Saeeda. 2006. Leading Multiethnic Schools: A New Understanding of Muslim Youth Identity. *Educational Management, Administration and Leadership* 34 (2): 215-237.

Michael Kiefer and Irka-Christin Mohr

The Pros and Cons of Islamic Religious Education in German Schools

Introductory Remarks

The debate about bringing Islamic religious education to German schools is far from new. As early as the late 1970s, it had become evident that many Muslims who had come as temporary workers were in Germany to stay. This also meant that they would wish to practise their religion in their new home. Up to then, they had been content with improvised prayer rooms and poorly trained imams, but now, plans to build proper mosques took off, and demands for the introduction of Islamic RE for the growing number of Muslim pupils in Germany's schools were voiced. The federal states' education systems were generally receptive to the idea, and in North Rhine-Westphalia – the state with the largest population of Muslims – plans to launch Islamic RE were developed as early as 1979. However, it quickly became clear that there was no institutional partner on the side of the Islamic community able to fill the role that the Basic Law assigns religious communities in the co-responsibility for religious education in public schools. Clear rules concerning membership were the primary unmet requirement to qualify as a religious community in this sense. So as not to allow the project to lose momentum entirely, several states – including Bavaria, Baden-Wurttemberg and North Rhine-Westphalia – launched more modest model projects to provide a provisional Islamic RE until the matter could be resolved. By now, these projects – many of them quite successful – have taken on a remarkable permanency. After more than a decade, we are no nearer replacing them with 'proper' Islamic RE than we ever were.

The following theses will address the pros and cons of Islamic RE in the light of the empirical results of our research work (Mohr; Kiefer 2009).

1) Thesis: Islamic religious education is a vital instrument to ensure equal status.

Religious Education is a regular curricular subject at public schools in Germany. This status is enshrined in Article 7, Paragraph 3 of the Basic Law, where it is defined explicitly as a regular school subject administered in joint responsibility by the state and the religious communities. Though the exact interpretation differs from state to state, and two of them – Bremen and Berlin – represent exceptions from the rule, regular Protestant and Catholic religious education is provided nationwide from Hanover to Sindelfingen and Cologne, with some cities also offering it to Jewish or Orthodox pupils. Wherever enough children of a given religious community are enrolled at a school, their parents have the legal right to confessional RE. In order to provide this in the constitutionally defined manner, though, the state needs an institutional partner to cooperate with. To date, no Muslim organisation has been able to meet the stringent requirements that German constitutional law makes of a properly constituted religious community. That is the reason why Muslim children in Germany for decades have been reduced to attending Christian RE or a secular substitute lesson except where model projects provided unilateral Islamic religious education provisionally in the absence of a formally constituted religious community to work with. Many school authorities are now offering either a provisional Islamic religious education on a confessional basis or a non-confessional form of Islam Studies in the sole responsibility of the state.

Pros: Observations of this form of Islamic RE show that it is welcomed by Muslim pupils and parents, teachers and non-Muslim pupils as an instrument of creating equality even in its current provisional form. It provides the normality and equal treatment universally desired and provides a place inside German schools for the Islamic tradition. This represents not only formal, legal and institutional recognition, it is felt to be a meaningful personal gesture of acceptance towards neighbours, fellow students and colleagues. The degree to which formal Islamic RE as a school subject is able to create a sense of belonging is illustrated by the statement of parents interviewed in the course of a study on the experimental project in Lower Saxony. They stated that "visiting Islamic religious education (…) can prevent Muslim children from becoming outsiders because Christian children also have Christian religious education" (Uslucan: 56).

Cons: The positive impact outlined above is entirely due to the institutional status accorded Islamic RE within the school system. Neither the actual content or quality of the classes nor the question whether any form of confessional religious education is appropriate for a public school in Germany today are addressed. In practice, the provision of RE in many federal states has changed greatly over the past decades. Affiliation with a religious community is frequently nonexistent or a mere formality, and in many cases it proves impossible to define 'belonging' to a religion with any certainty. Even parents and children who are members of a recognised religious group frequently choose attendance or nonattendance in religious education classes of a specific confession based on factors such as the teacher providing it, the desire to dialogically engage with different world-views, or the choice of close friends rather than automatically opting for 'their' form. The position forwarded in defence of confessional RE that only a solid grounding in one's own tradition allowed an open and respectful attitude towards other beliefs may well need reappraisal in the light of the reality of pluralism in modern life patterns. The "own tradition" is far less likely today to be living faith handed down from parent to child in a family, to be reflected and critically examined in religious education classes. Beliefs are increasingly individual rather than communal and acquired in a process of reflection rather than accepted as part of a traditional lore. Institutionalising an Islamic religious education alongside those of the other established faiths may provide a pragmatic short-term solution to providing equal recognition. The move would place it in the same position as all these forms of confessional RE, though: increasingly on the defensive in the face of mounting questions of legitimacy. It also poses the question which children are to be considered 'Muslim'. Can children with a migration background from a Muslim country automatically be assumed to share a Muslim religious identity? Should the school contribute to socialising them into one? This equally applies to all other forms of confessional RE in public schools, of course, whether it is for children from Catholic, Protestant, Orthodox or Jewish backgrounds. The model in itself is subject to legitimate questioning both in terms of its educational value and its place in today's society. Its roots, after all, lie in the mid-twentieth century, a time when the nascent Federal Republic was still a biconfessional, majority-Christian country with pervasive religious traditions. Today's society is characterised by value pluralism, extensive immigration, and great diversity in life patterns. A model that segregates pupils into confessional groups is a hindrance to dialogue and an obstacle to peaceful coexistence. Despite the legal situation the Basic Law enshrines, shared interreligious learning of the kind that the Hamburg model of *Religion für alle* has exemplified appears to be the more promising approach for an intercultural education that addresses the current reality and represents applicable ethical orientation in an authentic and accessible manner.

2) Thesis: Islamic RE replaces Madrassas.

During the early phase of the debate about Islamic RE in the 1980s and early 1990s, no Muslim voices were part of it. It was mostly the preserve of educators and sociologists, not Muslim migrants and their children. That is why at this stage we often encounter the argument that school-based Islamic religious education could serve to discourage parents from sending their children to an authoritarian, strictly catechetic religious instruction in so-called 'backyard mosques' (*Hinterhofmoscheen*). It was widely feared they would be inducted into a dogmatic form of Islam away from public scrutiny and control, whereas a school-based form of religious education would give them the opportunity to engage with religion openly and in a form compatible with plural society. Finally it was argued that not only would Islam be adapted to modern German society and the institution of the school, the arrangement would also allow the children to concentrate more fully on their educational careers and improve their future chances if they were no longer compelled to divide their time between school and mosque.

Cons: The early expectations were not fulfilled. In many cases, Muslim parents opt for religious instructions in mosques in addition to Islamic RE in school, viewing the two as compatible parts of an Islamic upbringing. The study on Islamic RE in Lower Saxony we referenced above shows that two thirds of parents are giving children religious instruction either at home or in the mosque alongside Islamic RE (Uslucan:30). The reasons quoted are manifold: Many parents are apparently unhappy with the scope and nature of the curricular content offered in school Islamic RE. Eleven percent of the respondents stated that their child had not learned anything new in the lessons, and 42 percent think they learned little (Uslucan: 29). The expectation of 'learning Islam' they express is one of acquiring the knowledge required to practice their religion. They frequently state they want the school to teach more prayer suras and hadith and placing greater emphasis on the distinction between *halal* and *haram*, the permitted and the forbidden (Uslucan: 31). These are the traditional tasks of Islamic education provided in the mosque. As long as the school cannot meet these demands, parents who wish for their children to receive a traditional induction into religious practice and do not feel competent to provide it at home will opt for mosque lessons. However, this idea of dividing tasks between the school and the family and religious community is hardly uncommon in other forms of religious education today. The schools' main focus traditionally was to provide knowledge in order to allow children to grow while the religious communities would provide values and instruction rather than factual content. This was expressed rather pithily – and untranslatably – as "*Die Schulen erziehen durch Bildung, die Religionsgemeinschaften bilden durch Erziehung*" (Heumann: 79). However, as Heumann shows, this traditional conception is becoming increasingly untenable even in Christian religious education. The more communities and families prove unable to fulfill their traditional educational role, the more the school is focused on as a forum of religious experience. Thus, we are seeing a revival of conceptions of religious education like the traditional form of *Evangelische Unterweisung*, which addressed the pupils as members of the Christian community and integrated prayer, song and Biblical stories into the lessons in more recent approaches whose primary aim is to lead pupils into communication with God (Heumann: 79).

Pro: Recent approaches that view religious education in school as a forum of evangelisation and the induction into religious practice must be understood in the context of the widespread loss of Christian social tradition. Children are increasingly less likely to be introduced into their religious practice or to have religious experiences as an integral part of their life. The assumption for Muslim children, on the other hand, has usually been that they are rooted in a living religious tradition and stand in need of a more reflected view which public school RE can provide. Uslucan's study from Lower Saxony shows that alongside a majority for whom this is largely true, about one quarter of Muslim children did not receive any form of religious socialisation: They were never at a mosque and their parents do not pray (Uslucan: 31). Muslim religious educators have been arguing in favour of an inductive, preaching approach for both groups. The former would be able to connect their religious upbringing with what they learn in school while the latter would receive their induction into religious practice in the RE classroom. If this development – paralleled by a strong current in Christian RE – were to become dominant, Islamic religious education in school may yet turn into full replacement for instruction at the mosque.

3) Thesis: Islamic RE fosters an Islamic identity in a largely non-Muslim environment.

The expectations that Islamic RE meets are manifold, but all stakeholders agree that one of its purposes is to facilitate the creation of an identity. The first curriculum for Islamic RE in Germany, developed in North Rhine-Westphalia in the 1980s, stressed the development of a Muslim or Islamic identity in a predominantly non-Muslim environment as a key task of the subject. The exact same expression is found in its successor of 2007 (MfSW-NRW 2007). Most Muslim parents agree with the position. The study by Uslucan records a strong majority stating they were sending their children to Islamic RE "Because we are Muslims ourselves and want our child to get to know his own religion" (Uslucan: 55). "A further relevant motivation was to acquire knowledge about culture and religion in order to counteract alienation, but also the fact that the parents themselves felt they lacked the time or knowledge to provide this to their children" (Uslucan: 55).

Pros: Any confessional religious education serves to establish an identity by its very nature. Its pupils are grouped into a specific community and instructed in its ways, up to age 14 even by parental fiat, regardless of their own personal wishes and sense of affiliation. Teachers have repeatedly reported children in their classes who are unaware that they are Muslims or what it means to be a Muslim. They only learn to assume this identity for themselves in the course of Islamic RE. Among the generation of their parents, the concern that is predominantly voiced is that the children might lose their religion under the influence of a mainly non-Muslim, Christian or secular civilisation. We find expressions such as that they might become *alienated* from the older generation, they might *forget* Islam, and that they had to *preserve* their Islamic identity. This line of argument reveals two key convictions: 1. that the children already possess a religion they are in danger of losing, and 2. that they need a protected space inside a non-Muslim environment to develop, grow and even live their religious identity. This desire among Muslim parents to see their children's identities strengthened is mirrored and modified in the official curricula. The aim of public schools is specifically to foster a controlled form of Islamic identity that is compatible with modern plural society. The addition "in a non-Muslim environment" that has persisted in the curricula of North Rhine-Westphalia from day one certainly owes less to parental fears of alienation than to the desire of the German state to adapt Islam to its plural and democratic society.

Cons: Aside from the fact that any confessional religious education both presupposes and then reproduces the religious identities it purports to foster, the aim of an Islamic identity as it is formulated for Islamic RE can be criticised on its own terms. It begs the question what the children are supposed to actually learn. Are they to become, as the North Rhine-Westphalia curriculum of 1986 puts it, "good" Muslims? A classroom discussion about what being a good Muslim actually entails would require the topic to be debatable openly, without self-censorship and limitations. Or are they to learn to understand the expectations of society and the older generation? In that case, the experimental Islamic RE in Lower Saxony must be regarded as a resounding success, since more than two thirds of the pupils polled state that it has helped them to better understand their parents (Uslucan 2007: 30f).

4) Thesis: Islamic RE helps Muslim children realise that Muslim does not equal Turkish.

Many young people from a Turkish background tend to conflate the ideas of Islam and Turkishness to the point of espousing the view only Turks can be 'real' Muslims. An Islamic RE would place them side by side with pupils from Arab, Iranian or German backgrounds laying equal claim to an Islamic identity, or they might even be instructed by a teacher of German descent, which challenges their traditional mental habits or at least inhibits their ability to lend ready expression to them. A religious education teacher is less suitable for definition as the "Other" and far less easy to dismiss and insult as a "German" than a maths or sports teacher would be.

Pros: Islamic RE demonstrates the universal character of Islam as a religion with adherents of very different national and ethnic backgrounds. Unlike the instruction provided by the – frequently ethnically and linguistically homogenous – mosque communities, school RE includes people from a variety of backgrounds and can thus be effective at creating a degree of intra-religious integration, provided that the curriculum is designed to mirror this plurality. Chauvinist and reductionist interpretations of Islam such as that propagated by part of the Ülkücü-movement (Grey Wolves, see Innenministerium NRW 2004, S.7) can thus be dismissed early.

Cons: The impact of a subject with two lessons a week is being greatly overestimated here. Nationalist interpretations of Islam need to be addressed at the root. The indoctrination that many mosques and Turkish associations provide should certainly be accorded closer attention than is currently the case. Spreading a chauvinist flavour of Islam needs to become unacceptable to Muslims and non-Muslims alike. This also extends to the field of curriculum development, where we see considerable room for improvement in terms of reflecting theological and cultural diversity. So far, the representation of Islam in religious education has largely been limited to its Sunni form, and here mostly to the type practiced in Turkey. This limited focus allowed an intrareligious Muslim dialogue in the classroom only by happy coincidence rather than making it a cornerstone of the educational concept.

5) Thesis: Islamic RE offers children a protected space within which they can develop a reflected approach to their own faith safe from criticism and attempts at indoctrination.

Modern conceptions of religious education regard the school as a neutral forum within which students are at liberty to engage with their faith free from dogmatic limitations and taboos.

Pros: Religious instruction in mosques is not always limited to reading the Qur'an and learning ritual practices. Frequently, teachers there impart a rigid morality and a questionable system of ethical judgement defined by the opposing poles of *haram* and *halal*. Religious education in a school context does not dictate morality and allow pupils to freely and critically engage with the corpus of their tradition(s). Its goal is not to inculcate a religiosity that conforms to traditional precepts, but the ability to reflect religious thought critically and independently.

Cons: A modern Islamic educational paradigm that reflects on its tradition and inculcates individual thought as a value is still in its infancy. As yet, it cannot inform school curricula and practice. Currently, Islamic religious education is very much taught on an ad-hoc basis. Teachers often find themselves inadequately supported by theory in their conflicts with mosque communities and parents. Whenever the goals or methods of Islamic RE meet resistance, children are taken out of the class. A school subject on its own cannot replace the overdue reform of an outdated and authoritarian madrassa culture.

6) Thesis: People are only able to practice tolerance and enter into dialogue once they are securely at home in their own religion.

In the debate on religious education, especially teachers have repeatedly stressed that tolerance towards other religions can only become a sutainable attitude once pupils have found their own religious home.

Pros: To many individuals, the modern globalised world above all appears unbearably confusing and invasive. Its political, cultural and economic developments have become so complex that their workings are incomprehensible to laypeople. Faced with this reality, an increasing number of people are now seeking out their social, religious and cultural roots. This quest for self-localisation can thus be understood as an effort to create certainty in a society characterised by plural values. The role of religion is central to this endeavour. It can offer explanations and clear norms that gives people stability and orientation. That makes it an important element of creating and stabilising individual identities and enabling decisionmaking. These are the foundations of dialogue and tolerance. Only someone who knows his own religion can recognise and define differences and commonalities with others and enter into a reasoned dialogue on them with people of other faiths.

Cons: A homogenous social environment is certainly no good school for constructively engaging with people of different beliefs and faiths. It simply offers no opportunities to learn how. Handling diversity can only be practised among people who hold different beliefs. A firm religious conviction, on the other hand, is no precondition for a constructive dialogue. Successful interreligious and intercultural learning takes place every day, inside and outside the school, with and without confessional religious education. Indeed, it needs to be pointed out that 'firm' convictions can become an obstacle to dialogue. A strong certainty that some beliefs are right, and thus others wrong, can create barriers that hinder or prevent dialogical exchanges.

7) Thesis: Islamic religious education fosters democratic attitudes and prevents extremism.

The impact of the mainly negative image of Islam created in the media on the debate about Islamic RE is painfully obvious. Fears of jihadism and political Islamism are evident at every turn. Politicians at both the federal and state level have come to view Islamic religious education as a tool to counter the radicalisation and political instrumentalisation of the Islamic faith (Kiefer 2008, 83-95).

Pros: In the opinion of teachers, the media habits of many pupils from migration backgrounds are worrying. Through satellite television and the internet, they have ready access to information and entertainment transporting antisemitic and Islamist views. One instance of this are the popular programmes – available in Germany, too – of the Lebanese TV station Al Manar and the Turkish broadcaster TV5 (Kiefer: 83 – 95). Both stations broadcast entertainment programmes in the past years that clearly espouse antisemitic positions. An open debate on these is rare and usually cursory in families and mosques. It was demonstrated in middle school *Islamkunde* lessons in North Rhine-Westphalia that a debate on media coverage of the Israel-Palestine conflict can be a source of productive engagement in the classroom. In it, the multiperspectivity of the conflict can be rendered tangible. Through analysing media content, pupils can come to understand that simple patterns of guilty and innocent parties rarely do justice to the complexity of the real political situation on the ground or the perspective of those directly affected. Beyond this, Islamic RE can also counteract radicalising tendencies by thematising the plurality inside living Islam in all topics it addresses. Thus, pupils can see for themselves that absolutising religious truths can lead to grave conflicts. This insight is an important foundation for developing tolerance.

Cons: Islamic religious education in public schools suffers from being overloaded with every kind of expectation. Not only is it supposed to enhance the linguistic abilities of immigrant children, it must also help to integrate pupils and parents and foster the development of an Islam compatible with a plural society. Surely, a subject of two lessons weekly cannot come anywhere near doing justice to these ambitions. Islamic RE is not and cannot be responsible for fixing every problem in society. It is also clear that a government-sponsored school subject cannot be the appropriate instrument with which to modify the religious beliefs of pupils in any way, whether to make them fit a pluralistic society or not. This must be the preserve of the religious communities themselves. For the state to overstep this boundary would constitute a violation of its constitutional obligation to maintain a religiously neutral stance.

8) Thesis: Islamic RE develops German language skills.

Advocates of integration policies view Islamic religious education as an important linguistic and cultural learning tool especially in primary education. They see it as vital that it teaches pupils to debate Islamic questions in a German-speaking environment.

Pros: Most pupils attending Islamic RE come from migration backgrounds and many have a limited or almost or no command of German. By teaching the subject in German, it will contribute towards improving their language skills. It also becomes a place in which religious texts and concepts, individual experiences and memories and family traditions are translated into that language. This effort allows the children to feel at home in the German language and enter into a meaningful dialogue with their non-Muslim, German-speaking environment.

Cons: Teaching pupils adequate German cannot be considered a primary purpose of religious education. For one thing, it is wrong to think of Islamic RE as a kind of reservation for the children of foreigners in need of help. Actual classes are usually quite heterogeneous. Many of the pupils were born in Germany and have an excellent command of the language. Indeed, in many cases it is the teachers that require a professional development of their language skills before they can begin to undertake the demanding project of rendering Islamic issues into a new linguistic and cultural context.

References

Heumann, Jürgen. 2009. Religionsunterricht darf kein Gebetsunterricht sein! Anmerkungen zum Problem einer Gebetspraxis im evangelischen und islamischen Religionsunterricht. *TheoWeb, Zeitschrift für Religionspädagogik 8*, H. 2.

Mohr, Irka, Kiefer, Michael. 2009. *Islamunterricht, Islamischer Religionsunterricht, Islamkunde – Viele Titel – Ein Fach?*, Bielefeld.

Innenministerium des Landes Nordrhein-Westfalen. 2009. *Internetaktivitäten der Ülkücü-Bewegung – „Graue Wölfe"*, at: http://www.im.nrw.de/sch/doks/vs/gw_ohne.pdf (last accessed 19 December 2010).

Kiefer, Michael. 2008. Islamismusprävention in der Schule – Grundprobleme und thematische Ansatzpunkte in Nordrhein-Westfalen, in: Kiefer et al. (eds.) *Auf dem Weg zum islamischen Religionsunterricht,* Berlin 2008.

MfSW-NRW, Ministerium für Schule und Weiterbildung des Landes NRW: *Islamkunde in deutscher Sprache. Lehrplan für die Sekundarstufe I,* Entwurf, Düsseldorf 2007.

Uslucan, Haci-Halil. 2007. *Wissenschaftliche Begleitung des Schulversuchs „Islamischer Religionsunterricht" in Niedersachsen,* 2. unpublished interim report.

Alison Scott-Baumann

Developing Islamic Higher Education for a Secular University sector: Orientalism in Reverse?

There is a stubborn strand in civil society in Britain that is characterized by pervasive and divisive media coverage of Islam, and by cultural traditions living side by side but never meeting. There is of course harmony and progress too, but also much ignorance and scapegoating around issues of race, ethnicity, terrorism and immigration. Half a million of the approximately 2 million Muslims in Britain are of school-going age. British Muslims are predominantly a young population, and many are interested in faith observance and identity politics (Muslim Council of Britain 2007). Their desire for religious education is very difficult for a secular society to understand, and Muslim religiosity, for political reasons, is seen as suspicious and often related to terrorism. Here I wish to analyse some of the key issues arising from a two-year government funded research project that was funded from a 'counter-terror' budget, in terms of the process, and the implications of the process for the findings. I write as a woman philosopher with particular interest in the work of Paul Ricœur and in the ways in which we can use his work to address social justice issues. I am also interested in the seeming impossibility of enabling those with deeply religious ideas and those with deeply secular ideas to understand and tolerate each other, a problem with which Ricœur grappled for most of his long life. He believed that this struggle also takes place within each of us: he accepted that his faith was based on different premises from his philosophy and that his intellectual life was a 'sort of controlled schizophrenia' (Ricœur 1998). His development of dialectical thought was an attempt to mirror these polarities within us and create the conditions in which self-critical analysis could develop towards some sort of resolution of the tension. Cultural differences also lead to suspicion of the other, and Ricœur addresses the need to understand oneself better *through* understanding the other person.

For me the current location of this schizophrenia is in higher education; I believe there is a clear and pressing need to provide university education that will meet the needs of religious British Muslims. I also believe that such education must include debate that compares Islam with the West, necessitating critique and self-critique of both and by both, and that this East-West pairing also represents an artificial polarisation, which is a tenable position for me as a secular Christian to challenge. However, this case is not yet proven and in fact is being resisted in Britain and elsewhere, often by use of tacit Orientalist approaches. I will therefore also look, albeit briefly, at the British situation within the context of European Islamic developments at universities in continental Europe, using Orientalism and its reverse approaches to clarify the situation.

Despite protests from academics in 2006, one of the major research funding councils, the Economic and Social Research Council (ESRC) is collaborating with the Foreign and Commonwealth Office (FCO) to commission research into 'radicalization.' This has raised concerns about independence of research.[1] There is a risk that such research will distort perceptions of Islam in the same way that the media provide legitimation of the 'othering' that makes Islam symbolize everything that defines fear (Insted 2007). Ricœur however analyses ideology as a force that refuses to be accountable, and simply *is*: "At its three levels – distortion, legitimation, symbolization – ideology has one fundamental function: to pattern, to consolidate, to provide order to the course of action" (Ricœur 1991, 318).

I will discuss herein, in brief, issues that arise in our new research, which works with the concerns of the British Muslim communities and is, we believe, as independent as is possible. It demonstrates that the theological training of imāms is often of a good standard and yet such training may not take sufficient account of the needs within Muslim communities to understand and prepare their community for inevitable co-existence with the secular world.[2] From our research we found that the perception among many ʿulamāʾ and ʿālimahs, Muslim women, the young and the imāms/mujtahids in our interview sample, is that imāms/mujtahids, ʿulamāʾ and ʿālimahs could play a more significant role in their community, with the right training in pastoral matters and the right support from their government and their communities. I will begin by setting the context in which the research process took place.

Imāms/mujtahids[3] are seen as key figures in Muslim communities, however, currently there is great suspicion of the role of the imām outside those communities (Birt 2006). Various factors probably contribute to this suspicion; the clothes they wear are perceived by many as strange, the habit of some mosques to import their imām/mujtahid from abroad (who then preaches in the mother tongue of the majority of the congregation), the evidence provided by undercover filming in which imāms rail against the corrupt West and, of course, the fear of 'radicalization' (Geaves 2008). As part of their counter-terror agenda, several attempts have been made by the British government to resolve what they see as related problems within Muslim communities: imāms out of step with secular life, imāms capable of criticising British foreign policy, and imāms encouraging profound religiosity. It can be argued that these are attitudes that deserve to be considered, i.e. secular life may not be the only or even the best way to live, and foreign policy may need to be debated; yet this is not encouraged. The situation has been exacerbated by, and has in turn led to various 'othering' devices, whereby the mainstream British culture rejects the culture of the alien, frightening 'other.' We can define 'mainstream British culture' as a recognisable essence of Britishness,

---

1 http://www.timeshighereducation.co.uk/story.asp?storycode=206121; http://www.globaluncertainties.org.uk

2 This paper represents my own views, which may not be those of my co-workers. Research commissioned by Department for Communities and Local Governments, and launched by DCLG October 6, 2010. Research undertaken by Dr Mohamed Mukadum, Dr Alison Scott-Baumann und Dr. Sariay Contractor; http://www.communities.gov.uk/publications/communities/trainingmuslimleaderspractice.

3 Imām and mujtahid are the names often used by the Sunnī and Shīʿa communities respectively to identify their priest. In Britain, Sunnī, and particularly Sunnī Deobandi groups are the most noticeable for their education-related activities e.g. establishment of seminaries, called darul ulums for teaching theology and religious law, courses called darse nizami.

by this device of identifying the alien in our midst, the enemy within. This tension has both increased partnership between certain Muslim groups and the government, and also led to friction between government policing agencies and the Muslim communities.

In addition to the government policies on social cohesion, policies were developed to prevent violent extremism and terrorism, marked in 2003 by the Contest plan and renewed in 2009 with Contest 2.[4] The London bombings of July 7, 2005, led to the establishment of a Muslim working party called *Working Together to Prevent Extremism*. In 2006, Bill Rammell, Minister for Higher Education at DfES, setup a working party to look at *Islam in Higher Education.* Dr Siddiqui conducted the research and made it very clear that he would be prepared to investigate two areas; the teaching of Islam in universities, and the pastoral support provided on campus. His recommendations include the need to update the teaching of Islam, make it more relevant to the diversity within British Islam, and to ensure that Islamic experts with theological as well as secular understanding, are responsible for designing curricula and teaching them in universities. He also recommended the appointment of Muslim chaplains. His report, *Islam in Higher Education*, was used as a trigger for setting up working parties to look at such issues, and there is great potential for progress. Indeed continental European analysts of the Islamic scene see Britain as reasonably far advanced (Rudolph, Lüddekens and Uehlinger 2009, 18):

> Great Britain offers a relatively wide range of opportunities for imams, although as yet little is known about how well the training of candidates prepares them for the practical demands of everyday life. The transition from a specialist training to one that is more generally applicable seems to have been attempted only sporadically. This is happening in those (private) institutions that are relatively open to the world, and they seek validation through state funded universities as well as collaborating with adult education organisations such as NIACE for places. By this means there are job opportunities in schools, hospitals and prisons, although this happens less in the Muslims' own (more conservative) Mosque communities.[5]

Yet, I believe that progress is hampered by the politicized conflict between counter-terrorist ideologies and social cohesion ideas about citizenship and social justice, and this shows itself in unnecessary bureaucratic demands about quality assurance (Scott-Baumann 2003a). It is difficult to demonstrate institutional Islamophobia, even when one knows that bureaucratic barriers are being raised unnecessarily to obstruct progress.

---

4 http://www.guardian.co.uk/politics/2009/feb/17/counterterrorism-strategy-Muslims; http://www.security.homeoffice.gov.uk/counter-terrorism-strategy

5 author translation

Precogs and orientalism in reverse

Counter-terrorist policies are dominant in the current official attitudes, even when those attitudes are apparently based upon the desire for social justice and equity within the UK for all communities. In such policies, it is possible to detect a desire by the secular government to 'educate' Muslim communities, who are perceived to be out of step with the majority culture because they are 'too' religious and in danger of terrorist activity. As I discuss in a recent paper about the ḥijāb, this form of policing resembles that in the film *Minority Report*, as identified by Toscano (Scott-Baumann 2011). In the film, three humans (the three *Precogs*) are able to use great perceptive powers of foresight ('precognition') to detect the intention to carry out a crime, intentions still deep in the unconscious of the unsuspecting and unsuspected perpetrator. The *Precogs'* handlers can alert the police to this pre-criminal activity and thereby avert disasters. Similarly I believe there is a desire on the part of those who form the majority in Britain to detect *pre-terrorist* activity in the British Muslim community: girls in the ḥijāb and men in the traditional loose trousers and long tunic are perceived, both consciously, and at some deeply inaccessible pre-conscious level, as demonstrating their sympathy for terrorists, because the clothes they wear seem to constitute pre-terrorist activity. If we think like the *Precogs*, we can thereby give ourselves permission to be suspicious. If we believe that we know more than most people do (which is true of the *Precogs* in their science fiction world) we can decide to attribute these acts *potentially* to all Muslims. Using this line of thinking, we can argue that Muslim clothing reflects the behaviour of those who hold beliefs that are alien to 'the West.' The exotic clothing, devotional behaviour and the mindset they can evoke, can be understood within the context of Edward Said's *Orientalism*.

Edward Said's 1978 book *Orientalism* analyses the tendency among western observers to see the exotic (literally and metaphorically) in the Muslim world, and to perceive it as both weak and also so different, so as to be incommensurate with one's own culture. Despite the weaknesses that arise when one overstates one's case, Said's thesis leads us to an interesting discussion of the position that 'only *we* can understand *us*'. While he denies that it is tenable to argue that only *we* can understand *us*, it clearly plays a part in his argument, and must be taken seriously to a certain extent. How does Orientalism develop into Orientalism in reverse? Gilbert Achcar takes the idea of 'only us' being able to understand ourselves, applies it to Orientalism and critically analyses what he calls its reversal: the idea that Islamism is the only possible agent of modernization, and that the religion of Islam is the essential language and culture of Muslim peoples. I believe that this is attributed to Muslim communities and used to create wilful distortion by using extreme examples. It is also possible that Muslim communities apply the same way of thinking to those of other cultures and faiths, but that is not my concern in this paper. Exaggerated representations of Muslims are rooted in the belief that Muslims seek solutions that are alien to 'us'. Reverse Orientalism forms part of the British dilemma, because those who are not Muslims are encouraged to pay attention only to those aspects of UK Muslim life to which they can attribute the embodiment of extreme versions of Islam, such as honour killings and terrorist acts. What needs to be acknowledged is that these extreme acts are not characteristic of British Islam and are rejected by most Muslims. Moreover, British foreign policy is a source of much concern and anger within Muslim communities worldwide.

Muslim faith leader training research

Against the backdrop of controversial foreign policy and the fear of domestic terrorism, the British government has initiated a range of research projects with British Muslims (e.g. Pennant 2005, Lawrence and Heath 2008, Holden 2009). In spite of the atmosphere of suspicion, these are good projects that help to dispel the suspicion. Some Muslim community leaders have asked the government for assistance in the important area of imām/mujtahid training, which they believe will make a significant and sustainable difference in creating a more tolerant, safe and just society. The government responded by calling for a review:

> Britain's Muslims – especially second generation Muslims – tell us that the training of Muslim faith leaders, in addition to English language requirements, is critical and the Secretary for Communities will be announcing an independent review to examine with communities how to build the capacity of Islamic seminaries, learning from other faith communities as well as experience overseas. [6]

As a result I was invited to co-chair a review on imām/mujtahid training. My co-chair (Dr Mukadam) and I, proposed a title that did not include the word 'imām': we suggested 'Muslim faith leader training', since this would include men and women scholars, the ʿulamāʾ and ʿālimahs, as well as the imām/mujtahid who leads prayers in the mosque.[7] We worked with British Muslim communities and other stakeholders in schools, as well as in further and higher education to carry out independent academic research on the following objectives:

Objectives

a) To carry out a survey of training of Muslim religious leaders to consider the current and future demands/challenges of the various sections within the Muslim communities living in the UK, including the youth and women.
b) To understand the different models employed by various institutions for training religious leaders, identify elements of best practice and disseminate them.

---

6 The Hansard, 14th November 2007

7 In Shīʿa traditions, religious scholars and teachers study the hauza and may be called mujtahids, ʿulamāʾ and muballighīn, with the terms imām and marja reserved for very expert scholars; in Sunnī traditions, ʿulamāʾ and ʿālimahs are scholars who have successfully completed the five–seven year theological training known usually as darse nizami.

c) To explore the possibilities of collaborative initiatives so that trainees and/or graduates could pursue further and higher education qualifications leading to better employment prospects.

For this research, we worked with the British Muslim community to record current practices and consider new ways forward into education and higher education for Muslims including youth, girls and women. Crucial to this work was a mapping of existing good practice in collaborations between mainstream higher education i.e. universities, and further education institutions and seminaries, and analysis of alternative models both here and abroad. Clear evidence now exists that significant groups within the Muslim community understand how important it is to review Muslim faith leader training. As an integral part of our research we developed the dialogue about best practice and about changing processes for the better, and we endeavoured to make our recommendations acceptable to key decision makers in Britain's Muslim communities, as well as, controversially for some groups, giving a voice to the young and to women. The research demonstrates how strongly the British Muslim communities develop their citizenship programmes – and it also provides many examples of how different the religious viewpoint is from the secularist one. As Ricœur pointed out, this can create tensions *within* an individual. I will return to this in the fifth and final section, as it forms a core component in the Orientalist approach, and provides a practical example of Ricœur's assertion that religious faith is not compatible with philosophy and secular approaches.

There is at present little research on the UK seminaries (Gilliat-Ray 2005, 2006). Access to these seminaries for research purposes has been difficult, but we were able to visit 27 seminaries and colleges, most of which are Sunnī-Deobandi. Most of the Islamic scholars complete their religious training at the school or seminary at which they enrol for their secondary education. These *dārul ʿulūms* are registered with the government and are inspected regularly by Her Majesty's Inspectorate of Schools. The reports about the inspectorate's visits are posted on the Internet and are publicly available, yet many people seem unaware of this and an image of secrecy persists. Some seminaries offer conservative models of Islam and formal types of pedagogy. Some are developing more contemporary forms of teaching and learning, and Islamic experiences that can provide contextualisation for better understanding of the secular community. Models of training in other religious groups, and in Muslim communities abroad provided us with paradigms for future developments. This comparative study of various models of imām/mujtahid training, facilitated recommendations about a way forward to improve community understanding and social cohesion.

Methodology

A blended model of qualitative research methods was employed, building on the review team's research expertise and the specialist faith advice from the advisory group that comprises Islamic experts from each major denomination. The research team comprised the two co-chairs, a research assistant, Dr. Sariya Contractor, and a team of experienced investigators who were known to the institutions they visited. An initial survey by questionnaire (of a representative large sample of institutions) was developed with the help of an advisory board, representing different groups within Islam and different faiths. The data collected from the questionnaires provided a baseline for subsequent refinement of findings, so that a sample group of institutions could be further researched. Frequent consultation was an integral part of the five-phase structure, to facilitate transmission of research findings among groups within those Muslim communities who were willing to engage. We hope this will lead to acceptance of our interpretations and engagement with critical self-reflection. A range of means, including desk research, targeted interviews from other religious groups, and also valuable material from reliable international sources was used to compare models from other countries and faiths.

The process of such work, like other projects, is affected by the political and Orientalist agenda described above, making it difficult to gain trust. The Starkey Report (2010) is a cross party response to the government's policy called 'Preventing Violent Extremism' and reports that the policy is counterproductive and alienates the communities with which the government wished to work[8].The political pressure related to the need to justify foreign policies has led to extreme forms of policing, apparently justified by a growth in the terror agenda and facilitated by a steady erosion of civil liberties for all members of the UK population, although there seems to be no doubt that the Muslim population is the primary targeted group. There are several problems with this approach, not least of which is that this research review, like all the civil society projects of the Department for Communities and Local Government (DCLG) is funded by money from the counter-terrorist fund, 'Preventing Violent Extremism.' In fact the DCLG does support a great deal of excellent community work, much of which is not tainted by being funded under the rubric of anti-terror. Nevertheless, it remains true that the political agenda makes it appear as if Muslim communities are the ones who should be targeted, when in fact I would rate the far right racist groups as the real threat to civic unity.

Some findings in brief

What does an imām/mujtahid do?

An imām/mujtahid is usually seen as the figure in whom the mosque committee has vested their trust and responsibility. He leads prayers, delivers sermons and officiates at ceremonies such as marriages and funerals, while also making rulings about Islamic law. For historic reasons related to Britain's imperial past, the majority of religious scholars in Britain are of the Deobandi Sunnī tradition, from India and Pakistan. In fact, while the number of Barelwi Sunnīs in Britain is at least as great, the Deobandi groups are however well organised in terms of estab-

8 http://www.publications.parliament.uk/pa/cm200910/cmselect/cmcomloc/65/65.pdf

lishing Muslim seminaries. Their names are derived from the names of the places in India, where the founding institutions were started. Barelwis are often considered to be more Sūfī-oriented and Deobandis to be more traditionalist, but these distinctions are also contested. The Shīʿa Muslim groups are fewer in number, yet they have the only two university validated courses for mujtahid training in Britain, at Islamic College in London (with Middlesex University) and the Worldwide Khoja Shīʿa Ithna-Asheri Community (with the University of Winchester). An ʿālim (female ʿālimah) is a religious scholar who, in the Sunnī tradition, was trained in the *dars-e-Nizami* syllabus which was developed in the middle of the eighteenth century by Mulla Nizāmuddīn Sahalwi towards the end of the Moghul Empire in India. This syllabus covered civil service training in law and all issues regarding family matters including inheritance, and was used for about a hundred years to administer the affairs of the East India Company according to *ḥanafī* law (for Sunnīs, the most frequently used legal system). The tradition has persisted, although originally these were civil servants who were responsible for the spiritual needs of those in their care, to the extent that this was achieved through correct devotional habits and authentic interpretation of the laws. In Britain, the students of the modern version of these courses attend boarding school–type seminaries and also study National Curriculum subjects in a range of state controlled subjects (GCSE and Advanced level subjects), thereby balancing both the secular and the religious curricula, although they do not necessarily balance the secular and religious worlds. Those students who are qualified as ʿulamāʾ when they leave the seminary, are unlikely to become imām/mujtahids for two main reasons; one is that there are few imām/mujtahid posts attached to mosques available, the other is that the majority never want to become imām/mujtahids, but wish to study Islam in order to be better Muslims and citizens. They do wish to contribute actively to their communities and to explain Islam to others, so they perceive a need for acknowledgement of their expertise and opportunities for skills training. Moreover, and perhaps surprisingly, it is not necessarily considered essential for an imām/mujtahid to have studied the full ʿālim course.

Career priorities identified by a sample of Muslim faith leaders

- Professionalization of the imām/mujtahid post, including proper pay.
- Access to training after their *dars-e Nizami* studies.
- Union possibilities.
- Acknowledgement of their pastoral contribution .
- Option of degree qualifications.
- Opportunities for already trained ʿulamāʾ and ʿālimas to become active in the community, even though they are not the imām/mujtahid attached to the mosque.

Learning priorities identified by the Muslim community

- Progression is a major issue: exploration of the student life cycle has already shown that Muslim school children need encouragement, role models and the possibility of inclusion without suspicion into higher education.
- We need to build bridges with alternative educational groups such as *madrassahs*[9], through accreditation of prior learning, top-up modules and foundation courses. This will facilitate full participation in British society of young adults who study for many years in *madrassahs* and *dārul ʿulūms* and whose qualifications, being theological, are not recognised when they wish to play an active role in British culture and train to be a teacher, for example.
- Creating capacity for postgraduate training e.g. in teaching, social work.
- Validation and Quality Assurance (QA) issues in innovative UK work with private community colleges.

Teaching priorities identified by educators at school and university level

- Capacity building of academic courses; to embed Muslim projects in mainstream curriculum planning.
- Support academic futures for Muslim academics e.g. by incorporating their unique contribution to Islamic Studies into existing courses, creating momentum instead of reliance on few individuals.
- Create opportunities for developing modular courses in Islam e.g. by integrating small courses that can easily be accessed by, for example, a student of law, medicine or social work, to enhance their professional practice in a multicultural world.
- Better academic support for Muslims and others is necessary; networking will help to reduce the 'Lone Ranger' effect, to help academics and administrators working in isolation on important social cohesion projects

Research priorities identified by British academics, mostly Muslim

During work I did in 2007 with HEFCE (Higher Education Funding Council for England) it was clear from the academic community that 'branding' is an issue: prestigious major research centres may dominate the field, and research should create a better balance depending on areas of expertise:

- We must differentiate between primary and applied research.
- Teaching and Learning need developing in religious Islamic Studies.
- Research is needed to establish who is teaching which aspects of Islamic Studies in Britain.
- Comprehensive analysis of the pedagogy of Islamic Studies is necessary.

---

9 In Britain, *madrassahs* are usually classes run for children after school, by local mosques.

- It is vital to bring together classical and modern exegesis e.g. to explore Islamic law.
- Above all, research can facilitate engagement of the academic community.

In addition, as mentioned above, there is a clear and present tendency within certain sections of the research funding system to define Muslims as part of a terror problem. This exaggerates the sense of Orientalism in reverse, implying that Muslims choose very different solutions to their problems than other people do.

Setting Britain within the EU Islamic context

The Siddiqui Report (2007) was commissioned by the British government. Dr Siddiqui advocated more clarity about what constituted Islamic Studies, and demonstrated clearly that it is often not taught by Muslim scholars, instead frequently by secular thinkers who are looking in at Islam from the outside. He recommended that secular and religious discourse should be brought together, which would mean providing Islamic theology in university courses. The government's response to the *Siddiqui Report* was to designate £1 million to the analysis of Islamic Studies, and to ask the Higher Education Funding Council for England (HEFCE) to study the matter. HEFCE's report, *International Approaches to Islamic Studies in Higher Education* 2008, was commissioned as a direct result of the Siddiqui Report, and covers Islamic Studies teaching in mainstream universities comprehensively. Islamic Studies, (HEFCE 2008, 7) is loosely described as covering Religious Studies, Middle Eastern Studies, languages, and other humanities and social science areas, mostly from the secularist approach that is often called Orientalist. Siddiqui demonstrated that Islamic Studies usually attracts university students who are not Muslim, and if they are Muslim, they are not seeking to become imāms/mujtahids or ʿulamāʾ. This is a different 'client base' from that of the *dārul ʿulūms* . In that sense the HEFCE report does not take further the debate initiated in *The Siddiqui Report*. Despite the inability of Islamic Studies to attract Muslim faith leaders, it is clear that Islamic Studies are seen in some quarters as a way of influencing British Muslim imāms/mujtahids and giving them a better understanding of secular British culture, and it is considered by some government agencies that this will reduce the risk of violent extremism (HEFCE 2008, 13-17). It seems, however, unlikely that an imām/mujtahid would want to study Islamic Studies, as it represents a syllabus that may be rich and varied, but lacks any religious content. As Siddiqui found:

> Current courses available at English universities with a more 'secular' focus were seen as worthwhile and having intrinsic value. However, they were not seen as being comparable as sources of learning about Islam to being taught by Muslim scholars of Islamic theology or to learning Islam at a well known Muslim centre of learning such as Al Azhar in Egypt (Siddiqui 2007, 89).

This respect for the Al Azhar institution exemplifies the importance of theological authenticity: the perceived authenticity of Al Azhar comes from its history and its experienced staff of theologians. A place such as Al Azhar, also has the capacity to provide intensive Arabic language teaching (both classical and modern) and various different approaches are followed to ensure authenticity. Firstly, British Barelwi ʿulamāʾ often go to Egypt to study at Al Azhar. Secondly, the Islamic College in London has various courses validated by Middlesex University and works with the university in Qom, Iran, to provide authentic scholarship and Arabic for its doctoral students who are studying for their theological Shīʿa qualifications.[10] Middlesex does not validate the mujtahid training, but they validate the courses that run parallel, so students have degrees and masters qualifications before they proceed to their doctoral theological studies. Thirdly, the Khoja Shīʿa Ithna-Asheri Muslim Community has recently achieved precisely that validation of the theological training. With the blessings of Ayatollah Sistānī and the support of the Bishop of Winchester, this Shīʿa group has achieved validation with the University of Winchester for a Masters level course for *muballighīn* (religious scholar as educator) to be based at the university in Damascus, and taught by experienced scholars of Damascus and also from within the British university system. Teaching will be in both Arabic and English. Thus they have achieved both religious authenticity and educational validation of qualifications (and the first cohort finishes in 2011). Britain is also home to a range of fast growing and reasonably well-established Muslim chaplaincy courses.[11] These are at diploma or certificate level, i.e. a lower academic level than the aforementioned validated programmes, yet the chaplaincy courses are providing valuable training in prison, hospital and university work. The Muslim chaplaincy course run by Dr Siddiqui at Markfield provides training for those who are already working as chaplains and for those with some community experience who wish to enter the field of chaplaincy.[12] This type of course offers training in pastoral care and relies upon an approach that resembles that of the father of counselling, Carl Rogers, who believed that 'active listening' enables those with problems to clarify difficult situations – to which they often know the solution, but need time, space and encouragement to articulate their solutions for themselves. This approach is very different from the setting down of limits, rules and legal interpretations that may be offered by a Muslim faith leader.

A Sample of European solutions

In Continental Europe, as in Britain, there is a wide range of different forms of faith teaching offered to Muslim children and adults: "This type of education … is controversial, because of the general opinion that extremist and fundamentalist

10 The Islamic College provides courses that are not exclusively Shīʿa in interpretation of Islam at degree levels, and become more explicitly Shīʿa at masters level and above.

11 Chaplains do not necessarily have the theological authenticity as they may be untrained, but they then receive training in counselling, tolerance and guidance for Muslims and others in hospitals, prisons and universities.

12 http://www.mihe.org.uk

views are taught and propagated exactly through some of these institutions" (Josza in Jackson et al 2007, 69). Yet there is also a growing acceptance that religion is re-entering the secular arena with renewed vigour, and that dialogue is vital if we are all to live together peacefully. Weisse points out that this has been reflected in the great European thinkers: not only in Ricœur from a strong faith base, but even Jürgen Habermas has come to see the possibilities of religion for developing mutual understanding (Weisse in Jackson et al, 2007, 9, regarding Habermas 2005). In order to establish whether there is such a major shift by secular societies towards discussion with Muslims in Europe, I first looked at France, the closest neighbour of Britain across the Channel.

The French government does not employ the rhetoric of the 'war on terror,' or invest in the 'counter-terror and radicalization agenda' as the British do.[13] Nor do the French use the term 'community' as the British do: they think in terms of secularism and apply urban policies to the Muslims.[14] It is the French commitment to '*laïcité*' that is the driving force behind the policy on Muslims in France. *Laïcité* is the definitive separation of church and state that came out of the French Revolution and underpins policy and legislation. The Sorbonne, and other sections of the University of Paris, when approached about developing imām/mujtahid training, refused on the grounds that it would compromise their '*laïque*' principles.[15] *Catholaïcité*, the term coined by Edgar Morin, refers to the belief that France is in fact still rooted in Roman Catholicism, and not lay and neutral. It is thus interesting that the *Institut Catholique* of Paris took up the challenge of imām/mujtahid training and developed a university diploma that is called *Interculturality, Secularism and Religions* and is open to all, although in practice it is attended by Muslims, mostly from outside France. Under the project management of Pierre Bobineau, the diploma course is based upon completely secular assumptions and taught by ten secular thinkers, looking at French law and culture. Four strands are covered: general culture, legal frameworks, religious culture with secularism and intercultural issues. The diploma course was set up in 2008 and two more are planned in Lille and Aix-en–Provence.

In Germany there is a considerable amount of activity, of which I give some examples here: Currently, the Turkish government sends imāms from Turkey, who stay for 2-4 years; it is felt that they may not integrate with German society, because they do not know the language and they do not understand the secular culture. This is not very helpful for German Muslims, yet the Turkish imāms are seen as being authentically Islamic, with well established theological backgrounds. The adult education centre in Offenbach, Hesse, is offering integration classes for imāms. The University of Osnabruck is providing a three-year degree

13 Meeting with Joseph Maïla, 19/10/09 Chef du pôle Religions, Ministère des Affaires Étrangères et Européennes, and David Behar, Pôle Religions

14 Meeting with Bernard Godard, 22/10/09 Bureau Centrale des Cultes, Ministère de L'Intérieur, Direction des Libertés Publiques

15 Meeting with Pierre Bobineau, 23/10/09 Directeur du Diplôme Universitaire, Interculturalité, Laïcité et Religions, Institut Catholique de Paris. I will use the word secular in place of *laïque*, although secular means non-religious, whereas *laïque* means assertively anti-religious. The British term 'lay' does not really have the force of the French *laïque*.

for imāms and hopes to develop a Masters degree. The Goethe Institute has developed a new course called 'Imāms for Integration' in collaboration with The Education Office for Migration and Refugees, and the German Association of Turkish Muslim Congregations (DITIB). This course includes 500 hours of German language instruction and twelve days of lessons on intercultural topics. In a bid to educate German-born Muslims to become imāms, there is a new imām/mujtahid school in Berlin, Karlshorst and the German government is planning imām/mujtahid training that will comprise a one year course (civic education, German language and dialogue with Christian churches) and a two year degree.

In July 2009, Zurich University published their final report on *Imām training and Islamic Religious pedagogy in Switzerland?* This forms part of NFP58, a major research programme on *Religious Communities, State and Society.*[16] The report was based on a series of interviews with Swiss Muslims and concludes that there is a strong majority voice in favour of imām/mujtahid training and a belief that consensus about the content of this training can be reached among the different groups of Muslims in Switzerland. The researchers (Professors Rudolph, Lüddekens and Uehlinger) also draw various conclusions from their overview of the European scene. Where the state takes the initiative and works closely with universities, they note that it is possible to put in place some form of secular imām/mujtahid training. Yet, to date, they point out that this training does not integrate the Islamic aspects with the secular aspects, and they cite the examples of Amsterdam, Leiden and Paris in this regard. (Rudolph, Lüddekens & Uehlinger 2009, 16). They believe that two features are decisive for success; the political will and being prepared to make the possible happen (Rudolph et al 2009, 18).

Vrije Universiteit in Amsterdam is offering courses in which the students develop their understanding of Islam as a religion, not as a cultural phenomenon and also learn about the particular skills they need to support the people in their charge when they graduate to responsible positions in their community:

> It also aims to soften the (unnecessary) boundaries between Islam/Muslims and the surrounding society; it is a matter of translation not only of the words but of the approach to the religious (Johansen 2006, 21).[17]

VU endeavours to show respect for Islam by offering theological training, although not as well as the Muslim students would wish: they told Schepelern Johansen that they wanted more theologically sound input.[18]

The European pattern

A pattern emerges from surveying a sample of European provisions: generally speaking European universities do not usually have Muslim academics on their staff and they do not offer theological study by Muslims for Muslims as part of

16 *Imam-Ausbildung und Islamische Religionspädagogik in der Schweiz?* In NFP58 Religionsgemeinschaften, Staat und Gesellschaft. mm_09jul21_schlussbericht_d.pdf http://www.zrwp.ch/fileadmin/user_upload/PDF/Imame_Schlussbericht_deutsch.PDF

17 Islam at the European Universities Report 11, Schepelern Johansen, 2006, p. 21

18 Ibid p. 23

their syllabus. European universities are beginning to offer courses for imām/mujtahid training, which are usually short courses in the history, customs and laws of the host culture, in the belief that this will enable the imām/mujtahids to support Muslims in that country.

Our research shows that several European countries are developing models that provide 'secular' education with some Islamic components that, in terms of quality and academic rigour, often fall short of the religious training that young Muslims seek. Nor do they necessarily facilitate the understanding of Western ways of thinking that is necessary for an imām/mujtahid (Johansen, 2006). I believe that the following issues arise in European (including British) models of Islamic Studies in universities:

- Perceived conflict between 'academic freedom' and 'faith based' thinking.
- Shortage of good Muslim scholars in mainstream universities to deliver Islamic Studies courses.
- Disagreement among Muslim groups about authenticity of teaching material.
- Tendency to provide exclusively secular materials with no room for discussion and comparison between faith and secular beliefs.

On the other hand there is also a trend towards replicating the perceived conditions of devotional priestly training that originates in the Indian subcontinent; we see this strongly established in Britain among some Sunnī groups, and also in Karlshorst in Berlin, where the new seminary discussed above has recently opened along similar lines. Much analysis that emerges from the European academy on both these developments (enhanced secular curricula and enhanced theological curricula) is, I believe, still profoundly Orientalist; it focuses on Islam as the different phenomenon, with the tacit assumption that 'the West' is the benchmark, and the Muslims are the strange others who, moreover, want to stay the way they are. Critique of Western culture is thereby safely 'off-limits' because 'we' are not like 'them'. Our research suggests that the UK can improve upon current models by *integrating* both high quality religious training (delivered by Muslim Islamic experts) and useful practical skills for daily life in the UK. This necessitates open and fair discussion of the differences between secular cultures and religious approaches. Such an approach would be one means of ensuring that the future leadership of Muslim groups and their university tutors will be more 'aware of' and 'comfortable with' theological thinking and how it differs from daily British society. For this to be workable, British society needs to be willing and able to give a clear account of itself, of what constitutes Britishness and of how different groups can live together peacefully. Moreover, it is clear that some Muslim religious leaders wish to become university tutors.

Even if this were to become accepted as a way forward, there is still the problem that Ricœur identified: how can those with deep religious convictions relate to those who are less committed? Perhaps the first step is to acknowledge the boundaries that demarcate certain ways of thinking from others. The next step is to establish courses that provide teaching on different approaches to life. The third step is to establish courses that combine theological teaching with exercises in practical life skills.

The British solution: Foundation degrees

Another possible approach is to use the foundation degree, a relatively new British workplace-based degree. We believe that the foundation degree[19] has the potential to facilitate a fusion between theology and life skills such as counselling. Partnerships between employers and universities are vital to the development and running of a foundation degree. A foundation degree must be validated and awarded by an institution with degree-awarding powers. Employers must be fully involved in order to have full impact on design, delivery and learning outcomes and also need to co-fund the degrees. In this context, there may be a variety of employers; the mosque committee is one that springs to mind, yet there are also potential employers, who are keen to work with the Muslim community e.g. local businesses.

Islamic Science training can be mapped onto the UK University academic structure and therefore should be considered for validation as a degree.[20] Foundation degrees can be considered as one appropriate vehicle, and this is already being achieved for Muslim social work (Chester) and training of Christian clergy (Gloucestershire). Counselling, pastoral care and interpersonal skills have been identified by Muslims in our research as necessary skills, and can be incorporated into the curriculum for the Islamic Sciences that is taught for ʿālim/ʿālimah training, using a broadly modular structure and practical work placements as with the foundation degree. The mosque, the *dārul ʿulūm* and especially the broader British workplace can provide work placements for trainee imām/mujtahids and ʿulamāʾ and ʿālimahs. It is possible to add a year of study to the foundation degree and thereby gain an honours degree, and clearly careers guidance must be provided to facilitate decision-making. Throughout the foundation degree, and particularly in the final, honours year, there will be the opportunity to focus on future pathways into teaching, chaplaincy, imām/mujtahid work and social work, for example. Cultural differences must also be addressed, during work placements.

Learning in the workplace will form an integral part of the foundation degree: undertaking work placements and internships in specialist community settings to learn about imām/mujtahid work and the law: British, European and Sharīʿa, child psychology, counselling, pastoral care, women and children, teaching, social work etc. Generalist modules for all students will be taken at a local institution of Further Education or Higher Education and will typically take place for seven hours a week. They will include: Comparative studies of Law: British, European and Sharīʿa, Civic structures in Britain, Explaining my faith, Understanding other faiths, Working in the Muslim community, Working in the wider community, Faith and Society: Working Together and Reflective Practice.

---

19 http://www.fdf.ac.uk/

20 Validation gives legitimacy to a course of study as a recognized qualification; in this case at degree level. University of Gloucestershire validation approval was given to Ebrahim Community College 2007, plans which then floundered for financial reasons. University of Winchester has validated Masters level muballighīn education.

Collaborative partnerships between Muslim colleges and state funded universities

While several universities already have appropriate and active expertise, only three partnerships exist between universities (Gloucestershire, Middlesex and Winchester) and those offering Muslim faith leader training courses (Markfield, Islamic College and Khoja Shīʿa Ithna-Asheri Muslim Community respectively). Two of these have university accreditation, as discussed above. The ʿālim/ʿālima, *dars-e Nizami* and Islamic Sciences training courses are NOT validated by UK institutions, yet there is a palpable desire for professionalization of the Muslim faith leader's role. Given the Orientalism in reverse, which assumes that secular study can be added on to theological learning without engaging with it directly, it is necessary to create an organisation that will oversee the new developments. As suggested by the British Prime Minister in 2007, an academic Centre of Excellence must be setup with regional hubs. This will be staffed by scholars from a range of backgrounds within Islam and from the secular tradition too, in order to facilitate understanding and conduct high level research and to educate imām/mujtahids, and community leaders such as ʿulamāʾ and ʿālimahs. Emphasis will be given to supporting Muslim institutions in working with universities to obtain validation. It is very important to develop capacity with the higher education sector for supporting Muslim institutions in satisfying United Kingdom Border Agency requirements for compulsory licensing of Muslim institutions, which depends on accreditation, which in turn depends on validation [21]

Existing excellence as identified by this report will be consolidated and enhanced. As part of its remit, the centre will work with clusters of interested Muslim religious groups to explore collaborative partnerships and a curriculum for the development of multi-purpose training that can lead to a range of professional routes; imām/mujtahid, social worker, counsellor, chaplain, teacher etc. Using collaborative partnerships between HEIs and Islamic institutions, it will become possible to provide foundation degrees and chaplaincy training and a range of different skills such as counselling and pastoral care.

Those who go on to become imāms/mujtahids are faced with a complex situation: is an imām/mujtahid an office holder, called and, in effect, appointed by his God, or an employee of the mosque, authorised by the mosque committee, or both? Added to this is the fast changing modern world that swirls around minority communities and can create even more confusions about roles; should an imām/mujtahid also be able to play football with the young men in his charge, should he be a team leader in the mosque, and if so, who should be in his team? How can he be true to his faith while also presenting his people to the modern world? Our research demonstrates that there are imāms/mujtahids who function at all these different levels, but many require training to be able to develop their role, and such support will increase the tension between devotion to God and secular modernity: "The test …will be whether it is possible to develop patterns of mutuality in ministry and vocation that are more true to the covenant re-

---

21 http://www.ukba.homeoffice.gov.uk/sitecontent/documents/employersandsponsors/pbsguidance/

lationship between God and humanity than they are to Western legal and civic constructs" (Ison 2005, 7). This statement demonstrates the common difficulties that face ministers of religion; there is a tendency to see the devotion to religious practice that is characteristic of a devout Muslim as being unique to Islam, but the statement above is from a Christian vicar and seems to be true of those who lead spiritually and theologically in a secular world, regardless of their religion.

Our work with Muslims, both male and female, convince us that more needs to be done to give Muslim girls and women increased access to religious training of the same calibre as boys and men. We see this in the prison service, for example; of the 203 Muslim prison chaplains currently employed in HMPS, only 18 are women and only two of the 18 are ʿālimahs. The prison service cannot provide training to become an ʿālim or ʿālima, but the ʿālimahs receive equal status with the men in their work with women prisoners, and are called imāmah/mujtahida if they have good theological knowledge and pass all the standards required for prison chaplaincy.[22]

Conclusions

Our research report contains practical recommendations that have been discussed with and approved by as many groups as possible within the UK Muslim communities.[23] The recommendations are based on the research findings, and include suggestions of models for the training of imām/mujtahids and scholars that would be appropriate to the UK context, if policy-makers and citizens would stop behaving like *Precogs*. It is hoped that working relationships and networks have been created by the development of community links for future projects. Only time will tell. Recommendations are also made regarding links between mainstream further and higher education and Muslim seminaries.

Currently, most Islamic study in Britain is offered in *madrassas* and *dārul ʿulūms* , i.e. traditional religious teaching in a protected environment. This leads to qualifications that are neither understood nor acknowledged by the British higher education system. There are institutes, colleges and *dārul ʿulūms* in Britain that combine seminary-type teaching with more western approaches to the curriculum, and it is also these with which we hope we will be collaborating. Expertise from these institutes and colleges can enhance the curriculum of the 'mainstream' universities and create productive juxtaposition with aspects of the curriculum that celebrate a range of civilisations, developing links between academics working within Muslim institutes and those in 'mainstream' universities.

It has also become clear from our research that there is excellent work being done by imāms and others in Muslim educational institutions to promote community cohesion and the multi-faith identity that is the reality of Britain today. Much

---

22 11/11/09 Discussion with Ahtsham Ali, Muslim Advisor, Her Majesty's Prison Service HQ

23 Since the report's launch by government in 2010, consultation has continued with Higher Education Academy funding. See Perspectives at www.islamicstudiesnetwork.ac.uk

of this could not take place without government funding. Such work can also be enhanced by collaborative ventures between universities and Muslim institutions, to create validation pathways. Higher education should attempt to provide a transformative experience for students, and an ethical community that facilitates debate and discussion about the complex and problematic world we live in. Yet the secularism in British universities assumes a very different mindset from that of the devout Muslim, and this has proved insurmountable in many situations, such as many anecdotally reported refusals by British universities to validate Islamic programmes.[24] This can be attributed to a form of Orientalism in reverse, whereby the secular community believes that the religious Muslim chooses solutions that are alien and cannot be incorporated into state funded, secular universities. There is also within some Muslim communities a form of Orientalism in reverse, whereby validation of religious courses by secular universities may be seen as a form of contamination. Indeed, Ricœur kept faith and secularism separate, not only because he did not wish to preach his own faith too insistently but also in order to show us that theology and secular philosophy *are* different; "my two allegiances always escape me, even if at times they *acknowledge* one another" and the best we can achieve is a resting place somewhere between them, depending on the issues at stake (Ricœur 1998, 150).[25] However, it is therefore all the more important to try and acknowledge these boundaries, talk about them and compare and contrast the solutions we believe to be workable for the dilemmas posed by daily life. Similarly, faith and suspicion can work as polarities; each can both validate the other, show up the weaknesses in the other and try to help us derive moral strength from such oscillation (Scott-Baumann 2009, 174). Ricœur also proposed that we take action to demonstrate our commitment to our ideals, even when they are in conflict with each other. For him, writing was a powerful action, and he was also an activist, demonstrating his commitment to human rights and liberty on many occasions (Scott-Baumann 2009, 1, 53, 171). The most important lesson that we can take forward is the need to be active in the real world.

Activism

What practical joint projects can we develop now, through a Centre of Excellence, in order to facilitate a bringing together of these different, even opposed areas?

- The university sector needs to increase *training of Muslim teachers, theologians and academics, including women*, so as to make a career possible in teaching both in schools and universities.

---

24 I have personally witnessed the collapse of two such attempts, such as the one I describe optimistically, before it failed (Scott-Baumann 2007), and have been told of several more.

25 Critique and Conviction p.150. my translation: 'elles se font signe mutuellement', seems to me to be more than a nod in this context. Translated from Paul Ricœur, *La Critique et la Conviction*, 1995, p. 228.

- We can *expand on alternative routes into teacher training for the teachers in the dārul ʿulūms:* There is a programme for the Assessment Only route into teaching, run by the University of Gloucestershire with the Association of Muslim Schools.
- Teacher training in Arabic is a good approach, because of the increased understanding that communication can bring. We can find practical application of this in Ricœur's work about translation (Ricœur 2006), in which he shows the value of translation as a way of understanding the other, and also as a paradigm that we should follow in philosophy and in our lives.
- We need to *develop validation pathways* that will make it possible for young Muslims to gain qualifications from many years of study in *madrassas* and *dārul ʿulūms* that will allow them the choice of parity in the higher education system, as identified by Khan-Cheema in 1991 and by Siddiqui in *Islam at Universities in England: the Siddiqui Report* (2007).
- We can *develop citizenship strategies* in schools for educating pupils from different faith groups to work together. These can benefit from successful projects already taking place in UK *dārul ʿulūms* and schools (Scott-Baumann 2003b).
- Research bodies need to consider *research that challenges prevalent ideological assumptions* about Muslim communities and develops evidence-based work to support social cohesion, and modern philosophy applied to these issues.
- We can *work with government groups* e.g the Department for Communities and Local Government.

We can create opportunities for *giving a voice to the unvoiced or misrepresented*, as Paul Ricœur argues:

> I am more and more coming to see that the emergence of a single, worldwide civilisation, with the problems that this poses, constitutes one of the most important concerns for reasoned reflection. To recapture the full range of the meaning of our humanity and to open up the maximum number of possibilities for every person is a challenge for thinkers in every human discipline. The divergences of our economic and political systems should not be seen as a threat but as a locus for an expanding and continuing dialogue on basic human issues. (Ricœur 1974: ix)

Perhaps we can also consider that secular approaches may not be the only or even the best way of living, thus opening up possibilities for dialogue. Islam in Europe is developing in response to its own perceived needs and also in response to the secular world that surrounds it. Cultural differences are so apparent that it is necessary to discuss them, even if we find the differences too problematic to resolve easily. Moreover, the world is experiencing problems of great magnitude. Most of them cannot, I believe, be blamed upon the Muslim world. On the contrary, real conversations among equals would be very helpful to all groups: consumerist obsessions, alcohol and drug abuse, obesity, fertility problems and ecological damage are doing much more harm to the world than terrorism. If we are suspicious of the motivations of those who feel bound to cultural habits, such as modest clothing, we should also be suspicious of the secularist ideologies that promote immodest clothing in others. Islamic Sciences courses can be validated within a British and European academic network, to work towards Islam within Europe, and this will facilitate more open debate about secularist excesses. Using modern philosophy, such as that of Ricœur, will enhance the European educational networks in conjunction with Muslim communities, other faith communities and those of no faith, with special focus on the views and aspirations of young people, tomorrow's Europeans.

References

Achcar, Gilbert. 2008. Orientalism in Reverse. *Radical Philosophy* 152: 20-30.

Birt, Jonathan. 2006. Good Imam, Bad Imam: Civic Religion and National Integration in Britain post-9/11. *The Muslim World* 96 (4): 687-705.

Department for Communities and Local Government (DCLG). 2010. *The training and development of Muslim Faith Leaders: Current practice and future possibilities*; http://www.communities.gov.uk/publications/communities/trainingmuslimleaders practice

Geaves, Ron. (2008) Drawing on the Past to Transform the Present: Contemporary Challenges for Training and Preparing British Imams. *Journal of Muslim Minority Affairs*, 28 (1): 99-112.

Gilliat-Ray, Sophie. 2005. Closed Worlds: (Not) accessing Deobandi Dar ul-uloom in Britain. *Fieldwork in Religion* 1 (1): 7-33.

Gilliat-Ray, Sophie. 2006. Educating the Ulama: Centres of Islamic Religious Training in Britain. *Islam and Christian-Muslim Relations* 17 (1): 55-76.

Holden, Andrew. 2009. *Religious Cohesion in Times of Conflict: Christian-Muslim Relations in Segregated Towns*. New York/London: Continuum.

Habermas, Jürgen. 2005. *Zwischen Naturalismus und Religion: Philosophische Aufsätze*. Frankfurt am Main: Suhrkamp.

Higher Education Funding Council for England. 2008. *International Approaches to Islamic Studies in Higher Education.* http//:www.hefce.ac.uk/Pubs/rdreports/2008/rd07_08/

Insted Consultancy for the Greater London Authority. 2007. *The Search for Common Ground: Muslims, non-Muslims and the UK media.* http://www.insted/co/uk/islam.html and http://www.London.gov.uk/mayor/equalities/docs.co

Johansen, Birgitte Schepelern. 2006. *Islam at the European Universities*. Research Report of University of Copenhagen. www.ku.dk/Satsning/Religion/indhold/pdf/Imamrapport2.pdf

Jackson, Robert, Siebren Miedema, Wolfram Weisse, & Jean-Paul Willlaime, eds. 2007. *Religion and Education in Europe: Developments, Contexts and Debates*. Muenster: Waxmann.

Laurence, James and Anthony Heath. 2008. *Predictors of community cohesion: multilevel modelling of the 2005 Citizenship Survey.* London: Department of Communities and Local Government Publications. www.communities.gov.uk

Muslim Council of Britain. 2007. *Towards Greater Understanding – Meeting the needs of Muslim pupils in state schools.* http://www.mcb.org.uk/downloads/Schoolinfoguidancev2.pdf

Pennant, R. 2005. *Diversity, Trust and Community Participation in England.* Findings 253. London: Home Office Research, Development and Statistics Directorate. http://www.homeoffice.gov.uk.rds/pdfs05/r253.pdf

Ricœur, Paul. 1974. *Political and Social Essays*. Trans.and ed. David Stewart and Joseph Bien. Athens: Ohio University Press.

Ricœur, Paul. 1991. *From Text To Action: Essays in Hermeneutics II*, Trans. Kathleen Blamey and John B. Thompson. London: The Athlone Press.

Ricœur, Paul. 1992. *Oneself as Another*.Trans. Kathleen Blamey. Chicago: Chicago University Press.

Ricœur, Paul. 1998. *Critique and Conviction. Discussions with François Azouvy and Marc de Launay.* Trans. Kathleen Blamey. Cambridge: Polity Press.

Ricœur, Paul. 2006. *On Translation*. Trans. Eileen Brennan. London: Routledge.

Said, Edward. 1978. *Orientalism: Western Conceptions of the Orient*. New York: Random House.

Scott-Baumann, Alison. 2003a. Teacher Education for Muslim Women: Intercultural relationships, method and philosophy. *Ethnicities* 3 (2): 243-61.

Scott-Baumann, Alison. 2003b. Citizenship and Postmodernity. *Intercultural Education* 14 (4): 355-66.

Scott-Baumann, Alison. 2007. Collaborative Partnerships as Sustainable Pedagogy: Working with British Muslims. In *Greener by Degrees: Exploring Sustainability through Higher Education Curricula*, eds. Caroline Roberts and Jane Roberts, 306-15. Cheltenham: GDN http://www.glos.ac.uk/shareddata/dms/FF071DBEBC-D42A039FF8B1E4A2EE4606.pdf

Scott-Baumann, Alison. 2009 *Ricœur and the hermeneutics of suspicion*. New York/ London: Continuum.

Scott-Baumann, Alison. 2011. Unveiling Orientalism in Reverse. In *Islam and the Veil*, eds. Theodore Gabriel and Rabiha Hannan. New York/ London: Continuum.

Scott-Baumann, Alison and Akram Khan-Cheema. 2001. A Case Study in Widening Participation with British Muslims. *Journal of Learning and Teaching* 6(1): 6-8.

Siddiqui, Ataullah. 2007. *Islam at Universities in England: The Siddiqui Report*. London: Department for Innovation, Universities and Skills.

Weisse, Wolfram. 2007. Introduction. In *Religion and Education in Europe: Developments, Contexts and Debates*, eds. Robert Jackson, Siebren Miedema, Wolfram Weisse, & Jean-Paul Willlaime, 9-25. Muenster: Waxmann.

Glossary

ʿaqīda – creed; statement of belief.

Barelwi – The Barelwi tradition in India is a popular and Sufi tradition in South Asia. It is associated with Mawlānā Ahmed Raza Khan (d.1922), the founder of the madrasah, Manzare Islam in Bareilvi, India.

Dar al-ʿulūm – literally, a "house of sciences"; a seminary, name given to institutes of higher Islamic learning (South Asia).

Deobandi – the name of a place in northern India; reference to the reformist school founded there in 1857 and which has been followed in other similar institutions in India and elsewhere.

Eid – Muslim festivals at the end of Ramadan, and the end of pilgrimage (hajj).

Fiqh – Islamic jurisprudence; rules deduced from the Qur'an and Sunna.

Ḥāfiẓ – someone who has memorized the Qurʾān or earlier, *ḥadīth* collections.

Halal – permitted or allowed according to Islamic law (fiqh).

Hanafi – relating to one of the juridical schools in Sunni Islam, relating to its epynomous founder Abu Hanifah.

Howzeh – a seminary, associated with higher Islamic learning in Iran.

ijtihād – juridical deductive reasoning based on the Qur'an, Prophetic statements and consensus; has also been used to refer to independent, creative thinking in modern Islamic thought.

Imam – a leader in a mosque; also used by Shi'ites to refer to the descendents of the Prophet Muhammad and the rightful successors of the Muslims.

Islamization – a philosophy of Islamic education which proposes to transform modern intellectual disciplines through the values of Islam.

Kafāʾa – suitability and legitimacy of an Islamic marriage in terms of status.

kuttāb – basic Islamic learning institutions (sometime also *maktab*).

madrasah – a school, literally a place of learning, used especially for higher Islamic learning.

madrassah – see madrasah, this spelling used particularly among Asian Muslims, in reference also to basic Islamic learning.

maktab – as *kuttāb.*

mīlad – (also mawlūd) birthday of the Prophet (is celerated by some Islamic groups but contested by others).

Muharram – first month of the Islamic calendar which marks the Islamic new year.

mujtahid – literally, someone who can apply deductive reason in Islamic law.

Nasheed music – Islamic vocal music sung a cappella or accompanied by percussion instruments.

Qawwali – indo-pakistani music genre over 700 years old and rooted in Sufism and Islamic mysticism.

Qāri – a reciter, in reference to a person who has master one or modes of recitation (of the Qur'ān).

Salafism – literally, a school of thought in Islam which gives preference to the way of the early, first Muslim (*salafī*); associated with Hanbalism and with Saudi Wahhabi thinking in modern society.

shaykh – literally, an older man, but also used for a teacher or master.

Shi'a – literally partisan; one of the major Muslim groups that believe the Prophet Muhammad was and should have been succeeded by his cousin and son-in-law ʿAlī, and his progeny with Muḥammad's daughter Fāṭima.

sunnah – custom, the way of the Prophet.

Sunni – followers of the *sunnah*; the majority of Muslim who opposed the Shiʿa and do not accept the Prophet's family as his successors.

Tablighi Jamaat – A proselytizing movement founded in India in the 1920s and which now has operations worldwide.

taqlīd – literally following, in reference to following the standards of jurisprudence of the past; opposite of *ijtihād* (juridical reasoning).

tarbiyyah – literally meaning the act of cultivation; referring to education or Bildung, the development of an individual.

taʿdīb – from *adab* (good habits); referring to the act of cultivating good moral habits.

taʿlīm – instruction; literally the act of transferring knowledge (*ʿilm*).

Authors

Aslam **Fataar** is a Professor and Departmental Head of the Education Policy Studies Department in the Faculty of Education at Stellenbosch University, South Africa.

Andreas **Hieronymus** graduated with a PhD in intercultural education. He is senior researcher and Director of the "Institut für Migrations- und Rassismusforschung" (Research Institute for Migration and Racism) in Hamburg, Germany.

Muhammad **Khalid Sayed** (MA, Religious Studies, University of Cape Town, 2010) currently works as Research Consultant for ETHICORE Advisory Solutions in Cape Town, South Africa.

Michael **Kiefer** (PhD, Islamic Studies) is a senior researcher in the field of Muslim religious education and Director of the "Agentur für participative Integration" (Agency for participatory integration) in Düsseldorf, Germany.

Irka-Christin **Mohr** (PhD, Islamic Studies) is a senior researcher and works on Muslims in Europe and on the topic of Islam and Education, Berlin, Germany.

Lubna **Nadvi** (PhD, Political Studies) is a lecturer and Political Analyst at the School of Politics, University of Kwa-Zulu Natal, South Africa

Inga **Niehaus** (PhD, Political Studies) is research coordinator at the Georg Eckert Institute for International Textbook Research in Braunschweig, Germany

Privatdozent Dietrich **Reetz** is senior research fellow at the Zentrum Moderner Orient and senior lecturer of political science at the Free University Berlin, Germany.

Alison **Scott-Baumann** (PhD, Education) is visiting Research Fellow at Lancaster University. She is a Reader Emeritus at the University of Gloucestershire and member of the Conseil Scientifique, Fonds Ricoeur in Paris.

Abdulkader **Tayob** holds the chair in Islam, African Publics and Religious Values at the University of Cape Town, South Africa. He is also Head of Department of Religious Studies, University of Cape Town.

Yusef **Waghid** is a Professor of Philosophy of Education and Dean of the Faculty of Education at Stellenbosch University, South Africa.

Wolfram **Weisse** is a Professor at the University of Hamburg. He is Director of the "Academy of World Religions" of the University of Hamburg, Germany.

Waxmann

Religionen im Dialog

Eine Schriftenreihe der
Akademie der Weltreligionen der Universität Hamburg

Band 1

Wolfram Weiße (Hrsg.)
Unter Mitarbeit von Dorothea Grießbach

Theologie im Plural

Eine akademische Herausforderung

2009, 214 Seiten, br., 19,90 €,
ISBN 978-3-8309-2084-7

Das Thema Religion hat Konjunktur: Es wird verstärkt darüber nachgedacht, wie Religionen sich in ihrem Beitrag für den Dialog zwischen Menschen, innerhalb von Gesellschaften und zwischen Nationen denken und gestalten lassen. Hierbei wird deutlich, dass unsere gewachsenen Voraussetzungen im Blick auf Religion sich dynamisch gestalten müssen. Dies betrifft gegenwärtig die Notwendigkeit, über die wissenschaftlichen Ansätze in der evangelischen und katholischen Theologie hinaus auch auf diskursfähige Theologien in den Weltreligionen zuzugehen.
Hiermit befasst sich dieses Buch. Initiativen für die Einrichtung von akademischer Forschung und Lehre sind vor allem auf die drei abrahamischen Religionen Judentum, Christentum und Islam gerichtet, beziehen aber auch z.B. den Buddhismus mit ein. Hierzu wird eine Reihe von bemerkenswerten Ansätzen an europäischen Universitäten vor, vorgestellt und analysiert.
Die Entwicklung von theologischen Ressourcen an europäischen Universitäten ist in den Anfängen begriffen, hat aber bereits nach wenigen Jahren eine große Dynamik entfaltet. Internationale Perspektiven weisen auf die Notwendigkeit des Dialogs der Religionen aus theologischer Sicht, beziehen neue Entwicklungen aus China mit ein und klären, wie religiöser Pluralismus im Kontext von Globalisierung verstanden werden kann, ohne religiöse und kulturelle Werte grenzenlos zu relativieren.

MÜNSTER · NEW YORK · MÜNCHEN · BERLIN

Band 2

Wolfram Weiße (Hrsg.)

Dialogischer Religionsunterricht in Hamburg

Positionen, Analysen und Perspektiven im Kontext Europas

2008, 260 Seiten, br., 19,90 €
ISBN 978-3-8309-2051-9

Der dialogische „Religionsunterricht für alle“ in Hamburg gewinnt zunehmend an Aufmerksamkeit. Die Schülerinnen und Schüler werden nicht nach unterschiedlichen religiösen und weltanschaulichen Hintergründen getrennt, sondern gemeinsam unterrichtet. Dabei lernen die Schülerinnen und Schüler Unterschiede nicht als Bedrohung des Eigenen wahrzunehmen, sondern Vielfalt als Bereicherung anzusehen und anderen Positionen mit Respekt zu begegnen.
In Hamburg selbst hat es in den vergangenen Jahren intensive Auseinandersetzungen über den Religionsunterricht gegeben. In diesem Buch werden Stellungnahmen dazu aus den Religionsgemeinschaften und aus der Politik vorgelegt. Ebenso kommen rechtliche Erwägungen von Experten zum Tragen. Schließlich werden neue empirische Studien und Analysen aus dem Praxisfeld vorgestellt.

Band 3

Wolfram Weiße
Hans-Martin Gutmann (Hrsg.)

Religiöse Differenz als Chance?

Positionen, Kontroversen, Perspektiven

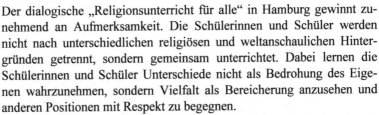

2010, 244 Seiten, br., 24,90 €
ISBN 978-3-8309-2342-8

Waxmann

Bei aller Dynamik in der Wertschätzung von Religionen sind indes mögliche Probleme nicht zu unterschätzen. Grundlegende Analysen und neue Antworten sind notwendig, damit die religiös-kulturelle Vielfalt eine Ressource für menschliches Zusammenleben und nicht einen Faktor für Missverständnisse, Spaltung und Feindschaft bildet.
In diesem Zusammenhang ergeben sich zwei Fragen: Zum einen ist eine Wahl darüber zu treffen, welches Verständnis von Religion und religiös inspirierter Identität leitend ist. Die zweite Frage richtet sich darauf, inwieweit „religiöse Differenz eine Chance“ darstellt. Dieser Frage wird in diesem Buch aus ganz unterschiedlichen Perspektiven nachgegangen.

Band 4

Ephraim Meir

Differenz und Dialog

Übersetzt von Elke Morlok

2011, 248 Seiten, br., 27,90 €
ISBN 978-3-8309-2511-8

Dieses Buch veranschaulicht die Ansätze der großen jüdischen Philosophen, Theologen, Bildungswissenschaftler und Psychologen der letzten Jahrhunderte. Namen wie Hermann Cohen, Sigmund Freud, Franz Rosenzweig, Martin Buber, Emmanuel Lévinas und Abraham Joshua Heschel gewinnen in einem großen Überblick und in faszinierenden Einzelanalysen Kontur und Gestalt. Die Schätze in diesen Ansätzen werden gehoben und bilden eine Ressource und Herausforderung für weiteres Nachdenken.
Ephraim Meir arbeitet in dieser Publikation mit der Dialektik von Differenz und Dialog. Damit vermeidet er, dass der Dialog als eine uniformierende, auf einebnende Harmonie ausgerichtete Denkbewegung verstanden wird, und damit erreicht er, dass dem Dialog in seiner grundlegenden Verwurzelung in der Differenz eine umso größere Urkraft zugetraut werden kann.
Die Publikation verbindet wissenschaftliche Theorie mit einem leicht verständlichen Stil und wendet sich sowohl an eine allgemeine Leserschaft als auch an ein wissenschaftliches Publikum.

MÜNSTER · NEW YORK · MÜNCHEN · BERLIN